m☀nday morning®

Amazing Alligators
and other Story Hour Friends

by Maxine Riggers, illustrated by Philip Chalk

REMOVED FROM COLLECTION 8562

WEST ISLIP PUBLIC LIBRARY
3 HIGBIE LANE
WEST ISLIP, NEW YORK 11795

D1472442

ABOUT THE AUTHOR

Maxine Riggers has led story hours in Nez Perce, Idaho for the past eight years. Drawing on her background as a kindergarten teacher, Maxine developed many ideas and activities for building the love of literature. AMAZING ALLIGATORS AND OTHER STORY HOUR FRIENDS, which grew out of popular programs presented at her local library, is Maxine's first book.

Publisher: Roberta Suid
Contributing Editor: Murray Suid
Production: Susan Pinkerton

Monday Morning is a registered trademark of Monday Morning Books, Inc.

Entire contents copyright © 1990 by Monday Morning Books, Inc., Box 1680, Palo Alto, California 94302

Permission is hereby granted to the individual purchaser to reproduce student materials in this book for non-commercial individual or classroom use only. Permission is not granted for school-wide, or system-wide, reproduction of materials.

ISBN 1-878279-11-4

Printed in the United States of America

9 8 7 6 5 4 3

CONTENTS

INTRODUCTION

In recent years, reading aloud has gained tremendous popularity. The reason is easy to discover. Parents, teachers, and others who care about children have become increasingly worried about the negative consequences of TV and other commercialized media. They believe children need entertainment that's more intelligent, nurturing, and uplifting. The story hour meets all these criteria, and more.

Storytelling, which in this book refers to reading or reciting, establishes a personal relationship that the mass media cannot provide. Children love hearing a story read or told by someone who is "live" and able to respond. A special bond is created between the storyteller and the children as they share laughter, ideas, and all sorts of unpredictable reactions.

If children are to develop a love for literature, they must read and be read to for the simple pleasure of the experience, without having to answer content questions or to make reports. This does not mean passivity. The joy of reading can—and should—involve a wide range of activities such as reciting, dramatizing, puppeteering, drawing, singing, and talking.

This book is meant to help you, the storyteller, create that rich kind of literary experience known as "whole language." Nine chapters, each dealing with a story-hour theme, provide information on almost 500 much-loved picture books suitable for children ages three to six.

At the core of each chapter is a Read-Aloud section that features eight to ten books. The write-up for each book includes a brief synopsis, a list of easy-to-make or easy-to-find materials for presenting the book, and simple activities to use before, during, and after the reading or telling. The activities, designed to add excitement and enrichment, include: games, poems, songs, finger plays, action verses, crafts, exercises, and creative dramatics.

Each chapter also contains a "More Books" section, which annotates about two dozen equally fine books. These are especially good for lap books. Of course, you can dream up your own enrichment strategies for these titles.

AMAZING ALLIGATORS is written for the storyteller working with a group of children in a classroom or library. However, parents will also find the book helpful in choosing books for their children. And, of course, many of the activities—especially those found in the crafts and snacks sections—can easily be adapted to the home.

CHOOSING BOOKS

Finding the right books is the single most important—and time-consuming—aspect of a story hour. It can also be one of the most rewarding tasks for the storyteller. That's because there are so many wonderful old books and so many wonderful new ones.

However, it doesn't matter if a book is an old classic or a recent prize winner. What does matter is whether you, the storyteller, like it. The book must touch your emotions. It might be wild, noisy and lots of fun. Or it might be warm and loving. But it has to do something to your heart. If it doesn't, chances are the book won't work with your children.

When choosing books, you might like to consider the following elements:

1. Plot—Does the story line make sense? Is it interesting? Will your children be able to understand it?

2. Illustrations—Is the artwork inviting? Are the pictures large enough for the children to see?

3. Style—Is the writing clear and easy to read? Is the vocabulary at the right level? (This doesn't mean, of course, that all the words be simple. One of the best ways to build vocabulary is to present children with new words,

which can be defined in context or by the storyteller.)

4. Theme—Does the book present a message with positive values? (This doesn't mean that all the characters will be "nice" or that a book must be preachy. It does mean that the overall impact of the book will illustrate the importance of values such as determination, creativity, cooperation, and integrity.)

Some of the books we'll discuss are available in large format editions. Children—and adults, too—are fascinated by these "big book" publications. These books are easier to see when working with large groups, and their size adds a dramatic touch. In addition, their large print makes them inviting to beginning readers. (Hint: If you find big books awkward to hold, try placing them on easels. Or invite the children to help you hold them up.)

To zero in on one or a few dramatic moments in a book, try making your own big story posters. This can be done by enlarging the pages at a copy store, or by drawing the pages freehand. Write the text on the back of the cards. You might sometimes present a scene from the middle of the book when you're introducing the story. Hold the picture up and ask a question like "What do you think is happening here?" Or "How do you think the character got into a mess like this?"

READING TO CHILDREN

Reading or telling a story can be a warm, enjoyable experience. However, there is no one best method to do it. You will need to   the experiment to see what works best for you. Perhaps the following hints will prove helpful as you experiment:

1. You should practice. Children's stories aren't necessarily simple. By reading the books aloud to yourself, you'll discover all sorts of things: words that may need explaining, points that need dramatic pauses, places where you'll want to invite the children to help you tell the story—for example, by making sounds. If you have the talent, you might also use your

rehearsal time to develop distinctive voices for the dialogue of different characters. Finally, even if you carefully practiced a story at home, if possible review it briefly just before presenting it.

2. Make the children physically comfortable. Have them sit on the floor or provide pillows or "magic carpets." Make sure everyone can see you, the book, and any props you will be using.

3. Be natural. Although you will be sharing the stories with a group, the key relationship is one-to-one. You can establish this by making eye contact with each child.

4. Establish the mood by a short introduction. This introduction might give a hint about the theme or the characters or the setting. It could include a reaction that you had when first reading the story. For example, if it made you laugh, let the children know.

5. Tell the story with enthusiasm. While props and costumes can be a plus, sometimes little things—like a dramatic snap of the finger or a wink—will powerfully communicate your love of the story.

PRESENTING STORIES

For the sake of variety, and also to get the most out of each book, you might wish to know about—and practice—different methods for presenting stories. Here are six common approaches:

1. Reading from the Book
Show the illustrations as you read. Do not read a page, stop, and then show the art. You may lose the continuity of the story. Hold the book high enough for the children to see, and to your side near your shoulder. It's especially important to show the pictures when they contribute largely to the meaning of the story.

2. Telling the Story in Your Own Words
For preparation, read a story several times, until you are so familiar with it that you can easily convey it in your own words. Telling makes sense when the text is too long or too complex, or when the illustrations don't contribute much. Telling allows you to elaborate,

delete, or modify the story. Also, by dispensing with the book, you'll be able to maintain constant eye contact with the children.

Hint: There's no need to memorize a text. In fact, memorizing can cause problems, because if you forget a line, you may lose the continuity of the story.

3. Telling the Story Using Flannel board Cutouts

Stories with repetition lend themselves to illustration with flannel cutouts that stick to a flannel board. You can purchase ready-to-use flannel board figures. Or you can make your own by cutting characters from a duplicate book, gluing them onto flannel.

4. Telling the Story with Puppets

Children love to watch and use puppets. In your presentations, use the puppets to act out key scenes or whole stories. You'll find sources for buying puppets in the Resource section of this book. In the Crafts section of each chapter, there are also directions for making paper-bag puppets, finger puppets, and stick puppets.

For young children, it's often best not to use a puppet theater, which can distract them. For better results, hold the puppets in front of you as you tell the story.

5. Telling and Drawing

Some stories lend themselves to draw-as-you-talk illustrations. Often, this will involve beginning with a simple shape—say, the outline of a house—which you will make increasingly elaborate as the plot thickens. Do your drawing on the chalkboard or on poster paper.

6. Acting the Story

If you've always wanted to be a star, consider using props and costumes to dramatize a story. Be careful not to overact. The children should not become so interested in the theatrics that they lose track of the story. A sure antidote to hogging the limelight is for you to involve the children in the drama. Their acting can range from the very simple—like extras on a movie set—to more complex acting out of the story while you narrate.

ORGANIZING A STORY HOUR

Story hours inspire children to read by giving children the opportunity to hear stories that will be stored in their memories forever. These remembered stories serve as the foundation for understanding the ever-more-complex stories which the children will encounter as they grow.

But laying the foundation doesn't happen by magic. Successful story hours require careful preparation. That is what this book is all about.

Plan ahead to allow time to find the books you want. Learn the songs, finger plays, and verses. Practice the games and dramatic plays. Make plans for snacks and crafts. Set the stage by displaying books, stuffed animals, and posters—at the children's eye level if possible.

Hint: To illustrate posters and bulletin boards, copy the art from covers or inside pages. If you're a confident artist, you can do this freehand. If not, try using an opaque projector to project printed material onto blank paper; you can then outline the projected figure and add color.

Because most of the books deal with animals, you might wish to display live frogs, mice, rabbits, monkeys, or even piglets. Sources can include friends, young listeners, pet shops, nearby farms, or the zoo. Hint: alligators, bears, and elephants might present something of a problem.

On special occasions, create and wear the costume of a storybook character. If you are good at sewing—or know someone who is—you can find many commercially-prepared patterns. If you're really good, you can probably design your own. On the other hand, if you don't know a thimble from a bobbin, you might try to buy or borrow costumes. In any case, if the children seem to be more interested in what you're wearing than in what you're saying, you might consider putting the costume back into the trunk. The main rule is: Let the book be the star.

Use carpet samples as magic carpets for the children to sit on as they soar to storyland or to the place featured in your story hour—such as the swamp where the alligators live. Warn the children to watch out for jets, birds, stars, and the moon. Land safely in your destination and have the children remove the fluff from their ears. Now they're ready to listen.

If the story hour actually lasts one hour, you'll usually be able to read three to five stories. Read longer books first. Save the shorter ones for the end, when the children are beginning to tire. In between stories, include songs, poems, finger plays, action verses, exercises, and games. Be sure to include a little stretching before moving on to the next story.

Set the books out on shelves and tables where the children can find them at the end of the hour.

STORY HOUR ACTIVITIES

Crafts

Crafts are important because they allow students to have hands-on involvement with the stories. Consider the following criteria when choosing a craft project:

1. The craft should relate to the specific stories or verses you've been presenting.
2. The crafts should lead to open-ended play. Clearly, puppets, headbands, and masks encourage this type of activity.
3. The crafts should be simple. Complex crafts, while interesting, can take the focus away from the stories.

4. Don't spend a lot on crafts. Inexpensive projects not only evoke more creativity, they also enable you to spend more money on good books.

For preschool age children, some of the work can be completed ahead of time. For example, if you're going to make stick puppets, you can prepare the figures ahead of time and then have the children attach the bodies to the sticks. You might ask volunteers to help, since making crafts can be very time-consuming.

Dramatic Play

Dramatizing a story helps children develop oral expression and also enables them to identify with the characters. In addition, it teaches sequencing, cooperation, and working to accomplish a goal.

A few children will be reluctant to participate at first, but as they watch the other children, they will gradually enter into the fun. Encourage—but never force—children to participate. One way to build confidence is to give the shyer children the easier parts to play. Being a tree, for example, isn't very scary.

You'll find many specific suggestions for dramatizing stories in the pages ahead. But don't stop there. You're likely to spot many opportunities for impromptu acting as you work with the children. And you'll want to do lots of it simply because it's what children love to do best of all.

Exercises

Exercising creates body awareness and develops important motor skills. If you value this kind of activity, you'll discover countless exercise moments in the books. For example, a story about elephants may suggest a few seconds of energetic stomping, while a frog tale might get everyone up and hopping.

If you've got a tape recorder or record player handy, use it to provide exercise music. Or make your own music.

Finally, encourage the children to take turns being the leader. It's a non-threatening way to increase confidence.

Finger Plays and Action Verse

These small-scale dramatic activities can have a big payoff in terms of creativity and involvement. For example, children can enter into the lives of alligators simply by pretending they are swimming slowly in a swamp. They can become frogs just by sitting on imaginary lily pads and croaking. (If you don't believe it, put down this book for a moment, close your eyes, and croak.)

Introduce a finger play or action verse by reciting the text and demonstrating the actions. Invite the children to join you in saying the words and carrying out the motions. You may want to repeat the performance a few times if the children show interest.

While this book contains numerous finger plays, you can explore further with RING A RING O'ROSES, a 98-page book of plays from the Flint Public Library (see Resources).

Games

Games provide children with an involving way of learning how to follow directions, while also helping them develop motor skills.

Choose games that relate to the story-hour theme and that suit the capabilities of the children and the space available. Games that give everyone the chance to play are better than those that involve only a few players at a time.

Poems

Children of all ages love to hear poetry and to participate by chanting familiar lines. They especially enjoy poetry that features humor, strong rhythm, unusual rhymes, and plot. Short poems have the advantage of being easier to memorize.

Poetry can inspire all sorts of worthwhile activities. Here are just a few:

1. Have the children illustrate a poem. Display the illustrations on a bulletin board.

2. Make a craft related to the poem.

3. Tell a poem using flannel board characters.

4. Bring the poem to life through creative dramatics. Try wearing masks, especially when presenting scary or silly poems.

5. Help the children memorize a poem. Suggest that they perform it at home for their families.

6. Write original poems.

7. Hold a poetry reading during which older students will present classic and original poems. Serve tea and cookies—use real tea cups.

Remember to use the same techniques for reading poetry that you use in reading prose. Hand gestures, facial expressions, and voice modulations can all work together to build a life-long love of this vital form of literature.

All of the poems are by the author, unless otherwise credited.

Puppets

Puppets are one of the most ancient forms of communication. And yet they still hold our attention and imagination—as demonstrated by such up-to-date characters as the Muppets.

The best way to involve young children in simple puppet play is to first demonstrate the use of hand puppets while telling a story. Later, give the puppets to the children with little or no explicit instruction and watch what they come up with. Shy children who are reluctant to participate may be more outgoing with puppets.

Puppets are simple to make. You'll find many patterns and ideas in this book, but your own creativity can take you into uncharted—and exciting—areas. A good source for inspiration are everyday household objects—tin cans, paper milk cartons, socks, boxes, unwanted stuffed animals with the stuffing removed, and so on. Play around with all sorts of materials, and invite the children to work with you. Try many forms: hand puppets, stick puppets, finger puppets, even simple marionettes.

Folkmanis, Inc. is a good source for ready-made, high-quality, reasonably-priced puppets (see Resources).

Snacks

At the end of the story hour or after reading a long story, serve a snack that relates to the literature at hand. All of the snacks described in this book have been child-approved. (No use serving a snack that the children won't eat.)

Some of the snacks are, by definition, messy. Those work best when eaten at a table. If tables aren't available, lay a plastic tablecloth on the floor.

Since spills and other minor catastrophes are to be expected, you might wish to involve parents or older students as servers and bussers. Of course, the little kids should be given the opportunity to clean up after themselves.

Songs

Singing develops a sense of rhythm and rhyme. Songs that feature repetitions and catchy tunes work best because they can be learned quickly. Choose songs related to the stories or to the overall theme of the hour.

To teach a song, sing first while the children listen. Then repeat the song, asking them to join you. Explain that they can participate even if they don't know all the words.

Don't worry if Caruso wouldn't envy your voice. Singing brilliantly doesn't matter. What counts is clear articulation and enthusiasm. If you can play the piano or guitar, that'll add to the fun. If you can't, perhaps you can find an adult or student volunteer to back you up.

AMAZING ALLIGATORS

Alligators—with their giant jaws and terrific tails—are star material for any story hour.

You'll probably want an alligator puppet to help you dramatize the many splendid stories that follow. Make the one illustrated in the Alligator Crafts section of this chapter. Or purchase one from Folkmanis (see Resources).

Alligators and crocodiles are reptiles that belong to the crocodilian family. Because these creatures are closely related, both are included in this chapter. The most common alligator is the American alligator, which lives in the southeastern part of the United States. The Nile crocodile, which is the most famous species of crocodile, lives in Africa. Freshwater and saltwater crocodiles live in Australia.

If you live near a zoo where alligators are on display, you might arrange for a visit there.

Happy reading, and as they say around the swamp, "See you later, alligator."

Setting the Stage

Make an alligator—about as long as an adult human—from rolled paper following the illustration as a guide. Paint it, cut it out, and mount it on the wall. Include the heading: "Alligators Read Very Long Books."

Wear an "Alligator Country" hat when reading the stories. To any hat with a brim simply attach a band made from paper with the words "Alligator Country" printed on it. Purchase several inexpensive children's straw hats and attach similar bands. The children can wear them when they're reading alligator stories.

For an appealing 3-D display, tie a white bandage around the alligator puppet's mouth to indicate the alligator has a toothache. Set it alongside the book ALLIGATOR'S TOOTH-ACHE by Diane de Groat.

Show children how to turn their hands into alligators. Using a fine-pointed felt marker with washable ink, draw an eye near the knuckle of the index finger. Move the finger and thumb up and down to make the mouth open and close.

If you are using magic carpets, fly to the swamps of the Florida Everglades where the alligators live. Your "private" Everglades might be home to a few rubber alligators purchased from a variety store.

Bulletin Board Ideas

1. Enlarge the cover of an alligator book such as THERE'S AN ALLIGATOR UNDER MY BED. Color and mat for a dazzling display.

2. Make your bulletin board come alive by enlarging Monty from the cover of MONTY by James Stevenson. From inside the book, make copies of the duck, the rabbit, and the frog. Color, cut out, and pin the quartet to your board, illustrating their journey across the river. Use the heading: "Hurry up, Monty." Later, the children might play with these cut-outs as they retell the story.

3. Enlarge the lady and her purse from THE LADY WITH THE ALLIGATOR PURSE, adapted by Nadine Westcott. Color, cut out the lady, add the title, and mount on your board.

ALLIGATORS READ VERY LONG BOOKS

Read-Aloud Stories

ALLIGATOR SHOES
by Arthur Dorros (Dutton, 1982)

Story: Alvin Alligator is locked inside a shoe store overnight. He delights in trying on all the shoes, but is surprised when someone decides to buy alligator shoes.

Materials: (optional) products made from alligator skin or an imitation

Directions: Begin by explaining that sometimes alligator skin is used for making shoes, belts, and other objects. Try to find something that is made from alligator skin or an imitation.

If you think your students can understand the concepts involved, you might tell them that in the past large numbers of alligators were killed for their skin. In fact, there was a real danger no alligators would be left. Fortunately, because people got together and decided to protect the alligators, now there are plenty again.

THE ALLIGATOR'S SONG
by Robert Tallon (Parents Magazine Press, 1981)

Story: A lost alligator is attempting to find its way back to the sea. Eddie hears the alligator's melancholy song and offers his assistance.

Materials: alligator puppet, sailor's hat, alligator's tooth

Directions: Put a sailor's hat on the alligator puppet who then—with your help—begins to cry. Ask the puppet why he's crying. The puppet explains that he's lost and wants to go back to the sea. Ask the children if they would like to help the lost alligator.

When you come to the song, sing it in a melancholy tone using your own tune if you like. At the end of the story, show the children an alligator's tooth on a string that you've made from poster paper or from clay. Give a tooth to each child, or help each child make a tooth, as a souvenir of the story.

ALLIGATOR'S TOOTHACHE
by Diane de Groat (Crown, 1977)

Story: This wordless book tells about an alligator who has a terrible toothache but is afraid to go to the dentist.

Materials: alligator puppet with a bandage tied around his mouth

Directions: Show the children the alligator and invite them to guess what the bandage is for. Explain that the alligator has a toothache. Ask the puppet if he wants to go to the dentist. The puppet shakes his head no.

Ask the children why the alligator might not want to go to the dentist. Their answers will vary. You might also ask the children to describe visits to the dentist or to tell about "baby" teeth that came loose.

Present the story using your own words and encourage the children to help tell the story with you. Dramatize the actions such as knocking whenever the friends or the dentist knock on the door, or dialing the phone when the monkey calls the dentist. At the end of the story, mimic the alligator by folding your arms together and then having the children do likewise.

THE CHICKEN'S CHILD
by Margaret Hartelius (Doubleday, 1975)

Story: In this wordless book, a hen decides to hatch a lost egg, which turns out to contain an alligator. The hen grows to love her newly adopted hatchling until he decides to eat everything in sight.

Materials: hard-boiled egg

Directions: Explain that a mother alligator builds a nest as big as an open umbrella. In this nest she lays between 40 and 60 eggs. After covering the eggs with grass and mud, she guards the nest until the eggs hatch two months later. If she didn't protect them, a raccoon or skunk might eat the eggs. When the alligators hatch, they already know how to swim and hunt.

Show the children the hard-boiled egg. Ask them to pretend that this is the egg in the story you are about to tell. As you go through the wordless book, invite the children to help you invent the narration.

If possible, bring in an encyclopedia or magazine that shows alligators hatching. Then invite the children to pretend they are baby alligators. First they must make themselves very small and egg-shaped. Then as they start to hatch, one leg "breaks through," then the head, then another leg.

FREDERICK'S ALLIGATOR

by Esther Peterson, il. by Susanna Natti
(Crown, 1979)

Story: No one believes Frederick when he tells them he has an alligator under his bed, but he really does!

Materials: rubber alligator, shoe box

Directions: Put the rubber alligator in the box. Ask the children to guess what he might be doing there since alligators usually live in swamps. Explain that this alligator belongs to a young boy named Frederick.

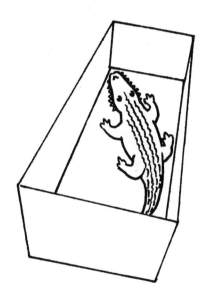

GATOR PIE

by Louise Mathews, il. by Jeni Bassett (Dodd, Mead, 1979)

Story: Two alligators, Alice and Alvin, discover a pie on a picnic table near the swamp. They decide to cut it into two equal pieces. However, when visitors arrive who also want to share, trouble develops.

Materials: alligator puppet dressed like Alice, alligator pie, paper plates

Directions: Dress the puppet in a purple skirt and bow. Have Alice tell the children how she and her friend Alvin found a large uncut pie.

As you present the story, use different voices—growling, sneering, demanding—for the different alligators. Rub your stomach when the alligators discover that this is their favorite pie—chocolate marshmallow. Show lots of excitement when the big fight is on.

When the reading is over, serve alligator pie (see Alligator Snacks). Also teach the song "Alligator Pie" (see Alligator Songs).

HESTER
by Byron Barton (Greenwillow, 1975)

Story: Hester is hosting a Halloween party. But before the guests arrive, she does a little trick-or-treating herself.

Materials: alligator puppet, small witch's hat and child-size broom

Directions: Dress the alligator puppet in a witch's hat. To make a simple hat, roll a sheet of black paper into a cone, crimp the bottom of the cone, and tape or glue the base to a round piece of paper, which will serve as the brim.

Introduce Hester to the children and let them guess why she's wearing a witch's hat. Place Hester on the broom. Now she's ready for Halloween night, and the children are ready to listen to the adventures of Hester as she goes trick-or-treating. The children will enjoy joining in when Hester says, "Trick or treat."

If possible, read this story near Halloween, so the children can join Hester in costume. Label the Hester puppet "witch" and help the children make labels that describe their costumes. If wearing costumes isn't feasible, at least encourage the children to describe their Halloween experiences.

THE LADY WITH THE ALLIGATOR PURSE
adapted and illustrated by Nadine Westcott (Little, Brown, 1988)

Story: This nonsense rhyme tells how Tiny Tim, who is ailing, gets a sure cure from the lady with the alligator purse.

Materials: poster of the lady with the alligator purse, pizza

Directions: Create a poster using the opaque projector or draw the lady freehand. Color and cut out.

Sing or say the verse as you show the illustrations, and invite the children to repeat the refrain, "...with the alligator purse."

Serve pizza as a special treat following the reading.

MAMA DON'T ALLOW
by Thacher Hurd (Harper & Row, 1984)

Story: Miles receives a saxophone for his birthday. When his mama says it's too loud to be played at home, he forms a swamp band that plays at the Alligator Ball. Things go well until the alligators decide they want "swamp band soup" for dinner.

Materials: saxophone

Directions: Ask the children what noisy activities they can't do at home. Then play a few notes on the saxophone to demonstrate its loudness. (If you've never played a saxophone, it's easy to make a tooting sound. Put your top teeth on the top of the mouthpiece; rest the wooden reed on your lower lip. Blow gently at first and then with greater force.)

As you present the story, use your voice to produce the sounds of the various instruments. Sing the musical phrases. Use a deep voice when the alligators are speaking and sing "Lullaby of Swampland" in a soft voice.

When the story is done, the children can sing "Mama Don't Allow" with you.

MONTY
by James Stevenson (Greenwillow, 1979)

Story: Monty the alligator decides he's not appreciated by the rabbit, frog, and duck who ride him to school everyday. When he goes on vacation, they soon discover that it's difficult to find a replacement.

Materials: crayons, markers, paper

Directions: Talk to the children about how they get to school—walking, biking, taking a bus, whatever. Ask if any of them would like to ride an alligator.

While reading MONTY, use a deep, slow voice for Monty. Kids will love to join in when you make Monty's "gug-guggle" snore.

After reading the book, pass out the art materials. Ask the children to draw pictures of animals they would like to ride to school. Mount the pictures on construction paper. The children can then make up stories about what it would be like to ride the different animals to school. As an option, you can do this activity using pictures clipped from nature magazines.

THERE'S AN ALLIGATOR UNDER MY BED
by Mercer Mayer (Dial, 1987)

Story: A young boy discovers an alligator hiding under his bed. He devises a way to get the alligator into the garage.

Materials: alligator puppet

Directions: Before the story hour begins, place an alligator puppet under your chair. When the children arrive, ask if any of them has seen an alligator under their bed. Raise your hand as if you have had that experience. Then ask if they have ideas about getting rid of alligators that are hiding.

By this time, the children may have noticed the alligator under your chair. During the reading, keep looking under it to see if the alligator is still there.

The children can participate by sharing their ideas for alligator bait. Be sure to yell "Mom" and "Dad" loudly when the boy calls.

When, at the end, you discover that the alligator is still under your chair, tell the children they should keep thinking about ways to get him to leave.

More Alligator (and Crocodile) Stories

Aliki. **KEEP YOUR MOUTH CLOSED, DEAR** (Dial, 1966)

Charles Alligator swallows a variety of household items until he finally learns to keep his mouth closed.

Aliki. **USE YOUR HEAD, DEAR** (Greenwillow, 1983)

Charles Alligator means well, but he always gets things mixed up even though his mother and father keep telling him to use his head. When his father gives him an invisible thinking cap for his birthday, the problem is solved.

Aruego, Jose and Ariane Dewey. **A CROCODILE'S TALE** (Scribner's, 1972)

In this Philippine folk tale, a crocodile fails to show gratitude to Juan, who has just saved the creature's life. Instead, the crocodile wants to devour Juan.

Aruego, Jose and Adriane Dewey. **ROCKABYE CROCODILE** (Greenwillow, 1988)

Two boars argue over who gets to babysit the crocodile baby. They settle the dispute by deciding to take turns.

Christelow, Eileen. **JEROME THE BABYSITTER** (Clarion, 1985)

Jerome the alligator is almost overwhelmed by Mrs. Gatorman's nine frisky alligators. In the end, Jerome gets his charges under control with a trick of his own.

Christelow, Eileen. **JEROME AND THE WITCHCRAFT** (Clarion, 1988)

After Jerome boasts about his baby-sitting abilities, his friends lure him to a deserted house to baby-sit Mrs. Witchcraft's two devilish children. These turn out to be his sister Winifred and her friend Lulu.

Cloudsley-Thompson, J., il. by Joyce Bee. **CROCODILES AND ALLIGATORS** (McGraw-Hill, 1977)

This nonfiction book written in storybook form documents the activities of these remarkable reptiles.

Dahl, Roald. **THE ENORMOUS CROCODILE** (Knopf, 1978)

An extra-large crocodile plans to eat some juicy boys and girls. Happily, his nasty plan fails.

de Paola, Tomie. **BILL AND PETE** (Putnam, 1978)

Bill the crocodile becomes good friends with a toothbrush bird named Pete, who saves Bill from becoming a suitcase.

de Paola, Tomie. **BILL AND PETE GO DOWN THE NILE** (Putnam, 1987)

Bill the crocodile and his friend Pete go on a class trip to a Cairo museum where they capture a thief.

Eastman, P. D. **FLAP YOUR WINGS** (Random House, 1977)

A young boy puts an alligator egg into a bird's nest. When the alligator hatches, the birds care for him as if he was their own. But he never does learn to fly.

Engel, Diana. **JOSEPHINA HATES HER NAME** (Morrow, 1989)

An alligator named Josephina wonders why she was given such a name. She learns that she's named for her Grandma's sister who had many wonderful adventures. Josephina then decides she is very proud of her name.

Engel, Diana. **JOSEPHINA THE GREAT COLLECTOR** (Morrow, 1988)

Josephina's passion for collecting things leads to a conflict with her sister.

Gross, Ruth. **ALLIGATORS AND OTHER CROCODILIANS** (Scholastic, 1976)

This nonfiction book describes the habits and environment of crocodilians in language that young children can understand.

Hoban, Russell. **DINNER AT ALBERTA'S** (Crowell, 1975)

Arthur Crocodile has very poor manners. When he visits his sister's friend Alberta for dinner, however, he decides that good manners are worth developing in order to make the right impression.

Hodeir, Andre and Tomi Ungerer. **CLEOPATRA GOES SLEDDING** (Grove Press, 1967)

Two crocodiles wish to include Cleopatra the giant turtle in their soup.

Kundardt, Edith. **DANNY'S BIRTHDAY** (Greenwillow, 1986)

Danny the alligator celebrates his fifth birthday while his father videotapes the entire party. Danny loves viewing the tape over and over again.

Lester, Alison. **CLIVE EATS ALLIGATORS** (Houghton Mifflin, 1985)

Each of a group of children is different in the way they dress, eat, play, shop, and go to bed. But whatever Clive does relates in some way to alligators. For example, he eats a breakfast cereal called Alligator Pops.

Minarik, Else, il. by Maurice Sendak. **NO FIGHTING, NO BITING!** (Harper & Row, 1958)

In this "I Can Read Book," two human children—Rosa and Willy—are always squeezing like alligators, while two alligators—Lightfoot and Quickfoot—are always fighting and biting like human children.

Morrison, Susan. **THE ALLIGATOR** (Crestwood House, 1984)

This nonfiction book, for older children, describes the habits, behaviors, and characteristics of the alligator.

Schubert, Ingrid and Dieter. **THERE'S A CROCODILE UNDER MY BED!** (McGraw-Hill, 1981)

Peggy can't go to sleep because there's a crocodile under her bed. Her father explains that crocodiles are too big to hide there. But Peggy has a surprise for her father when he does find a crocodile under her bed—one made of an egg carton.

Sendak, Maurice. **ALLIGATORS ALL AROUND** (Harper & Row, 1962)

This alphabet book depicts alligators performing different feats for each letter.

Shaw, Evelyn. **ALLIGATOR** (Harper & Row, 1972)

This nonfiction "I Can Read Book" provides fascinating facts about alligators and how they live.

Stevenson, James. **NO NEED FOR MONTY** (Greenwillow, 1987)

The animal parents decide that Monty is too slow in carrying their children to school, so they try other methods. When these other strategies fail, the parents realize that Monty is irreplaceable.

Strauss, Barbara and Helen Friedland, il. by Tershia d'Elgin. **SEE YOU LATER, ALLIGATOR...**(Price/Stern/Sloan, 1987)

This laugh-and-learn book features funny rhymes all beginning with "See you later..."

Waber, Bernard. **THE HOUSE ON EAST 88TH STREET** (Houghton Mifflin, 1962)

This is the first in a series of books about a lovable, city-dwelling crocodile named Lyle. Other titles from the same author and publisher include:

LYLE, LYLE, CROCODILE
LYLE AND THE BIRTHDAY PARTY
LOVABLE LYLE
LYLE FINDS HIS MOTHER

West, Colin. **HAVE YOU SEEN THE CROCODILE?** (Harper & Row, 1986)

The parrot, dragonfly, bumblebee, and frog ask each other if they have seen the crocodile. The answer is always "No," but the crafty crocodile is closer than they think.

Alligator Finger Plays

THE BIG ALLIGATOR

Suit actions to the words using your alligator hand. See the Introduction to this chapter for directions. Also, refer to the alligator games section for a game using this poem.

There was a BIG alligator,
Into the swamp he did plop.
He dove to the bottom,
Then he rose to the top.

He snapped at a hunter.
He snapped at a bee.
He snapped at a frog.
And he snapped at me.

He caught the hunter.
He caught the bee.
He caught the frog.
But he didn't catch me.

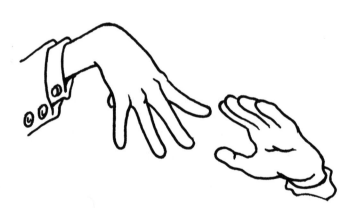

FIVE LITTLE MONKEYS

When performing the following verse, swing one hand with five fingers extended. With the other hand, make the alligator that snaps at the swinging fingers with the thumb and fingers coming together in a snapping action. Continue with four fingers extended, then three, etc., until all the monkeys are gone.

Five little monkeys
Swinging in a tree.
Five little monkeys say
"You can't get me."
Along comes Mr. Alligator
Fresh from a nap.
He's as hungry as can be
So his mouth goes snap.

Four little monkeys,
Swinging in a tree.
Four little monkeys say
"You can't get me."
Along comes Mr. Alligator
Fresh from a nap.
He's still hungry as can be
So his mouth goes snap.

Continue until there are no monkeys left. Then say, "No more monkeys swinging in a tree" to end the finger play.

More Finger Plays and Poems
"A Crocodile" and "An Alligator" p. 50 in MOVE OVER, MOTHER GOOSE by Ruth Dowell, il. by Concetta Scott (Gryphon House, 1987).

"The Alligator" p. 176, "Alligator Pie" p. 180, and "The Crocodile" p. 81 in THE RANDOM HOUSE BOOK OF POETRY FOR CHILDREN selected by Jack Prelutsky, il. by Arnold Lobel (Random House, 1983)

"The Crocodile's Toothache" p. 66 in WHERE THE SIDEWALK ENDS by Shel Silverstein (Harper & Row, 1974)

Alligator Songs

ALLIGATOR PIE

Sing the following song as an introduction to GATOR PIE by Louise Mathews, or before serving alligator pie as a snack.

Alligator Pie
by Maxine Riggers

Alligator pie, alligator pie,
I shout it once, I shout it twice.
Give me some al-li-ga-tor pie. Please.

OLD MACDONALD HAD A SWAMP

While singing the following song, put hands together to form an alligator's mouth; open and close them to make the snaps.

Old MacDonald Had a Swamp
(Tune: "Old MacDonald")

Old MacDonald had a swamp.
E-I-E-I-O.
And in the swamp he had a 'gator.
E-I-E-I-O.
With a snap, snap here,
And a snap, snap there.
Here a snap, there a snap,
Everywhere a snap, snap.
Old MacDonald had a swamp,
E-I-E-I-O.

More Alligator Songs

"The Crocodile," p. 38 in WEE SING SILLY SONGS by Pamela Conn Beall and Susan Hagen Nipp (Price/Stern/Sloan, 1983)

"Mama Don't Allow" in MAMA DON'T ALLOW by Thacher Hurd (Harper & Row, 1984)

THE LADY WITH THE ALLIGATOR PURSE (Tune: "Pretty Little Dutch Girl") adapted and il. by Nadine Westcott (Little, Brown, 1988)

"The Alligator's Song" in the book of the same title by Robert Tallon (Parents Magazine Press, 1981)

Alligator Games

ALLIGATOR HUNT

The storyteller stands in front of the children who repeat everything and follow the actions.

We're going on an alligator hunt.
Are you ready?
Ready!
Let's go.

I see a path.
   (Point finger.)
Let's walk down the path.
   (Slap hands on thighs.)
Stomp, stomp, stomp, stomp.
Stomp, stomp, stomp, stomp.

I see the rain forest.
   (Point finger.)
Let's walk through the rain forest.
   (Make arm motions as if pushing aside
   branches.)
Swish, swish, swish, swish,
Swish, swish, swish, swish.

I see a hill.
   (Point finger.)
Let's walk up the hill.
   (Move arms and legs as if climbing.)
Climb, climb, climb, climb
Climb, climb, climb, climb.

I see a puddle.
   (Point finger.)
Let's walk through the puddle.
   (Tip-toe through the water.)
Splash, splash, splash, splash.
Splash, splash, splash, splash.
I see another hunter.
   (Point finger.)
Let's run past the hunter.
   (Run in place.)
Run, run, run, run,
Run, run, run, run.

I see the swamp.
   (Point finger.)
Let's walk through the swamp.
   (Lift legs up high.)
Squish, squish, squish, squish,
Squish, squish, squish, squish.

I see the ALLIGATOR!
   (Point finger.)
Run fast!
   (Run in place.)

We made it!
   (Wipe brow.)

ALLIGATOR ROCK

Play rock and roll music while the children pretend they're alligators doing some rock and roll dancing.

THE LADY WITH THE ALLIGATOR PURSE PLAY

The storyteller reads THE LADY WITH THE ALLIGATOR PURSE while the children do the acting. If the children are willing, they can say the words. Props aren't necessary, but if you want to use them, you'll need:

    a bathtub (a large cardboard box should do)
    a telephone
    a hat
    a doctor's bag
    an alligator purse (see Alligator Crafts)
    a pizza (real or a photo from an ad)

Repeat the play as many times as necessary to make sure everyone has a chance to take a part. For an "after theater" snack, serve pizza (see Alligator Snacks).

THE BIG ALLIGATOR

This game requires space, so move outside or to the gym. If the play area doesn't have one, draw a circle large enough to contain all the children. One child, the BIG alligator, goes to the center of the circle, while the other children stay at the circumference. The children recite "The BIG Alligator" (see Alligator Finger Plays) as they walk around the circle. After the last line of the poem is recited, the child in the center races around tagging children. The children are not allowed outside the circle until they have been tagged. Continue this way until all the children have been tagged. Select another BIG alligator and play again.

Alligator Crafts

ALLIGATOR STICK PUPPET

Materials: green, red, and white construction paper; tongue depressors, glue, felt marker, puppet patterns, scissors, 10 inch pieces of yarn or string

Directions: Cut out the patterns as directed and follow the steps to create an alligator puppet that can open his mouth.

1. Glue white teeth on one side of head.

2. Glue red mouth on top of teeth.

3. Fold head in half on dotted line. Glue half of the string on one side of folded head, leaving the other half free at the top.

4. Glue tongue depressor to the other side.

5. Draw facial features onto the face pattern and glue on top of the side with the string on it.

6. Pull up on the string to make the puppet's mouth open.

ALLIGATOR BOOKMARK

Materials: green and yellow construction paper or felt, felt marker, scissors, glue

Directions: Use the pattern to cut bookmark from green paper or felt. Cut circles from the yellow material for the eyes, which are then glued into place. Draw on the other features with the felt marker.

Alligator book hooks may be purchased at children's educational supply stores or write to Creative Teaching Press (see Resources).

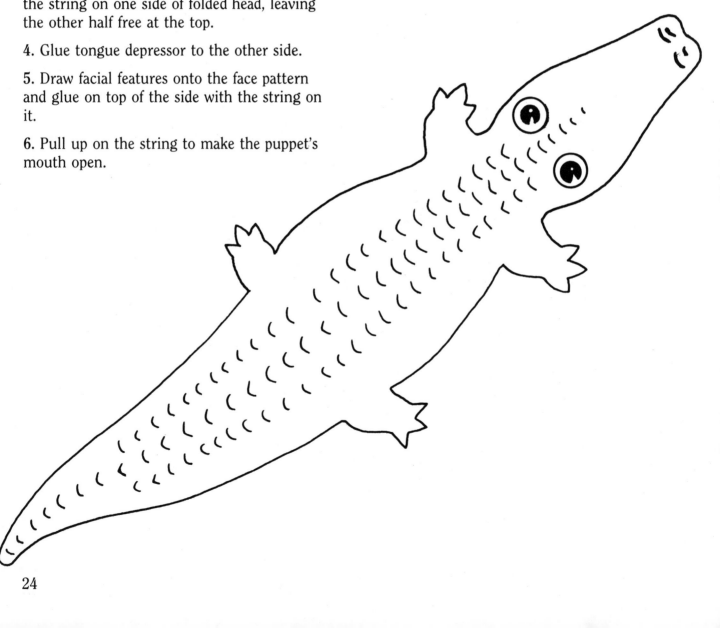

ALLIGATOR PURSES

Poster Paper Purse

Materials: poster paper, felt markers or water paint, scissors, stapler, yarn or cord

Directions: Use an opaque projector to enlarge the alligator purse from the book, or draw a pattern freehand. Color and cut out. Staple yarn or cord in place for the handle, making it long enough for the children to wear on their shoulders.

Felt Purse

Materials: one sheet 9½ x 11½ inch green felt, 7 inch piece of green ribbon, purse pattern, sewing supplies, scissors

Directions: Pin the pattern onto a double thickness of green felt. Cut out. Sew the pieces together on the sewing machine using a zig-zag stitch, leaving an opening as marked. Attach the ribbon by sliding it between the layers of felt at the ends of the opening. Stitch it in place. If you want eyes and teeth, hand stitch them with embroidery thread onto the purse, going through both thicknesses of the felt. Now your alligator purse is ready for carrying pizza (see Alligator Snacks).

ALLIGATOR HAND PUPPET

Materials: green, red, and white sturdy felt; pinking shears; scissors; 2 movable eyes; glue; sewing supplies; patterns

Directions:

1. Cut out the pattern pieces as directed on the patterns.

2. Use a zig-zag stitch to connect one of the mouths, C, to the body, A. Do not stitch across the body or you won't be able to slip your hand into the puppet.

3. Stitch the teeth, D, to the other mouth, C, using a straight stitch. The white teeth will extend beyond the mouth. On the same stitching line, sew the mouth and teeth, D and C, to the underside of the head, B.

4. Stitch the underside of head, mouth, and teeth, D, C, and B, to the body, A, along the stitching lines as indicated on the pattern.

5. Whip stitch the openings of the two red mouth pieces together.

6. Glue on movable eyes or ones made from yellow felt.

7. Place your thumb in the lower head and fingers in the top section, and your alligator is ready to talk, eat, or go on some fabulous adventure.

Alligator Stick Puppet Pattern Pieces

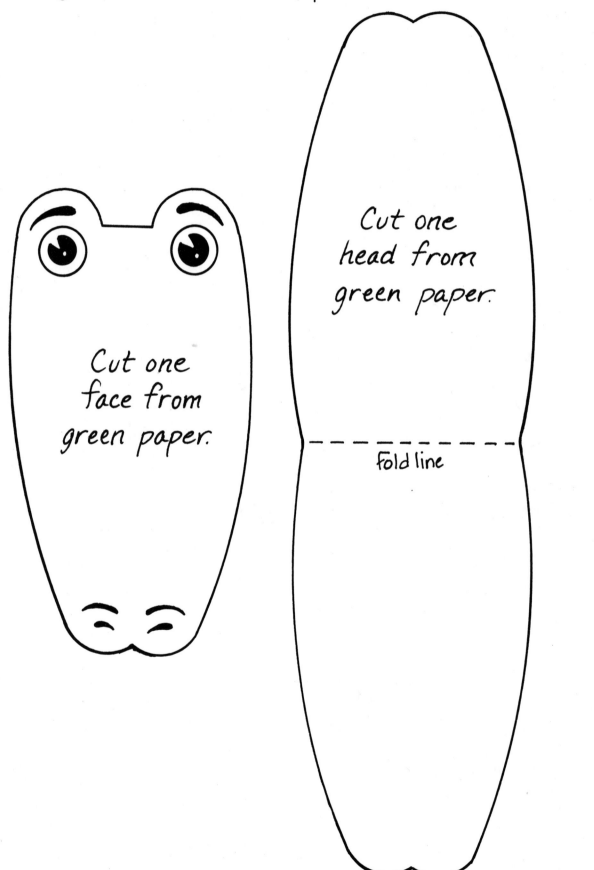

Cut one
face from
green paper.

Cut one
head from
green paper.

Fold line

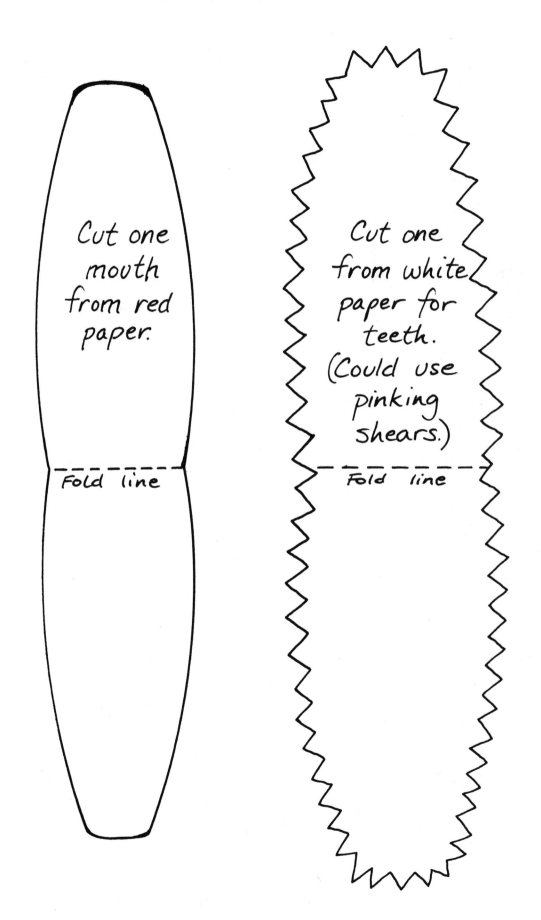

Cut one
mouth
from red
paper.

Fold line

Cut one
from white
paper for
teeth.
(Could use
pinking
shears.)

Fold line

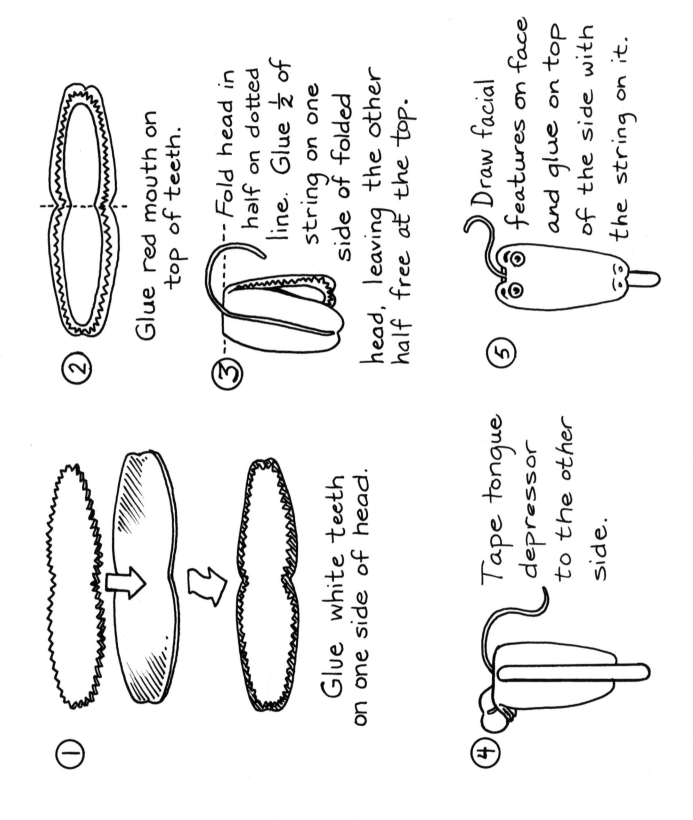

② Glue red mouth on top of teeth.

③ Fold head in half on dotted line. Glue ½ of string on one side of folded head, leaving the other half free at the top.

⑤ Draw facial features on face and glue on top of the side with the string on it.

① Glue white teeth on one side of head.

④ Tape tongue depressor to the other side.

⑥

Pull up on the string to make the puppet's mouth open.

Alligator Purse Pattern

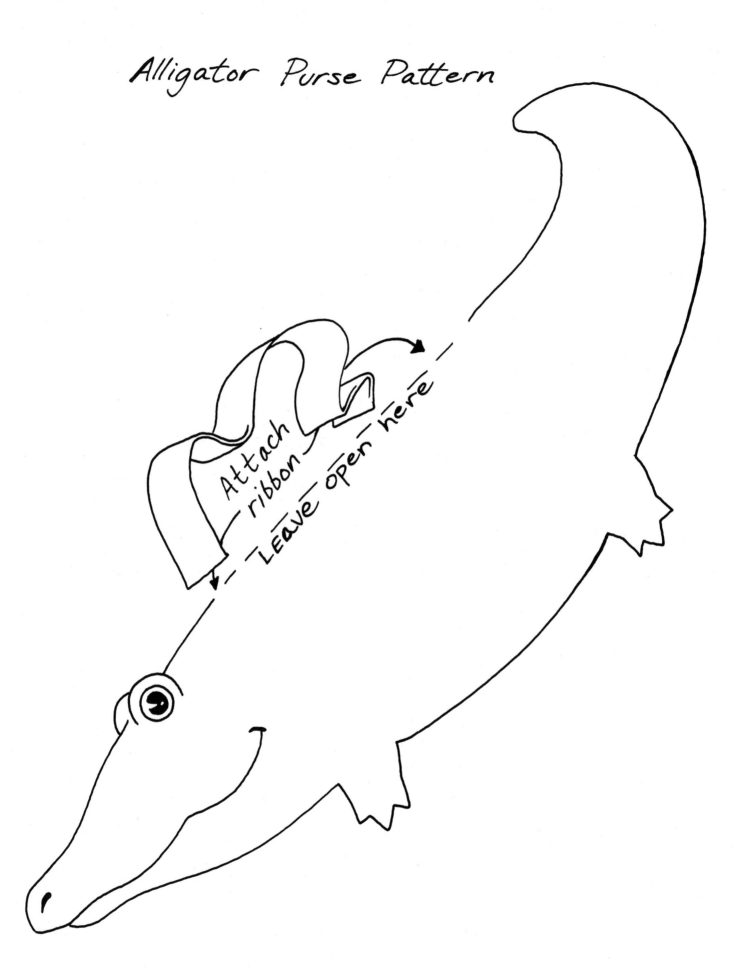

Alligator Hand Puppet

Alligator Hand Puppet

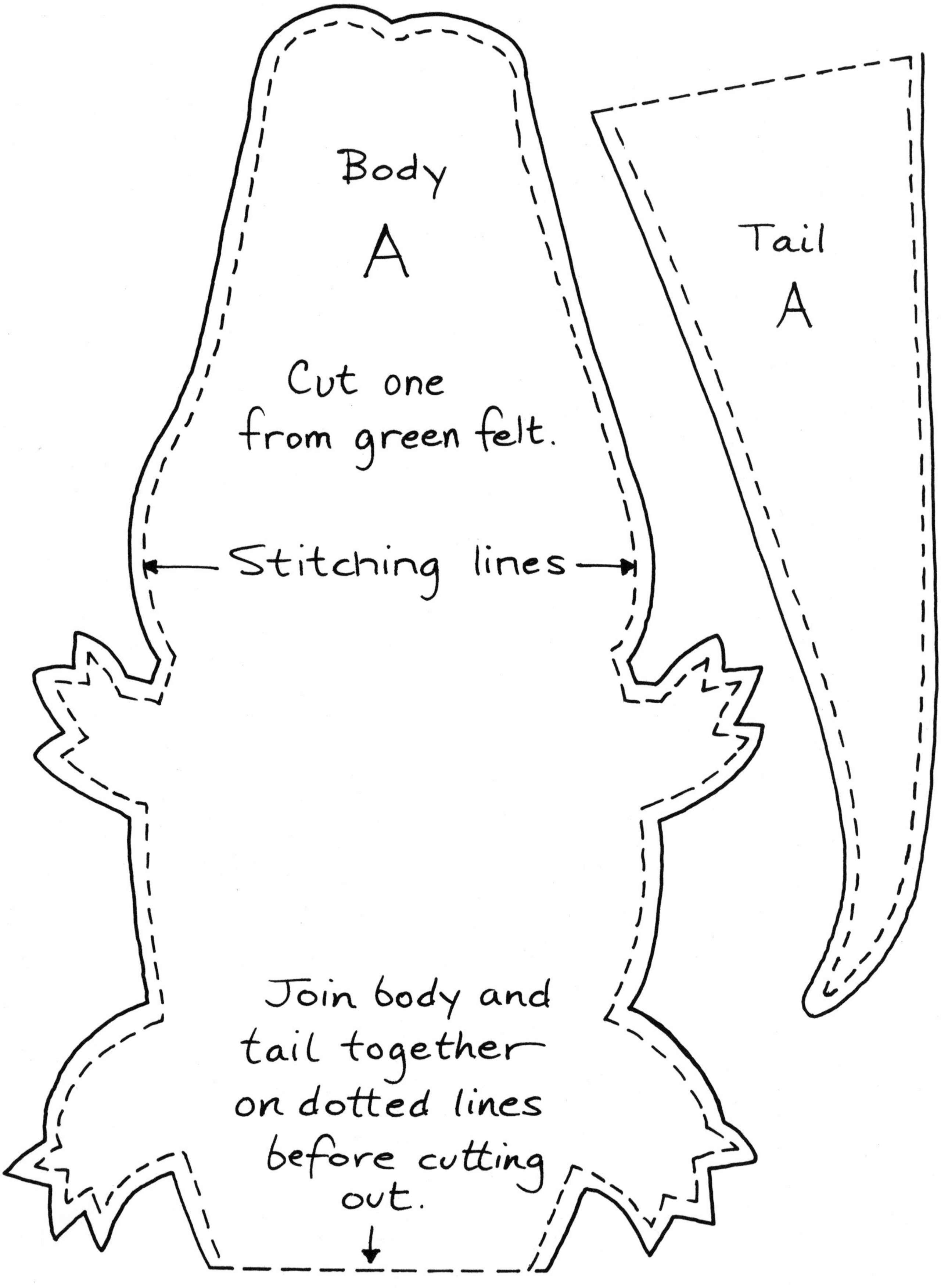

Body

A

Cut one
from green felt.

←— Stitching lines —→

Tail

A

Join body and
tail together
on dotted lines
before cutting
out.

Alligator Hand Puppet

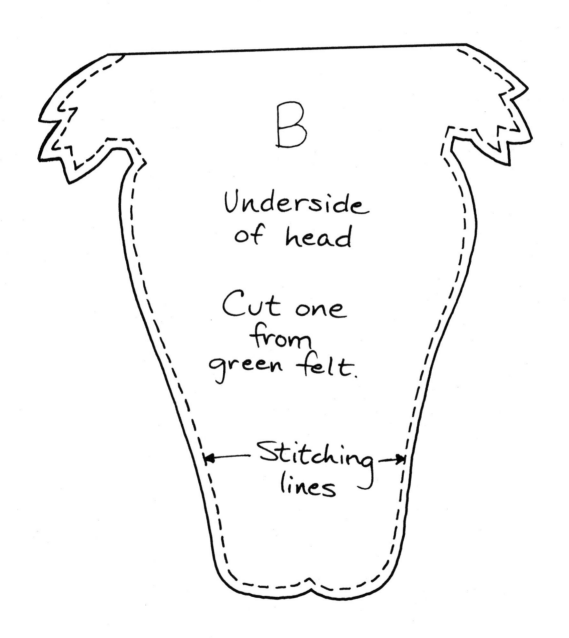

B

Underside
of head

Cut one
from
green felt.

Stitching
lines

Alligator Hand Puppet

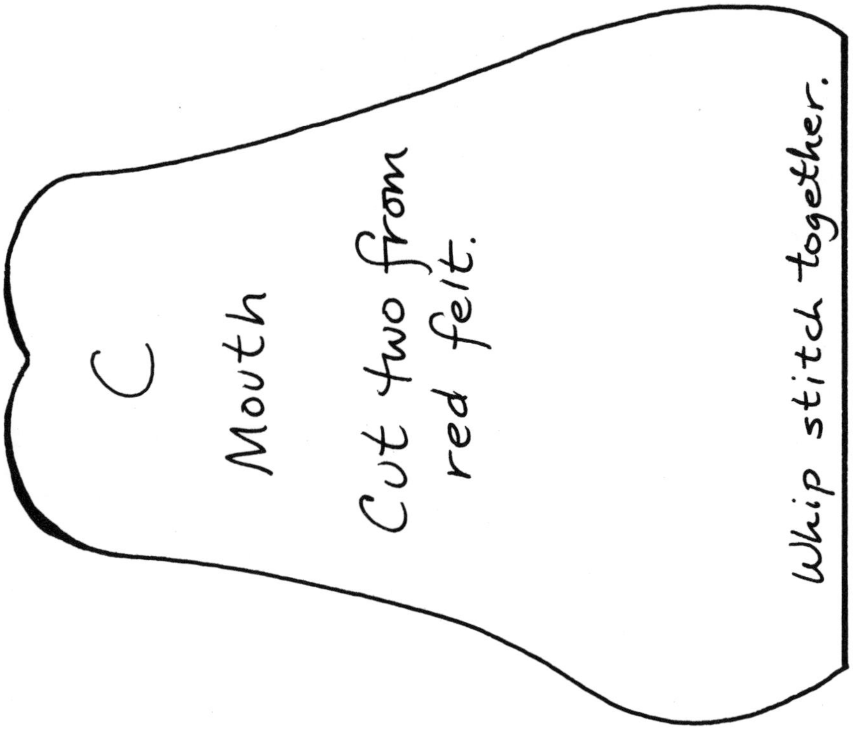

C

Mouth

Cut two from
red felt.

Whip stitch together.

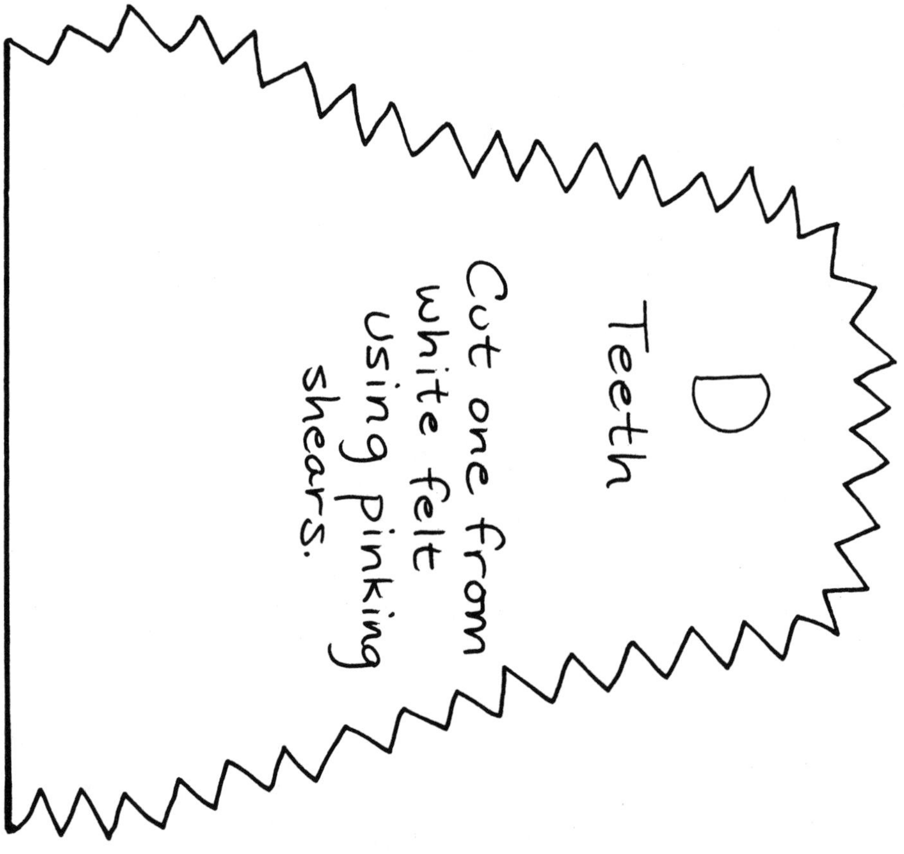

D
Teeth

Cut one from
white felt
using pinking
shears.

Alligator Snacks

ALLIGATOR PURSE PIZZA

1 pkg. flaky refrigerator biscuits
½ cup tomato sauce
1 tsp. oregano
grated mozzarella cheese
Toppings: mushrooms, pepperoni, sausage, hamburger, Canadian bacon, pineapple, peppers, olives

Preheat oven to 400 degrees. Pat each biscuit into a four inch circle and place on a lightly oiled baking sheet.

Mix the tomato sauce and oregano. Spoon some of this mixture onto each biscuit. Sprinkle with cheese and favorite topping. Bake on the middle rack for 8 minutes or until the crust is light brown. Yield: 10 individual pizzas.

ALLIGATOR PIE

3 six-oz. packages of chocolate pudding and pie filling
1 package miniature marshmallows
2 eight-oz. packages of whipped topping
3 sticks of prepared pie crust

Prepare three single pie crusts as directed on the package, or use your own favorite pie crust recipe. Bake in a 14 inch round cake pan or deep dish pizza pan. Cool. Prepare the pudding mix as directed for the pie filling. Cool. Fold the miniature marshmallows into the filling and pour into the baked pie crust. Refrigerate. Just before serving, add whipped topping. Don't forget to sing "Alligator Pie" before digging in.

ALLIGATOR COOKIES

Dough

¾ cup shortening	1½ tsp. vanilla
¾ cup butter	5 cups flour
2 cups sugar	2 tsp. baking powder
4 eggs	1½ tsp. salt

Frosting
1 package frosting mix
green food coloring
yellow candies

Mix shortening, butter, sugar, eggs, and vanilla thoroughly. Stir flour, baking powder, and salt together; blend with the shortening mixture. Chill at least two hours.

Preheat oven to 400 degrees. Roll dough about ¼ inch thick on lightly floured board. Trace the alligator pattern onto poster paper. Lay the pattern on the rolled dough and cut out using a sharp knife. Place on ungreased baking sheet. Bake 6 to 8 minutes. Cover with green frosting and use yellow candies for the eyes. Makes about 4 dozen.

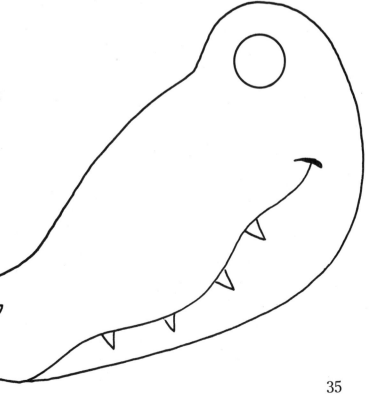

BEARABLE BEARS

Introduce bear story hours by telling the children about bears and their habits. There are brown, black, polar, and grizzly bears. Bears hibernate during the winter, and this is when the female bear gives birth, usually to two cubs. It takes two years for a cub to grow to adult size. A large bear can weigh about 1500 pounds, the same as a small car. Bears eat fish, roots, nuts, fruits, small mammals, and honey. They live in various parts of the world. Generally, bears are not ferocious, but they will attack people if provoked.

You can obtain a bear puppet—not of the teddy bear variety—from Folkmanis (see Resources). Use this puppet when giving children facts about bears, answering their questions, or telling some of the bear stories.

Some children may have seen bears in zoos or national parks. Encourage them not to be em*bear*assed when sharing their eyewitness accounts of these large, fascinating creatures.

Setting the Stage

Have a teddy bear parade. The children can make stand-up teddy bears (see Bear Crafts) and line them up on a shelf for the parade. Erect a sign saying "Teddy Bear Parade" near the bears, or have the first teddy bear carry a banner.

Find an old, tattered teddy bear at a garage sale, thrift store, or flea market. Cover his holes with patches and give him a ribbon or string necktie. Then enlarge and copy the poem "My Teddy Bear," by Margaret Hillert (found in READ-ALOUD RHYMES FOR THE VERY YOUNG selected by Jack Prelutsky). Mat the poem, rest it on a small table-top easel, and set the bear next to it. Read the poem to the children after they have seen the display.

Invite the children to bring in their teddy bears. Arrange the bears on a table or shelf with a sign that reads "Teddy Bear Land." Invite the children to tell about their bears.

Play the song "The Teddy Bears' Picnic" while the children are choosing bear stories to read or as an introduction to a bear story hour.

Bulletin Board Ideas

1. Use an opaque projector to enlarge and copy the illustration "Sharing a Good Book" onto poster paper. Color and mat it. Use this bulletin board to encourage children to read a book together.

2. Read HAPPY BIRTHDAY, MOON by Frank Asch. Draw or enlarge and color a leafless tree and a teddy bear poster similar to the illustrations in the book. Draw and cut out a black top hat and yellow moon. Pin the hat on a tree branch and the moon in the sky, as illustrated in the book. The bulletin board should be low enough so the children can move the moon while telling the story.

Sharing a "Beary" Good Book

Read-Aloud Stories

ASK MR. BEAR
by Marjorie Flack (Macmillan, 1986)

Story: Danny can't decide what to give his mother for her birthday. He asks a hen, a goose, a goat, a sheep, and a cow for advice, but none of them have good answers. Finally, he asks Mr. Bear, who tells him to give his mother a bear hug.

Materials: felt flannel board characters—hen, goose, goat, sheep, cow, boy, bear, and Danny's mother

Directions: Make the characters from the story into flannel board characters (see Bear Crafts). Move the characters on and off the flannel board as you tell the story. The children will enjoy giving some bear hugs as you come to the end of the story.

Encourage the children to use the flannel board characters themselves to retell the story. Two or more children can tell the story together. The children will also enjoy dramatizing this story. Refer to Bear Dramatic Play for tips.

BEADY BEAR
by Don Freeman (Viking, 1984)

Story: Beady Bear is a wind-up toy bear who decides he should live in a cave like real bears do. Beady Bear has a difficult time making the cave comfortable. Finally, his friend Thayer, a young boy, brings Beady Bear back home.

Materials: wind-up bear (or stuffed bear that you pretend to wind), pillow, flashlight, newspaper, blanket

Directions: It works well to tell this story in the first person as if you were Beady Bear. Use your own words and elaborate as much as you like. Begin the story by saying "I'm Beady Bear, a wind-up toy bear, and I belong to a nice boy named Thayer."

After reading the story once, use the bear, pillow, flashlight, newspaper, and blanket to retell the story. Invite the children to assist you. Leave the materials in the room and encourage the children to tell the story on their own.

THE BEAR'S TOOTHACHE
by David McPhail (Little, Brown, 1972)

Story: A bear with a toothache is sitting outside a young boy's bedroom. The boy invites him in and tries to help him pull the aching tooth. After much effort, the boy succeeds. As a reward, the bear gives the boy the pulled tooth.

Materials: "bear's tooth" made from clay (see Bear Crafts)

Directions: As you read this very funny story, feel free to elaborate on the text. For instance, instead of saying the bear chewed on "anything else he could find," you might say that "he ate a baloney sandwich, a chocolate pie, a bowl of strawberries, a bowl of potato salad, and five fried fish." (Actually, the bear is more interested in eating than in loosening his tooth.)

Practice the bear's painful cry to make the toothache seem real. The children will like to join you, of course, in making the anguished noise.

After reading the story, make a "bear's tooth" with the children.

BERTIE AND THE BEAR
by Pamela Allen (Coward-McCann, 1984)

Story: A bear chases Bertie. A queen, a king, an admiral, a captain, a general, a sergeant, and a dog then chase the bear. They each make a sound or play a musical instrument, and all together they make an incredible noise during a hilarious chase.

Materials: five simple musical instruments (see Bear Dramatic Play)

Directions: This is a great participation story. If you cue them, the children can make the sounds of the queen, the musical instruments, and the barking dog as they occur in the story. Or, use various musical instruments which different children can play during the chase. Because of the noise, you may wish to tell this story outside or at a time when other people won't be disturbed.

When reading about the bear, use plenty of facial expressions and body gestures. The children will probably like to act the bear's part, too.

After finishing the book, consider dramatizing the story. This may involve imitating the bear's poses. Using musical instruments can add to the fun.

CORDUROY
by Don Freeman (Viking, 1968)

Story: Corduroy is a toy bear who lives in the toy department of a big store. He searches in vain for a button missing from his green overalls. Then a little girl purchases Corduroy, sews a button on his overalls, and gives him a loving home.

Materials: teddy bear, overalls, button, needle and thread

Directions: Corduroy may be purchased from school supply outlets or from Trudy Toy Company (see Resources). Or create your own Corduroy by making a pair of green corduroy overalls for any teddy bear. Simply trace the outline of your bear onto paper to make a pattern for the overalls. Make the pattern ¼ inch larger for the seam allowance. Cut out and sew together. Attach straps and just one button.

Before the story hour begins, hide Corduroy's button somewhere in the room. After reading the story, introduce Corduroy to the children and explain that Corduroy has lost a button. Give the children clues to help them find the button, and after they find it, sew it on. Hug Corduroy and suggest the children also hug him, to make him feel welcome.

COUNTRY BEAR'S GOOD NEIGHBOR
by Larry Brimner, il. by Ruth Tietjen Councell (Orchard Books, 1988)

Story: Country Bear borrows apples, sugar, an egg, walnuts, cinnamon, and butter from his good neighbor. He later returns with a delicious apple cake to share with his friend.

Materials: large bowl, four apples, sugar, an egg, walnuts, cinnamon, butter, and other items called for in the recipe in the book

Directions: If you have access to an oven, bring the cake ingredients to story hour. Before reading the story, give the cake ingredients Country Bear borrows to different children. As you read the story, have the children put the ingredients in the large bowl as Country Bear borrows them. Then make the good neighbor cake. Put a blanket on the floor to eat the cake picnic style.

If you don't have an oven handy, prepare the cake ahead of time. The children could then help you frost it.

Later, provide play food and dishes for the children to "bake" with. Make chef hats for the children to wear (see Bear Crafts).

GOLDILOCKS AND THE THREE BEARS
retold by James Marshall (Dial, 1988)

Story: In this updated version, Goldilocks visits the bears' Victorian home while the bears are out riding bicycles. She creates pandemonium with the porridge, chairs, and beds, before escaping out a window when the bears return.

Materials: Goldilocks and Three Bears body puppets (see Bear Crafts)

Directions: Since most of the children will be familiar with the plot, you might pretend to forget parts or mix up the order, and invite the children to straighten you out. Also, encourage them to elaborate by inventing details, such as what Goldilocks is wearing, what the bears' house looks like, or what the bears see while bicycling.

Later, dramatize the story using tips in Bear Dramatic Play.

PEACE AT LAST
by Jill Murphy (Dial, 1980)

Story: Mr. Bear is tired, but he can't sleep because Mrs. Bear is snoring. He tries sleeping in Baby Bear's room, the living room, the kitchen, the garden, and the car, but all these places are too noisy. When Mr. Bear finally falls asleep, the alarm clock rings.

Materials: blanket, pillow, teddy bear dressed in pajamas

Directions: Dress a teddy bear in pajamas, preferably a green-striped outfit like the one worn by Mr. Bear. Use baby or doll clothes or make a pair. Introduce Mr. Bear to the children and let them hold him if they want to. Explain that Mr. Bear is tired and wants to go to bed. Make a bed for him with a pillow and blanket. Read the story. Invite participation by having the children make the various sounds as you move through the story. Children also delight in reading the phrase, "I can't stand this."

If you're a beginner at storytelling, this story is a good place to start. It's simple and the children love it. You'll be a great success.

A POCKET FOR CORDUROY
by Don Freeman (Viking, 1978)

Story: When Corduroy is visiting the laundromat, he hears Liza and her mother talking about pockets. Corduroy wants a pocket of his own, and while searching for one he's locked in the laundromat overnight. When Liza finds him, she makes a purple pocket for him, and gives him a name card to put in it.

Materials: name cards, purple fabric, safety pins, teddy bear, needle and thread

Directions: Dress a brown teddy bear in green overalls to look like Corduroy. Carry Corduroy in your arms and explain that you're going to the laundromat. Set Corduroy in a chair and ask him to be good while you do the laundry. Read the story. Use a soft loving voice for Corduroy's dialogue to depict his character. Make a purple pocket for Corduroy and sew by hand to his overalls while the children watch. Make a card with Corduroy's name on it for him to slide into his pocket.

Make enough purple pockets for all the children. Attach them with three safety pins and give each child a card with his name on it. Older children can make their own cards.

THE TEDDY BEARS' PICNIC
by Jimmy Kennedy, il. by Alexander Day
(Green Tiger Press, 1983)

Story: The teddy bears are having a picnic in the woods. They wear delightful disguises, play games, and have lots of marvelous things to eat. When all the activities wear them out, they go home to bed.

Materials: teddy bears, masks, costumes, recording accompanying the book (optional)

Directions: A recording is packaged with this book. Play the music as the children arrive for story hour. Explain that the song was made into a picture book.

Of course, you'll want to have a teddy bear picnic. Ahead of time, ask the children to bring their bears to the story hour. Bring a few extra bears for children who might not have one. Make costumes from old doll or baby clothes. Cut masks out of paper. Reserve a spot in the room for the picnic. Put up a sign saying "Teddy Bears' Picnic." Encourage the children to play with the bears as if they were on a picnic.

More Bear Stories

Alborough, Jez. BARE BEAR (Knopf, 1984)

A polar bear wears polar clothes, of course. And when the bear removes his boots, mittens, mask, and polar suit, he's wearing pale blue polar underwear.

Alexander, Martha. BLACKBOARD BEAR (Dial, 1969)

The big boys won't let a little boy play with them because of his size. However, when the big boys learn that the little boy is friends with a big, furry bear, they change their minds. Other stories about Blackboard Bear include:
> WE'RE IN BIG TROUBLE, BLACKBOARD BEAR
> AND MY MEAN OLD MOTHER WILL BE SORRY, BLACKBOARD BEAR
> I SURE AM GLAD TO SEE YOU, BLACKBOARD BEAR.

Appiah, Sonia, il. by Carol Easmon. AMOKO AND EFUA BEAR (Macmillan, 1988)

Amoko takes her teddy bear, Efua, with her everywhere. Efua is Amoko's best friend. However, when Amoko gets a new drum, she temporarily forgets about her bear until Amoko's father helps reunite the two.

Asch, Frank. BEAR'S BARGAIN (Prentice-Hall, 1985)

Bear longs to be able to fly just like Little Bird. Meanwhile, Little Bird wishes to be big like Bear. Thanks to their friendship and ingenuity, they help each other make their wishes come true.

Asch, Frank. BREAD AND HONEY (Parents Magazine Press, 1981)

One day at school Ben paints a picture of his mother, but on the way home an owl, a rabbit, an alligator, an elephant, a lion, and a giraffe help Ben change the picture to look like each one of them. Ben's mother likes the picture the way it is, and gives him bread and honey.

Asch, Frank. POPCORN (Parents Magazine Press, 1979)

On Halloween night, when Sam Bear's parents are out, he invites his friends to an impromptu party. Soon, there is a house full of popcorn. When Sam's parents return, they bring a special treat for him—popcorn. Other bear stories by Asch include:
> HAPPY BIRTHDAY MOON
> BEAR SHOW
> SAND CAKE
> MOONCAKE
> MOONGAME
> SKYFIRE

Banks, Kate, il. by Peter Sis. ALPHABET SOUP (Knopf, 1988)

When a boy objects to eating his alphabet soup, his mother tells him he is acting like a grouchy bear. The boy spells "bear" with the letters in his soup and a bear appears in the kitchen. Together, the two of them have some marvelous adventures as they spell other words which make the objects appear. Finally the hungry bear eats the alphabet soup.

Blocksma, Mary, il. by Sandra Cox Kalthoff. THE BEST DRESSED BEAR (Childrens Press, 1984)

A bear wishes to be the best-dressed bear at a dance. The fox, the kangaroo, the goat, and the cat help him choose the right clothes to make his wish come true.

Browne, Anthony. BEAR HUNT (Atheneum, 1980)

While in the forest, two hunters find Bear, but Bear knows how to escape from them. He's very clever as he uses his trusty pencil to draw his surprising escapes.

Browne, Anthony. **THE LITTLE BEAR BOOK** (Doubleday, 1989)

Bear goes for a walk in the woods where he meets Gorilla, Crocodile, Lion, and Elephant. Bear uses his fat magical pencil to draw what each of the four wants, and then Bear draws an opening through which he exits.

Bucknall, Caroline. **ONE BEAR ALL ALONE** (Dial, 1985)

This one-to-ten counting rhyme relates the adventurous activities of the bears during a busy day.

Carlstrom, Nancy, il. by Bruce Degen. **JESSE BEAR, WHAT WILL YOU WEAR?** (Macmillan, 1986)

This rhyming story describes what Jesse Bear wears at breakfast, at play, for lunch, at bath time, and at night. Another delightful Carlstrom book is:

    BETTER NOT GET WET, JESSE BEAR

Chambless, Jane. **TUCKER AND THE BEAR** (Simon & Schuster, 1989)

Tucker is a small boy who lives all alone in the forest. One day a bear comes and offers to help Tucker with his work if the bear can spend the winter with the boy. The situation doesn't work out very well, and when the first snow comes, the bear leaves. However, he returns in the spring and the two become good friends.

Freeman, Don. **BEARYMORE** (Viking, 1976)

In this book by the creator of Corduroy, Bearymore has trouble trying to hibernate because he worries about a new circus act.

Gackenbach, Dick. **HOUND AND BEAR** (Seabury, 1976)

Hound is always playing practical jokes on Bear, such as painting his window black so that Bear will think it's night when it's really morning. Hound finally decides it's better to be friends, and he gives Bear a special gift—a beautiful hat.

Gage, Wilson. **CULLY CULLY AND THE BEAR** (Greenwillow, 1983)

Cully Cully goes hunting for a bear to make a bear rug. When he finds a bear, he chases it. But then the bear chases Cully Cully. Around and around a tree they both go in an hilarious adventure.

Gordon, Margaret. **WILBURFORCE GOES ON A PICNIC** (Morrow, 1982)

One day Wilburforce goes on a picnic with his family. He plays in the pond and enjoys his picnic lunch. Then the wind and rain come and everyone hurries home.

Graham, Thomas. **MR. BEAR'S CHAIR** (Dutton, 1987)

When Mrs. Bear's chair breaks, Mr. Bear goes to the woods to chop a tree into wood to make her a new chair. She is very pleased, but as they sit down to dinner, Mr. Bear's chair breaks, and now he will have to make a new chair for himself.

Gretz, Susanna, il. by Alison Sage. **TEDDY BEARS CURE A COLD** (Four Winds Press, 1984)

William Teddy Bear says he is sick. The other teddy bears take his temperature, make his bed, bring him flowers, and serve him a chocolate pie. Finally, when William asks for a milkshake and chips, the other teddy bears realize he's really not sick any longer. Other teddy bear stories by Susanna Gretz include:

    TEDDY BEARS' MOVING DAY
    TEDDY BEARS GO SHOPPING
    TEDDY BEARS AT THE SEASIDE

Hague, Kathleen, il. by Michael Hague. **ALPHABEARS: AN ABC BOOK** (Holt, 1984)

Each letter of the alphabet introduces a teddy bear, telling—in rhyme—what he or she enjoys doing.

Hague, Kathleen, il. by Michael Hague. **NUMBEARS** (Holt, 1986)

A group of teddy bears introduce the first twelve numbers in a rhyme about their zany bear activities.

Hale, Irina. BROWN BEAR IN A BROWN CHAIR (Atheneum, 1983)

Because Brown Bear lives in a brown chair, no one notices him and he's always sat upon. Brown Bear asks for a pair of trousers, a shirt, shoes, a hat, and a yellow ribbon so that he'll be noticed. The clothes prove too uncomfortable, but his good friend Maggie offers a solution: she picks him up and holds him.

Hissey, Jane. LITTLE BEAR'S TROUSERS (Philomel Books, 1987)

Little Bear searches for his lost trousers. When he finds them, he discovers that the camel, the sailor, the dog, the rabbit, the zebra, the duck, and another bear have all found another use for his pants.

Hofmann, Ginnie. THE RUNAWAY TEDDY BEAR (Random House, 1986)

Tired of being just a toy bear, Andy's teddy bear runs away. But things aren't so great living with real bears, and after Arthur falls into the river, Andy rescues him.

Hofmann, Ginnie. WHO WANTS AN OLD TEDDY BEAR? (Random House, 1978)

Andy rejects the teddy bear which his grandmother sent him. In the night, Andy dreams about teddy bears. The dream teaches Andy to love the bear after all.

Isenberg, Barbara and Marjorie Jaffe, il. by Diane de Groat. ALBERT THE RUNNING BEAR'S EXERCISE BOOK (Clarion, 1984)

Albert Bear meets Violet Bear, and together they learn to do exercises that make them feel good and have healthier bodies.

Jackson, Ellen, il. by Margot Apple. THE BEAR IN THE BATHTUB (Addison-Wesley, 1981)

Andrew does not like to take baths. When his mother insists, he reluctantly goes to the tub. There, he's surprised to find a bear in the bath. At first, no one can get the bear to leave. Finally, Andrew gives the bear a bath, and the bear gives Andrew a bear hug before going away. Now Andrew decides he likes baths.

Jensen, Helen. WHEN PANDA CAME TO OUR HOUSE (Dial, 1985)

A large, lovable panda comes from China to visit an American girl. The panda teaches the girl about China and they play and sing together. They will remember each other forever because they have become best friends.

Jeschke, Susan. ANGELA BEAR (Holt, 1979)

After Angela buys magic crayons and draws a bear, the bear steps out of the picture. Angela and the bear become best friends until the bear falls in love with another bear at the zoo.

Kantrowitz, Mildred, il. by Nancy Parker. WILLY BEAR (Parents Magazine Press, 1976)

A young boy is uneasy about his first day at school. The boy expresses his feelings to Willy, his teddy bear. The boy decides to be brave, and so does Willy.

Kelley, True. BUGGLY BEAR'S HICCUP CURE (Parents Magazine Press, 1982)

Buggly Bear wakes up from his winter nap with the hiccups. His friend Forrest Moose tries many cures for Buggly's hiccups. Unfortunately, Forrest gets the hiccups himself after he cures Buggly.

Maris, Ron. ARE YOU THERE, BEAR? (Puffin, 1984)

In a dark bedroom, several toys search for a toy bear by calling out, "Are you there, Bear?" Bear is found using a flashlight to read a book and all the other toys in the room want Bear to read them a story. Another good book by the same author is:
HOLD TIGHT, BEAR.

McCloskey, Robert. BLUEBERRIES FOR SAL (Viking, 1966)

Sal and her mother go to blueberry hill to pick berries. The berries go "kuplink" as they land in the pail. Shortly, the mother and daughter meet a mother bear and her cub. The encounter is friendly, and each pair is able to get all the blueberries they want.

McKee, David. **I HATE MY TEDDY BEAR** (Clarion, 1982)

Though John and Brenda say they do not like their teddy bears, both brag that they have the better bear. Meanwhile, the two bears confide in each other about what they can and cannot do. In the end, the two children show that they really do love their bears.

McLeod, Emilie, il. by David McPhail. **THE BEAR'S BICYCLE** (Little, Brown, 1975)

A boy and his bear have some exciting encounters as they travel around town on their bicycles.

McPhail, David. **THE DREAM CHILD** (Dutton, 1985)

The Dream Child and Tame Bear experience magical adventures as they sail along in a winged boat.

Minarik, Else, il. by Maurice Sendak. **LITTLE BEAR** (Harper & Row, 1957)

This picture book contains four short adventures about Little Bear— "What Will Little Bear Wear?" "Birthday Soup," "Little Bear Goes to the Moon," and "Little Bear's Wish."

Muntean, Michaela, il. by Doug Cushman. **BICYCLE BEAR** (Parents Magazine Press, 1983)

Bicycle Bear has had great success delivering little and big items. Now, however, he has a whale to deliver, and it won't be easy.

Murphy, Jill. **WHAT NEXT, BABY BEAR?** (Dial, 1984)

Baby Bear takes an imaginary trip to the moon in his cardboard box rocket. After being joined by an owl, Baby Bear survives stormy weather and enjoys a lunar picnic. Baby Bear finally returns home, happy and satisfied with his fantastic adventure.

Patz, Nancy. **SARAH BEAR AND SWEET SIDNEY** (Four Winds Press, 1989)

Sweet Sidney and Sarah Bear are an affectionate elderly bear couple. Sweet Sidney tries his best to convince Sarah Bear that spring has come and it's time to wake up.

Rosen, Michael, il. by Helen Oxenbury. **WE'RE GOING ON A BEAR HUNT** (Macmillan, 1989)

This recent retelling of the old camp favorite features a man, four children, and a dog who all look for the bear. When they find the bear, they retrace their steps and end up in bed under the covers.

Sivulich, Sandra, il. by Glen Rounds. **I'M GOING ON A BEAR HUNT** (Dutton, 1973)

In this version of the above tale, the reader participates with a boy who's going on a bear hunt. The pretend actions include walking through tall grass, crossing a bridge, meeting the bear, and then retreating, with the actions quickly done in reverse order.

Stoddard, Sandol, il. by Lynn Munsinger. **BEDTIME FOR BEAR** (Houghton Mifflin, 1985)

Small Bear thinks of various excuses to avoid going to bed. When Big Bear becomes exasperated, she decides to rock Small Bear. However, it's Big Bear who falls asleep first.

Waber, Bernard. **IRA SLEEPS OVER** (Houghton Mifflin, 1972)

Ira, a young boy, is invited to spend the night with his friend Reggie. Ira wants to bring his teddy bear with him but is afraid Reggie will laugh. All ends well when each boy discovers that the other sleeps with a teddy.

Wahl, Jan, il. by William Joyce. **HUMPHREY'S BEAR** (Holt, 1987)

One night Humphrey's toy bear grows to human size and wakes Humphrey. Together the boy and the bear set off in a magical sailboat for some extraordinary adventures.

Weinberg, Lawrence, il. by Paula Winter. **THE FORGETFUL BEARS** (CLARION, 1981)

The Forgetful Bears plan a picnic, but forget the food. Later, they remember that they forgot to get Grandpa. They want to go back, but they forget where their house is. This hilarious adventure continues until they finally have a picnic they will never forget.

Winter, Paula. **THE BEAR & THE FLY** (Crown, 1976)

In this wordless picture book, three bears are smugly enjoying their dinner when a fly intrudes. Trying to swat the fly, Father hits each family member. After the room is totally wrecked, the fly leaves through the very window that he entered in the first place.

Wood, A. J., il. by Chris Forsey. **THERE'S A BEAR IN MY BED** (Modern Publishing, 1987)

When Ben goes to bed one night, he finds a big, furry bear sleeping in his bed. The bear is very friendly and they tell each other stories until the bear must continue his journey to the North Pole.

Worthington, Phoebe and Selby Worthington. **TEDDY BEAR POSTMAN** (Puffin, 1981)

Teddy Bear Postman delivers letters and parcels to people on Christmas Eve. Everyone is happy to see Teddy Bear Postman as he brings Christmas cheer. Other teddy bear books by the same authors include:

TEDDY BEAR BAKER
TEDDY BEAR COALMAN
TEDDY BEAR GARDENER

Bear Songs and Poems

THE DANCING BEAR

Fill in the name of a child in your room or any other name that you think the children will like. During the singing, perform the various actions.

_____, the Dancing Bear
(Tune: "Bingo")

There was a bear
Who loved to dance
And _____ was his name.
Left foot, tap, tap, tap.
Right foot, tap, tap, tap.
Both paws, clap, clap, clap.
And _____ was his name.

There was a bear
Who loved to dance
And _____ was his name.
Turn, turn, all around,
Bend and touch, touch the ground.
Jump, jump, up and down,
And _____ was his name.

FUZZY WUZZY

Fuzzy Wuzzy was a bear;
Fuzzy Wuzzy had no hair
So Fuzzy Wuzzy wasn't fuzzy. Was he?
—Anonymous

ALGY MET A BEAR

Algy met a bear,
A bear met Algy.
The bear was bulgy,
The bulge was Algy.
—Anonymous

More Bear Songs

"The Bear Went Over the Mountain" p. 12 in EYE WINKER TOM TINKER CHIN CHOPPER by Tom Glazer (Doubleday, 1973)

While you're singing this song, walk in place and put your hand on your forehead as if you're looking for something. On the second verse, turn in the other direction and keep on looking.

More Bear Poems

"Bear in There" p. 47 in A LIGHT IN THE ATTIC by Shel Silverstein (Harper & Row, 1981)

"Grandma Bear" p. 36 in RIDE A PURPLE PELICAN by Jack Prelutsky, il. by Garth Williams (Greenwillow, 1986)

"My Teddy Bear" p. 53 in READ-ALOUD RHYMES FOR THE VERY YOUNG selected by Jack Prelutsky, il. by Marc Brown (Knopf, 1986)

"Wild Beasts" p. 19 and "Furry Bears" p. 13 in POEMS TO READ TO THE VERY YOUNG selected by Josette Frank, il. by Eloise Wilkin (Random House, 1982)

"Polar Bear" p. 60 in THE RANDOM HOUSE BOOK OF POETRY FOR CHILDREN selected by Jack Prelutsky, il. by Arnold Lobel (Random House, 1983)

Bear Poem Books

BEAR HUGS by Kathleen Hague, il. by Michael Hague (Holt, 1989)

BEAR IN MIND, poems selected by Bobbye S. Goldstein, il. by William Pene du Bois (Viking, 1989)

THE TEDDY BEAR BOOK by Jean Marzollo, il. by Ann Schweninger (Dial, 1989)

Bear Finger Plays and Action Verse

TEDDY BEAR, TEDDY BEAR

Teddy bear, teddy bear,
    (Tip back and forth at waist, arms
    out like a teddy bear.)

Go upstairs.
    (Climb.)

Teddy bear, teddy bear,
    (Tip back and forth.)

Say your prayers.
    (Fold hands in prayer position.)

Teddy bear, teddy bear,
    (Tip back and forth.)

Turn out the light.
    (Pull an imaginary string.)

Teddy bear, Teddy bear,
    (Tip back and forth.)

Say good night.
    (Lie down . . . shhh.)

A BEAR EATS HONEY

A bear eats honey,
    (Eat.)

And it goes to his tummy.
    (Rub stomach.)

He thinks it's quite yummy.
    (Smile contentedly.)

But the bees don't think it's funny,
    (Wiggle fingers wildly around.)
Bzzzzzz.

FIVE LITTLE BEARS

In the following finger play extend a finger each time a bear is mentioned, or use the bear glove (see Bear Crafts). The fingers of the other hand are the bees who scare away the bears.

There was a little bear whose name was Sue.
Another came to see her, and that made two.
Two little bears quickly climbed a tree.
To find another, and then there were three.
Three little bears were fishing from the shore,
Where they met another, and that made four.
Four little bears found a busy beehive.
Another joined in, and then there were five.
Five little bears ate honey in the sun.
Out came the bees—bzzzzzzzzz
And then there were none.

A BEAR IN A CAVE

Read "A Bear in a Cave" (below) while the children imitate the bear's actions. This activity gives children a chance to stretch between stories. Note: If there's too much action for your room—e.g., the somersault—modify the reading.

A bear crawls out of a cave.
He stands up and stretches and yawns.
He looks in every direction and turns around.
He lumbers off to the river where he catches
    a fish with his paw.
He eats the fish in one gulp.
He turns a somersault and stands up to
    stretch.
Then he crawls back into his cave for another
    nap.

More Finger Plays and Action Verse
"Let's Go On a Bear Hunt" p. 52 and "Honey Bear" p. 42 in RING A RING O' ROSES (Flint Public Library, 1988)

"Amanda is a Panda Bear" p. 36 and "Pierre the Bear" p. 47 in MOVE OVER MOTHER GOOSE! by Ruth Dowell, il. by Concetta Scott (Gryphon House, 1987)

Bear Games

THE TEDDY BEARS' PICNIC

After reading THE TEDDY BEARS' PICNIC, play the games the bears play while on their picnic—basketball, baseball, hide and seek, and sack races. Play "The Teddy Bears' Picnic" record and let the children move to the music. The words suggest interesting actions, and the children will love the catchy tune.

WHERE'S THE BUTTON?

After reading CORDUROY, send all of the children save one out of the room. The remaining child hides several buttons in the room. The other children then come back and look for the buttons. The first child to find a button hollers "Button, button, I've found the button!"

BEAR HUG TAG

Choose a designated area where the children can run. It's best to play outdoors or in a gymnasium. The children pretend they are bears. Depending on the size of the group, choose one or two children to be "it." They chase the other children who try not to get tagged. The children are safe and cannot be tagged if they are giving another child a bear hug. The bear hug may last only to the count of three, and then the "bears" must find other bears to hug. A child who is tagged becomes "it."

ALBERT'S EXERCISES

Exercise along with Albert as you read THE ADVENTURES OF ALBERT, THE RUNNING BEAR. This book is full of exercises, so you have plenty of choices. Pretend you're a bear doing the exercises and wear a headband like the one Albert's friend Violet wears. Simple headbands can be made by sewing strips of stretchable terry cloth together.

BEAR POSES

Pretend to be the bear in BERTIE AND THE BEAR. Play recorded classical music and follow the storyteller as she imitates the bear's poses. Give the children an opportunity to create their own poses. This exercise develops a sense of balance and an appreciation of one's own body. Photocopy and display the pages showing the bear's poses for the children to imitate.

Bear Dramatic Play

GOLDILOCKS AND THE THREE BEARS

The storyteller presents the story while small groups of children perform the actions and the dialogue. Follow the directions in Bear Crafts to make body puppets for the characters. The activity will be more fun if you provide a few props: the three bowls, a table, three chairs (of different sizes), and three blankets to suggest the three beds.

ASK MR. BEAR

You will need eight actors: six for the animals plus one each for the boy and his mother. The mother and boy are in a house, which can be a designated spot in the room. The bear is in the forest—you might draw a paper tree—and the other animals stand in a pathway which can be marked by strings or yarn. As the storyteller narrates the story, the children dramatize the actions.

BERTIE AND THE BEAR

Nine children are needed to present this story. Ahead of time outline the path the characters will follow during the chase. The storyteller introduces each character who makes the appropriate sound. If possible, provide simple costumes and musical instruments: a toy drum, rhythm band instruments, a harmonica, blocks, even spoons for clanging.

Bear Crafts

STAND-UP TEDDY BEAR

Materials: brown construction paper, scraps of different colored construction paper, felt marker, glue, scissors, patterns (see below)

Directions: Cut the head from brown construction paper. Double another piece of brown construction paper and cut the body. (Use white or black paper to make polar or black bears.) Cut the paws, ears, eyes, and nose from scraps of colored paper. Draw the mouth with a felt marker. Glue the head to the body and the bear is ready to stand up and join a teddy bear parade. Clothes, ribbons, or any special decorations can be added to make the bear uniquely yours.

ASK MISTER BEAR FLANNEL BOARD CHARACTERS

Materials: various colors of felt, scissors, patterns

Directions: Make patterns for the hen, goose, goat, sheep, cow, bear, boy, and mother by placing a sheet of paper on top of the pictures in the book and tracing them. Cut out the patterns. Pin the paper cutouts onto felt and cut out. These simple felt characters can be moved according to the action of the story. Face the animals toward the boy when they are talking to him and face them the other direction as they walk away.

BEAR GLOVE PUPPET

Materials: brown cotton garden glove, ten ½ inch tan pompons, ten small wiggle eyes, tan and black felt, glue, narrow ribbon, batting

Directions: Tightly stuff the top 1½ inch of each finger of the glove with batting. Tie the ribbon into a bow around the fingers at the base of the stuffing. Cut nose from tan and black felt as illustrated. Glue on the eyes, nose, and the pompons for the ears. Insert your hand into the glove to use for a finger play or to create your own counting rhyme. Encourage the children to use the glove themselves.

THE BEAR'S TOOTHACHE TOOTH

Materials: homemade clay (see below)

Directions: To make about two dozen teeth, mix in a bowl 2 cups flour, 1 cup salt, 1 cup cornstarch. In a separate bowl blend 1 cup water and 1 tsp. glycerin. Gradually add liquid to dry ingredients, stirring constantly. Add more water if necessary. Knead dough for about five minutes until it's soft and pliable.

Create your own bear's tooth as a model for the children. Then give each child a small amount of clay to mold into a bear's tooth. When the teeth have shape, identify each one with the child's initial.

Place on a cookie sheet and bake at 275 degrees for one hour. Allow the teeth to cool an hour in the oven to eliminate cracking. They can be baked later at home if you don't have an oven handy.

You might choose to substitute modeling clay for baked clay. Modeling clay does not get hard and can be used over and over. In either case, leave the teeth on display for a few days.

COUNTRY BEAR'S GOOD NEIGHBOR CHEF'S HAT

Materials: white wrapping tissue paper, white lightweight tag board or construction paper, glue, scissors, stapler

Directions: For each hat cut a 20 inch circle from tissue paper. Cut a 4 x 23 inch band from white paper. Staple the band together. Put glue along an inside edge of the band. To make the fluffy top, gather the edges of the tissue circle as you place it on the glued edge of the band.

These hats, which make children feel like they're real chefs, can also be used with any food-related story.

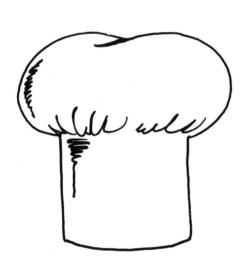

GOLDILOCKS AND THE THREE BEARS BODY PUPPETS

Materials: four 2 foot x 3 foot pieces of poster board, scissors, paint, chalk or felt markers, ruler

Directions: Five inches from the top of the poster board cut a hole eight inches long and seven inches wide. Seventeen inches down from the top cut two 3 inch holes for the arms. Draw and color the figures using the illustrations as your models. Cut out the characters. These sturdy puppets can be used again and again as children take turns dramatizing the story.

Three Bears Body Puppets

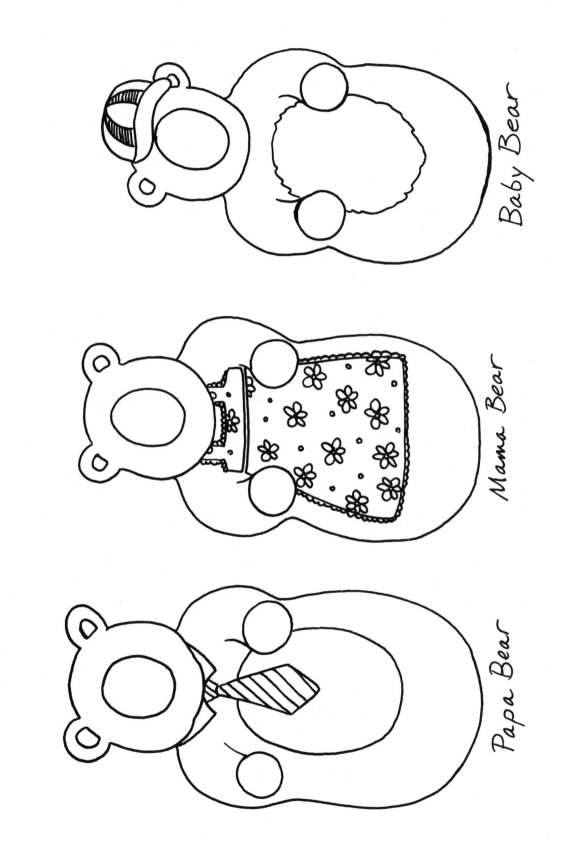

Papa Bear

Mama Bear

Baby Bear

Bear Snacks

TEDDY BEAR COOKIES
Follow the directions for making Alligator Cookies in the Alligator Snacks section. Roll the dough about ¼ inch thick. Place the bear pattern on top of the dough and use a knife to cut out. Bake. When cool, decorate or frost.

TEDDY BEAR CAKE
Enlarge the teddy bear cookie pattern to cover a 9 x 13 inch cake pan. Follow the directions on a cake mix to make your favorite cake. Remove from pan when cool. Lay the pattern on the cake and cut out. Frost and decorate to make him look like your favorite teddy bear or one of the bears in a book you've read. For example, you could use green frosting to simulate Corduroy's overalls.

GRAHAM CRACKER TEDDY BEARS
Serve graham cracker teddy bears available at grocery stores. Fill a small bag with a handful of crackers and give one bag to each pair of children. The children count the bears and divide the contents equally. A snack is better when it's shared with a friend.

BREAD AND HONEY SANDWICHES
After reading BREAD AND HONEY, have the children pretend to be bears and eat bread and honey sandwiches.

BLUEBERRY MUFFINS
Read BLUEBERRIES FOR SAL. Serve blueberries from a pail like Sal's. Or, for a less messy treat, serve blueberry muffins.

ENTERTAINING ELEPHANTS

Elephants, the largest land animals, have long entertained, enthralled, and enchanted adults and children. They are revered for their great strength, amazing memory (not simply a myth), and defiantly regal character. It is perhaps a tribute to the elephant's complex intelligence that despite its having been domesticated for a few thousand years, much of its behavior in the wild remains a mystery.

Next to the elephant's size (they may reach nearly twelve feet at the shoulder), and the elephant's appetite (a typical zoo elephant will daily consume ninety pounds of hay, three pounds of oats, forty-six pounds each of carrots and lettuce, a handful of vitamins, a quarter cup of salt, and fifty gallons of water), children find the trunk the elephant's most intriguing feature. The elephant's ability to handle water, dust, food, and baby elephants with what is essentially its nose is certainly worth a trip to a zoo or circus to witness. Failing this, a short film, video, or nature magazine photo-essay will help introduce children to these most entertaining creatures.

Setting the Stage

Make a sign for a stuffed toy elephant or for a paper cutout elephant. Attach a string to the sign so that it will hang around the elephant's neck. The sign should say, "Read an Elephant Book Today."

Place a thin book—or a book jacket—in the trunk of a stuffed elephant or elephant puppet.

Post a "Welcome Elephants" banner, made by hand or using the computer.

Make an elephant library out of a cardboard box that's big enough to hold all of your elephant books. Cover the box with plain paper and draw windows and a door. Over the door print the word "Elephant Library." Leave the top open so that the books can easily be taken out.

Bulletin Board Ideas

1. Reserve a spot on the bulletin board for elephant jokes. Here are a couple to start your collection.

> What do elephants get when they have a cold?
> A runny trunk.

> Why is the elephant sitting on the ice cube?
> He doesn't want to fall into the punch.

> Where are elephants found?
> They are so big, they almost never get lost.

Invite the children to add their own jokes which they can collect from their friends and parents. Older children can discover elephant jokes in library joke books.

2. Enlarge Babar by using an opaque projector to put an image onto poster paper. Outline, color, cut him out, and pin him and his name onto the board. You and the children can search for all the Babar stories and list many of the titles on the board. Have a "Babar Day" or "Babar Week" during which you read only Babar stories.

3. Enlarge the "Read in a Tub" illustration. Then color, cut and pin it up for some giggles.

Read A Book

In The Tub

Learn To Swim

Read-Aloud Stories

ALISTAIR'S ELEPHANT
by Marilyn Sadler, il. by Roger Bollen
(Prentice-Hall, 1983)

Story: Much to Alistair's displeasure, an elephant follows him home from the zoo. The elephant is a big bother to Alistair but by the time he returns him to the zoo, they have become friends.

Materials: paddle ball game, handkerchief, spray bottle with water (optional)

Directions: Show the paddle ball game to the children, and demonstrate how to play it. Count how many times you can bounce the ball on the paddle without missing. Explain that you are going to read a story that involves paddle ball and that children will have a chance to play the game later.

While reading the story, use a nasal voice for the mother when she shouts at Alistair. When the elephant cries, bring out a handkerchief and use it to dry your elephant tears. When the story mentions rain, spray a fine mist using the spray bottle.

ALL IN ONE PIECE
by Jill Murphy (Putnam, 1987)

Story: Mr. and Mrs. Large are trying to get ready to go to a dinner party; however, their four young elephants insist on helping, making it very difficult for the parents to get away.

Materials: stuffed elephant plus a dress, beads, flower, earrings, and purse

Directions: Tell the children that the elephant, Mrs. Large, was invited to a party. She wants to get dressed so she can look her very best. As you explain the background, dress the elephant in the dress, beads, and earrings. If possible, have a variety of accessories on hand so that you can ask the children to suggest which ones the elephant should wear.

Pin a flower on the dress and give her a purse to carry. The children will think it's funny to see an elephant being dressed—and they're right.

Set Mrs. Large where the children can see her as you read the story. Use an exasperated voice when Mrs. Large talks to her children, and a begging voice for her children.

BUT NO ELEPHANTS
by Jerry Smath (Parents Magazine Press, 1979)

Story: Grandma Tildy reluctantly agrees to let a cold elephant into her home. But when the elephant takes Grandma Tildy and her friends to a warm climate, she gladly welcomes all elephants.

Materials: "Welcome Elephants" banner

Directions: Make a "Welcome Elephants" banner. Letter by hand or use a computer. Put up the banner as you talk to the children about what they might do if an elephant came to their house. Would the elephant be invited in?

As you read the story, ask the children to help you by repeating the refrain, "But no elephants," every time Grandma Tildy shouts this phrase.

When the happy bird in the story sings, sing a little song of your own, for example, "You Are My Sunshine." Invite the children to join in.

THE DREAM OF THE LITTLE ELEPHANT
by Ruth Bornstein (Seabury Press, 1977)

Story: The little elephant lives in the land of the big elephants. With the help of a white sea bird, the waves, the wind, a flower, a worm, a stone, and a tree, the elephant finds his own homeland.

Materials: none required

Directions: The little elephant can't make any noises. All he can do is sing, so all his dialogue should be sung as you're telling the story.

Be ready to make the wonderful sounds that fill the book, for example, the "ooooooooh" of the wind's "strong breath."

Also, look for action words that can be dramatized. Act out the elephant's sadness, fear and joy.

A LEMON-YELLOW ELEPHANT CALLED TRUNK

by Barbara Softly, il, by Tony Veale (Harvey House, 1970)

Story: Trunk asks his small animal friends to play hide-and-seek with him, but it's very difficult for a big, yellow elephant to hide.

Materials: the Lemon-Yellow Elephant (see Elephant Crafts)

Directions: Ask the children where they like to hide when playing hide-and-seek.

Show the elephant to the children, explaining that it's different from all other elephants in the world. One side is gray and the other side is yellow. Ask the children which side would be better at hiding.

After reading the story, serve the lemon-yellow elephant cookies (see Elephant Snacks).

You might also organize a hide-and-seek game based on the book. First, make a large lemon-yellow sign that says: "Trunk." Then have children take turns trying to hide while holding the sign aloft. This game could be played before or after the story is read.

FIVE MINUTES' PEACE

by Jill Murphy (Putnam, 1986)

Story: While taking her morning bath, Mrs. Large seeks peace and quiet from her three energetic elephant children.

Materials: stuffed elephant or elephant puppet, shower cap, tonette (or song flute)

Directions: Put the shower cap on the elephant. Ask the children why the elephant might be wearing the cap. If you are using an elephant puppet, let the puppet talk about her plans for finding some peace and quiet. Explain that mothers occasionally need time to themselves.

While reading the story, use different voices for the mother and her children. Play—or have someone else play— "Twinkle, Twinkle, Little Star" on a tonette when Lester plays the music for his mother. Ask the children to sing along. Serve toast and marmalade after the story.

THE MYSTERY BEAST OF OSTERGEEST
by Steven Kellogg (Dial, 1971)

Story: In this retelling of a classic tale, a mysterious beast sails into the town of Ostergeest. The king calls on six blind professors to classify the strange animal which, in reality, is an elephant. In the end, a young boy with an alphabet book—and not the experts—solves the mystery.

Materials: an alphabet book with a picture of an elephant on the "E" page

Directions: Introduce this story by reading an alphabet book in which an elephant illustrates the letter "E." (If you can't easily locate such a book, make your own.)

Stop after you've read that page and explain that you know a story about a little boy who solved a mystery by reading an alphabet book.

In THE MYSTERY BEAST OF OSTERGEEST, you'll notice the clever writing on the signs that appear throughout. Don't stop to read them when you're first presenting the book, or else you'll lose the flow. But when you've read the story through, go back and share these witty illustrations with your children.

THE TINIEST ELEPHANT
by Jack Kent (Doubleday, 1979)

Story: Floyd is the tiniest elephant in the circus. Because nobody notices him, he goes to live with the mice.

Materials: Floyd's note (copied from the book), tiny elephant stick puppet (use pattern below)

Directions: Introduce this story by singing the first verse of "Do You Know the Elephant?" (See Elephant Songs.) Explain that you're going to tell a story about an elephant living in Circus Lane.

When reading the story, use the stick puppet to suggest Floyd's travels. Have the children repeat the phrase, "But nobody noticed." Take out Floyd's note at the appropriate moment.

At the conclusion of the story, teach the children the rest of "Do You Know the Elephant?"

Later, pin Floyd's note on the bulletin board as a reminder of the story.

More Elephant Stories

Azmon, Edward. **A HUNT IN THE JUNGLE** (Lion, 1971)

Chin Cham visits the jungle to capture an elephant for the zoo; however, he soon changes his mind about what to do with the elephant when he arrives back home.

Boynton, Sandra. **IF AT FIRST...** (Little, Brown, 1980)

A determined little mouse tries again and again to move a lazy elephant up a hill, only to discover that when the job is done, there are more elephants who want to be moved up.

Burton, Marilee. **THE ELEPHANT'S NEST** (Harper & Row, 1979)

This wordless book contains four whimsical animal stories in which a bird hatches baby elephants, who learn to fly. They even live in a kangaroo's pouch.

Caple, Kathy. **THE BIGGEST NOSÉ** (Houghton Mifflin, 1985)

Eleanor's friends tease her about having the biggest nose in school, but eventually she finds a solution to her problem when she realizes Betty the hippopotamus has the biggest mouth.

Chorao, Kay. **GEORGE TOLD KATE** (Dutton, 1987)

George enjoys fooling his little sister Kate about cleaning her room, going to school, and moving to a new house.

Cole, Joanna, il. by Ned Delaney. **ARE YOU FORGETTING SOMETHING, FIONA?** (Parents Magazine Press, 1983)

Fiona has trouble remembering everything, but her family helps her remember when it's time for her to go to her exercise class.

Cutler, Ivor, il. by Helen Oxenbury. **ELEPHANT GIRL** (Morrow, 1975)

A little girl playing in her yard digs into the ground and uncovers an elephant living there. They soon become good friends.

Day, Alexandra. **FRANK AND ERNEST** (Scholastic, 1988)

Frank and Ernest, a bear and an elephant, manage a diner, and soon learn all about food language. "Moo juice" is milk, "paint a bow wow red" means "put catsup on a hot dog," and "nervous pudding" is jello.

de Brunhoff, Jean. **THE STORY OF BABAR, THE LITTLE ELEPHANT** (Random House, 1961)

In the forest, a little elephant is born and named Babar. When Babar's mother is killed by a hunter, Babar goes to the city to live, but eventually returns to the forest where he marries Celeste and becomes the king. Other stories about the same elephant include:

THE TRAVELS OF BABAR
BABAR THE KING
BABAR AND HIS CHILDREN
BABAR AND FATHER CHRISTMAS
BABAR'S FRENCH LESSONS
BABAR COMES TO AMERICA
BABAR'S SPANISH LESSONS
BABAR LOSES HIS CROWN
BABAR'S TRUNK
BABAR'S BIRTHDAY SURPRISE
BABAR VISITS ANOTHER PLANET
BABAR AND THE WULLY-WULLY
BABAR SAVES THE DAY

de Brunhoff, Laurent. **BABAR'S LITTLE CIRCUS STAR** (Random House, 1988)

As the smallest elephant in the family, Isabelle is very dissatisfied until she's asked to perform at the circus.

Delton, Judy, il. by Lynn Munsinger. THE ELEPHANT IN DUCK'S GARDEN (Whitman, 1985)

Duck and Bear struggle to remove an elephant from Duck's garden.

Gamerman, Martha, il. by Alexandra Wallner. TRUDY'S STRAW HAT (Crown, 1977)

Trudy wants a straw hat just like the one her friend Wanda has. When her parents don't think she needs one, Trudy sets out to find a way to get one herself.

Gammell, Stephen. ONCE UPON MACDONALD'S FARM (Four Winds, 1981)

MacDonald doesn't have any cows, horses, or chickens on his farm, so he tries farming with elephants and other circus animals.

Hadithi, Mwenye, il. by Adrienne Kennaway. TRICKY TORTOISE (Little, Brown, 1988)

In folk tale tradition, the little sporty tortoise tricks the big elephant who is a bully and a boaster.

Hoffman, Mary. ELEPHANT (Random House, 1984)

Photographs and descriptive dialogue depict the physical characteristics, habits, and behavior of elephants.

Kent, Jack. THE BIGGEST SHADOW IN THE ZOO (Parents Magazine Press, 1981)

Goober the elephant loves his shadow and is quite distressed when it disappears. He tries many strategies to get it back.

Kent, Jack. MR. ELEPHANT'S BIRTHDAY PARTY (Houghton Mifflin, 1969)

Mr. Elephant has trouble remembering anything until his friends give him a birthday party that he'll never forget!

Klein, Suzanne, il. by Sharleen Pederson. AN ELEPHANT IN MY BED (Follett, 1974)

A young boy finds an elephant and wants to keep him. At first, he can't figure out what to do with the elephant, but finally the boy decides to put him in his own bed.

Lapp, Eleanor, il. by John Richards. HEY, ELEPHANT (Steck-Vaughn, 1970)

An elephant walks away from the zoo and ends up in James's garden. James keeps the elephant in his bedroom, and his busy parents never realize the elephant is there.

Leydenfrost, Robert. TEN LITTLE ELEPHANTS (Doubleday, 1975)

This counting rhyme features ten elephants who go out to play but keep having accidents, until there is just one left.

Lobel, Arnold. UNCLE ELEPHANT (Harper & Row, 1981)

When Mother and Father Elephant are lost at sea, Uncle Elephant decides to care for his young nephew.

Mahy, Margaret, il. by Patricia MacCarthy. 17 KINGS AND 42 ELEPHANTS (Dial, 1987)

The king, riding the elephants through the jungle one night, has a wild, wet time while meeting the jungle animals.

Matthews, Morgan, il. by Susan Miller. WHICH WAY, HUGO? (Troll Associates, 1986)

When an elephant, who repeatedly runs away, develops sore feet, a turtle offers some good advice.

Mayer, Mercer. AH-CHOO (Dial, 1976)

This small, wordless picture book features the adventures of an elephant whose sneezes cause several catastrophes.

Pearce, Philippa, il. by John Lawrence. EMILY'S OWN ELEPHANT (Greenwillow, 1987)

While visiting the zoo, Emily finds a small elephant in need of a home. She provides him a comfortable place in her family's shed.

Reinarch, Jacquelyn, il. by Richard Hefter. ELEPHANT EATS THE PROFIT (Holt, 1977)

Elephant has trouble making a profit in his supermarket because his enormous appetite compels him to constantly eat.

Riddell, Chris. **THE TROUBLE WITH ELEPHANTS** (Lippincott, 1988)

A little girl plays with her stuffed elephant while grumbling about how real elephants might cause problems such as crowding her out of bed, eating her food, and sliding down the banister.

Sanchez, Jose and Miguel Pacheco, il. by Nella Bosnia. **ELEPHANT** (Fisher Publishing, 1983)

This nonfiction book, also available in Spanish, explains the habits and characteristics of elephants.

Saxe, John, il. by Paul Galdone. **THE BLIND MEN AND THE ELEPHANT** (McGraw-Hill, 1963)

In this retelling of a classic tale, six blind men set out to learn about the elephant. Because each touches a different part, there are six different opinions about what an elephant is like.

Seuss, Dr. **HORTON HATCHES THE EGG** (Random House, 1940)

Horton the elephant sits on a lazy bird's egg despite all sorts of hazards. When the egg hatches, it's an elephant with wings.

Smath, Jerry. **ELEPHANT GOES TO SCHOOL** (Parents Magazine Press, 1984)

Grandma Tildy and her friends are in trouble when the school bus breaks down, but the children are delighted when Elephant carries them to school on his back.

Standon, Anna and Edward Standon. **A FLOWER FOR AMBROSE** (Delacorte, 1964)

Clumsy Ambrose cries when he gets into trouble. However, when his tears make wilted flowers grow, he's happy again.

Stock, Catherine. **ALEXANDER'S MIDNIGHT SNACK: A LITTLE ELEPHANT'S ABC** (Clarion, 1988)

Alexander the elephant wakes up thirsty and goes to the kitchen for a drink of water. There, he creates a terrible mess as he eats, while journeying through the ABC's.

Thomas, Patricia, il. by Wallace Tripp. **"STAND BACK," SAID THE ELEPHANT, "I'M GOING TO SNEEZE!"** (Lothrop, 1971)

This rhyming story features the adventures of an elephant who has to sneeze. The little mouse scares his sneeze away. But that doesn't entirely save the day.

Tresselt, Alvin and Wilbur Wheaton, il. by Tom Uroman. **AN ELEPHANT IS NOT A CAT** (Parents Magazine Press, 1962)

Pieter Vanderloon has the best corn mill in Holland, but that changes when he brings home an elephant to chase two mice away.

Weiss, Leatie, il. by Ellen Weiss. **MY TEACHER SLEEPS IN SCHOOL** (Frederick Warne, 1984)

Because Mrs. Marsh, an elephant teacher, is always in her classroom before the students arrive and after they leave, a student named Mollie decides Mrs. Marsh lives and sleeps in the school.

Young, Miriam, il. by Robert Quackenbush. **IF I RODE AN ELEPHANT** (Lothrop, 1974)

A young boy imagines all the wild and wonderful adventures he would have if he could ride an elephant.

Elephant Poems

MY ELEPHANT

Use the pattern below to make a very small elephant from pink paper. Read or recite the poem, and then show the children the little elephant that shrank. After teaching the poem to the children, invite them to make their own miniature elephants.

My Elephant

My elephant is pink.
I wrapped him in fake mink.
I bathed him in the sink.
And hoped he wouldn't shrink.
But he did.

WAY DOWN SOUTH

Copy this poem and the one below it in large print and pin them onto a bulletin board. After reading the poems aloud, have the children create illustrations.

Way Down South

Way down south where bananas grow,
A grasshopper stepped on an elephant's toe.
The elephant said, with tears in his eyes,
"Pick on someone your own size."
—Anonymous

The Elephant Carries a Great Big Trunk

The elephant carries a great big trunk;
He never packs it with clothes.
It has no lock and it has no key,
But he takes it wherever he goes.
—Anonymous

More Elephant Poems

"The Elephants" by Dorothy Aldis and "Circus Elephant" by Kathryn Worth in CIRCUS, CIRCUS (Knopf, 1982)

"An Elephant…" in A DAY OF RHYMES selected and illustrated by Sarah Pooley (Knopf, 1987)

"Beside the Line of Elephants" p. 59 and "Ele-telephony" p. 192 in THE RANDOM HOUSE BOOK OF POETRY FOR CHILDREN selected by Jack Prelutsky, il. by Arnold Lobel (Random House, 1983)

Elephant Finger Plays and Action Verse

ELEPHANT, ELEPHANT

Elephant, elephant, go to the circus.
  (Walk in place.)
Elephant, elephant, show your tusks.
  (Put head between arms.)

Elephant, elephant, stand on your toe.
  (Stand on toe.)
Elephant, elephant, shake your head "no."
  (Shake head.)

Elephant, elephant, go to the zoo.
  (Walk in place.)
Elephant, elephant, they want to see you.
  (Open eyes wide.)

Elephant, elephant, come home to me.
  (Beckon.)
Elephant, elephant, there's peanuts and tea.
  (Eat.)

THE BIG ELEPHANT

The elephant swings his big trunk.
Swing, swing, swing.
  (Swing arms back and forth.)

The elephant flaps his big ears.
Flap, flap, flap.
  (Put hands on side of head and flap.)

The elephant stomps his big feet.
Stomp, stomp, stomp.
  (Stomp feet.)

If I were big, I'd be an elephant, too.
  (Point to self.)

WHAT DOES AN ELEPHANT DO?

An elephant walks very slowly.
  (Take big, slow steps.)

He's quite enormous.
  (Stretch arms out wide.)

And he's very tall.
  (Reach arms up high.)

He has a big mouth.
  (Open mouth wide.)

He's noticed wherever he goes.
  (Make glasses with fingers.)

And I sure like his funny nose.
  (Extend arms together in curling position to form a trunk. Move up and down while snorting.)

More Finger Plays

"Five Little Elephants" p. 28 in RING A RING O'ROSES (Flint Public Library, 1988)

"Oliver the Elephant" p. 40 and "Penelope Elephant" p. 41 in MOVE OVER, MOTHER GOOSE by Ruth Dowell, il. by Concetta Scott (Gryphon House, 1987)

Elephant Songs

TWO ELEPHANTS WENT OUT TO PLAY

Learn this simple song for a trunk-load of fun. The leader stands with one child behind him holding the child's hand. Everyone sings the first verse while the leader and child walk around. They cup their hands around their mouths when they call, "Elephants, elephants."

Two more elephants join the line, and everyone counts to check that there are four. The four elephants walk around as before while singing the second verse.

Continue this way until everyone has joined the line of elephants. At this point, the children drop their hands and turn one arm into an elephant's trunk by curving the hand slightly and lifting the arm while making an elephant call: a guttural sound that comes from between nearly closed lips.

If everything goes right, it'll sound like a real herd of elephants. In fact, because of the volume, you might want to perform this song outside.

DO YOU KNOW THE ELEPHANT?

Divide the children into two groups standing opposite each other. One group sings the first verse while looking at the other group in a questioning manner. The second group answers by singing the second verse. Then everyone sings the third verse.

In this chapter's Read-Aloud section, you'll find suggestions for using this song with THE TINIEST ELEPHANT.

Do You Know the Elephant?
(Tune: "The Muffin Man")

Oh, do you know the elephant,
The elephant, the elephant?
Oh, do you know the elephant
Who lives in Circus Lane?

Oh, yes I know the elephant,
The elephant, the elephant,
Oh, yes I know the elephant
Who lives in Circus Lane.

We all know the elephant,
The elephant, the elephant,
Oh, yes we know the elephant
Who lives in Circus Lane.

Two Elephants Went Out to Play
by Maxine Riggers

Two elephants went out to play upon a bright and
Four.....
Six....
etc.

sunny day. They had such a lot of fun, they called for two

more friends to come. Elephants. Elephants.

Elephant Games

HIDE THE LEMON-YELLOW ELEPHANT

Make the Lemon-Yellow Elephant following the directions given in Elephant Crafts. Play hide and seek with it. One person hides the elephant while the other children are out of the room. The child who then finds it gets to hide the elephant the next time. To make sure everyone has a chance to hide the elephant, include a rule that each player may hide the elephant only one time.

BE AN ELEPHANT

Begin this activity by reciting the following verse:

I'm a huge elephant,
And I take huge steps so slow.
Are you ready to play a game?
Then let's go.

The children pretend they're elephants by imitating the leader who does the following actions:

1. Walk around very slowly on all fours, using your arms as front legs.

2. Balance on one foot like a circus elephant.

3. Form an elephant's trunk by clasping your hands together and letting your arms hang down in front. Move your "trunk" up and down while making a guttural sound.

4. Pick up real or pretend peanuts or other objects with your "trunk."

After reading several elephant stories, the children may have other ideas about elephant behavior. Let them add to the game by suggesting actions.

HOLDING HANDS

Read the poem "Holding Hands" p. 11 in READ-ALOUD RHYMES FOR THE VERY YOUNG selected by Jack Prelutsky, illustrated by Marc Brown (Knopf, 1986).

Pretend to be elephants who are holding "hands" by holding their tails. One hand serves as the "trunk" and the other as the "tail." Form a line of elephants who prance around as if they are in the circus ring. Encourage the children to recite the poem with you as they perform.

Elephant Crafts

ELEPHANT FINGER PUPPET

Materials: elephant pattern, gray construction or poster paper, scissors, black felt marker

Directions: Copy the elephant pattern onto gray paper, draw the features as illustrated, and cut out. Cut out the small circle. To use the puppet, stick the index finger through the hole to make the elephant's trunk.

Encourage the children to put on their own puppet shows. They can retell the stories or pretend to be elephants having conversations.

ELEPHANT FOLD-OUT PUPPET

Materials: gray construction paper, Popsicle stick, felt marker, glue, scissors, tape

Directions: Cut a 5 x 9 inch rectangular piece of gray paper. Fold into thirds and cut the corners at an angle as illustrated. Unfold. The middle section becomes the elephant's face and the outside sections the ears.

Draw small elephant eyes. Make the trunk by cutting a strip of paper 6 inches long with the width tapering from 1 inch down to ½ inch at the end. Fold the trunk in accordion style and glue the larger end to the face of the elephant. Darken the narrow end of the trunk to indicate the opening.

Tape a Popsicle stick to the back of the head. Fold the ears on top of the folded trunk. When it's opened, the trunk will fall into place.

The children will enjoy folding and unfolding the elephant to see the trunk move.

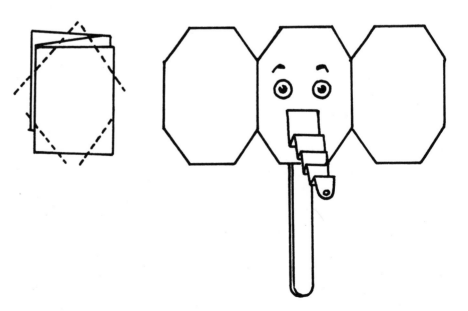

PAPER CUP ELEPHANT

Materials: 16 oz. paper cup, elephant ear pattern, scissors or cutting tool, felt marker

Directions: Use the ear pattern to trace and cut out ears on two sides of the cup as illustrated. Fold the ears out. Draw eyes, mouth, and a circle for the trunk on the bottom of the cup. Cut out the circle.

    Insert your hand into the cup, placing your middle finger through the hole to form the elephant's trunk. To make the elephant's legs, insert the index and fourth fingers through the openings made when the ears are folded out. You now have a very versatile elephant who can walk around and stretch his trunk at the same time.

BABAR'S CROWN

Materials: gold construction or tag paper, scissors, stapler

Directions: Follow the directions for making the crown given in Frog Crafts with two modifications: first, omit the red circles, and second, include the peaks all the way around the crown.

Wear this crown when reading the Babar stories. Also, let the children wear the crown when they are dramatizing the stories.

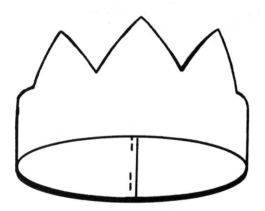

LEMON-YELLOW ELEPHANT PUZZLE

Materials: yellow and gray construction paper, elephant pattern, scissors, rubber cement or paper glue, felt marker, envelope

Directions: Copy the elephant pattern onto yellow and gray paper. You'll need one sheet of each color. Draw the features onto the elephant and cut out. Glue the two pieces together using rubber cement or glue.

For young children, draw in the dotted lines which they can follow while cutting the puzzle pieces. Older children will be able to cut without lines.

Store the puzzle pieces in an envelope marked "Lemon-Yellow Elephant Puzzle." Use the craft in conjunction with Barbara Softly's book, A LEMON-YELLOW ELEPHANT CALLED TRUNK. Of course, the same technique can be used to create puzzles featuring other storybook characters.

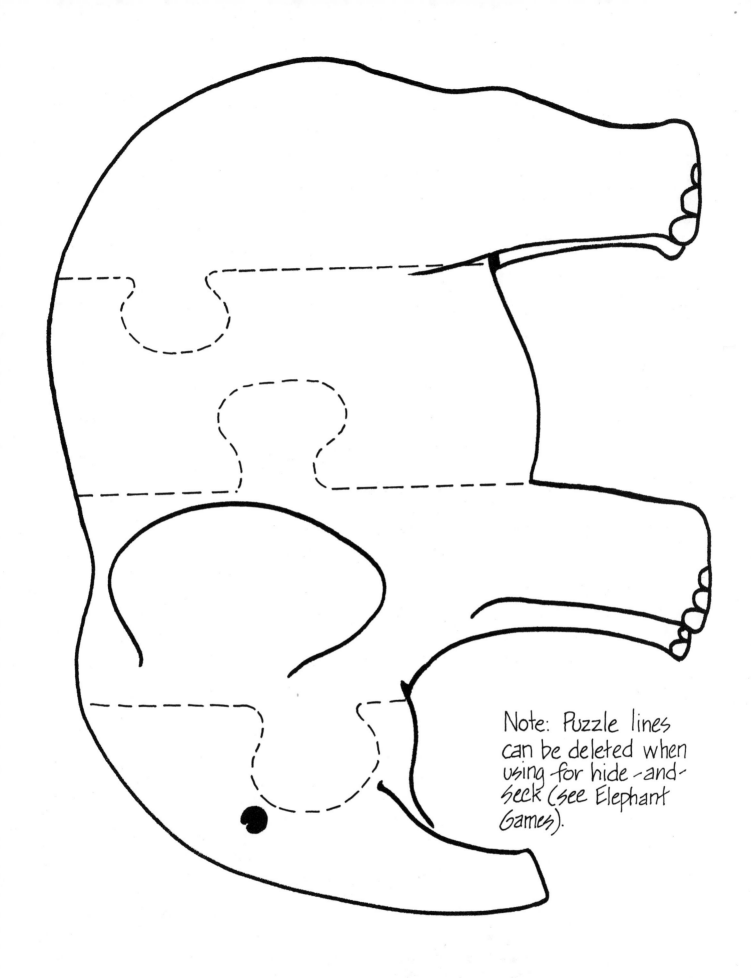

Note: Puzzle lines can be deleted when using for hide-and-seek (see Elephant Games).

Elephant Snacks

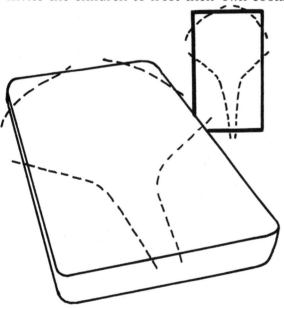

PEANUTS

Serve unshelled peanuts in small paper bags or cups. Because the shells make a mess, you may want to eat the peanuts outside. Either way, keep a broom and dustpan handy.

LEMON-YELLOW ELEPHANT COOKIES

Follow the recipe used for making Alligator Cookies in Alligator Snacks. Transfer the elephant pattern onto heavy paper and place on the rolled-out dough. Use a sharp knife to cut around the edge of the pattern. Bake the cookies. Prepare yellow frosting. Invite the children to frost their own cookies.

ELEPHANT CAKE

Whip up your favorite cake batter. Bake in a 9 x 13 inch pan. When the cake is completely cooled, use the patterns to cut out the ears and head as illustrated. Arrange the elephant on a tray or cookie sheet. Prepare a fluffy white frosting and color with gray food coloring. Frost the entire elephant on the top and sides. Decorate with black string licorice for eyebrows and wrinkles. Use candies for the eyes.

You may substitute yellow food coloring to make the Lemon-Yellow Elephant, or green coloring to make the little elephant in THE DREAM OF THE LITTLE ELEPHANT.

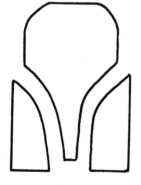 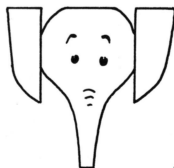

1. Cut
2. Arrange*
3. Smooth Edges
4. Ice & Decorate

* Top corners can be used as tusks.

74

Pattern For Cake

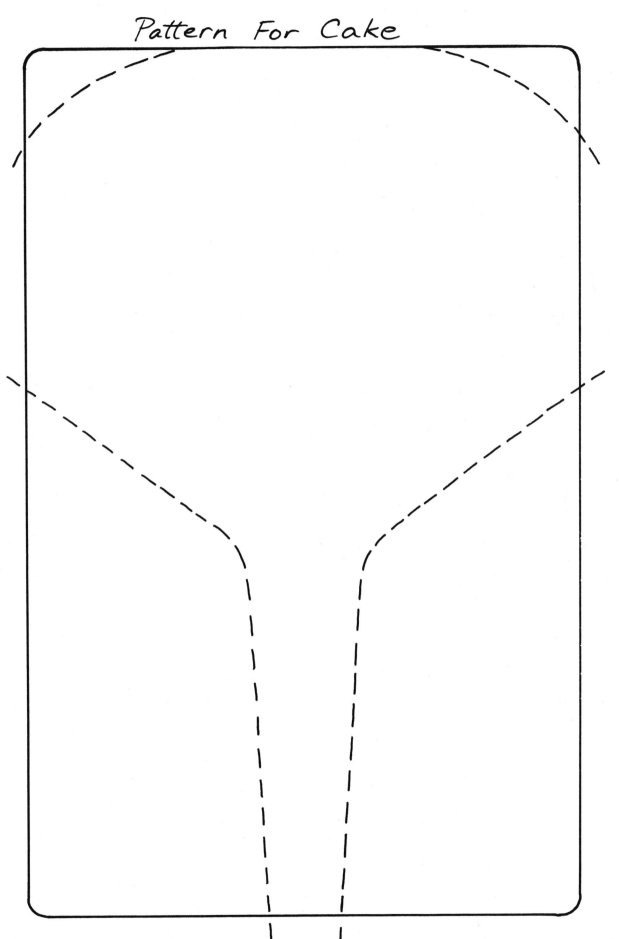

FRIVOLOUS FROGS

Frivolous frogs are fabulous characters for some fantastic story hours and some "un*frog*getable" experiences. Plan these story hours during the warm months when frogs are available, so the children can bring them to the classroom or library—a great way to liven up the room. If you don't live in an area where frogs are readily available, try purchasing one from a pet store. Hop to it, or you might be accused of not having the "*frog*giest" idea what to do.

Setting the Stage

You will need a frog puppet for these story hours. You may construct the paper bag puppet using the instructions in the Frog Crafts section of this chapter. Or you can purchase one from Folkmanis (see Resources).

If you're using magic carpets, fly to Frogville to discover the frivolous frogs hiding in the books. Listen for the croaking. The children can croak as they land in Frogville.

Ask the children this silly riddle: "Why do frogs croak?" The answer: "Because they don't know any words."

Designate a shelf or table as Frogville. Construct a Frogville sign and stick it in clay to make it stand up. Ask the children to bring their pet stuffed frogs to live in Frogville. The variety and colors make a great display.

Bulletin Board Ideas

1. Using the illustration here as a guideline, create a frog in the leaping position. Aim him toward a stack of books.

2. Make a poster of a book cover or a frog character. Use the opaque projector or draw it freehand. Color with chalk, paint, or felt markers.

3. Order a "Frog and Toad" poster from the Peaceable Kingdom Press (see Resources).

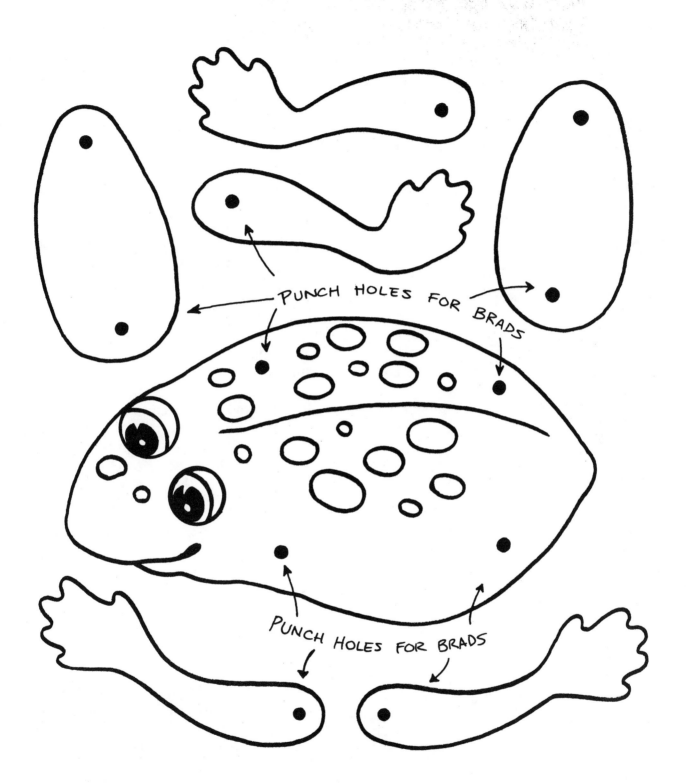

PUNCH HOLES FOR BRADS

PUNCH HOLES FOR BRADS

Read-Aloud Stories

THE CATERPILLAR AND THE POLLIWOG
by Jack Kent (Prentice-Hall, 1982)

Story: The caterpillar boasts that she will turn into a beautiful butterfly. The polliwog decides to watch very carefully in order to learn how to become a butterfly.

Materials: flannel board, frog life-cycle patterns, green felt or construction paper, felt marker, glue, scissors

Directions: It's best to use this story when live polliwogs or caterpillars are available for classroom observation of their life cycles. In spring polliwogs can be found in ponds, while caterpillars are abundant in the late summer or fall.

Introduce the story by constructing and displaying the frog life cycle on the flannel board. Leave it up for the children to look at and play with.

FROG AND TOAD ARE FRIENDS
by Arnold Lobel (Harper & Row, 1970)

Story: Five short adventures show how two wonderful friends, Frog and Toad, solve their problems.

Materials: Frog and Toad puppets (see Frog Crafts)

Directions: Become familiar enough with the story so that you can tell it while using the puppets. The puppets fit on the middle and index fingers, one on each hand with the palms facing outward, thus enabling you to bend the fingers to move the puppets.

Use a different voice for each puppet. Move them around in a way suggested by the story.

If you have time for only one story, show the book to the children to interest them in the other tales. After letting the children play with the puppets, invite them to put on their own puppet shows. Older children will probably want to make their own puppets.

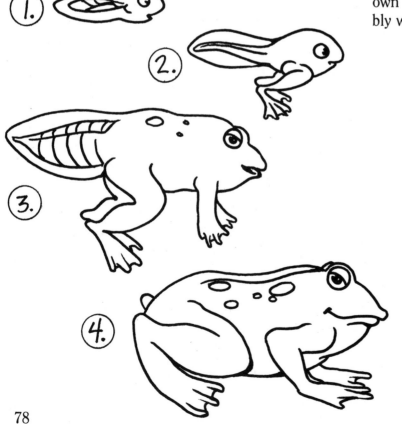

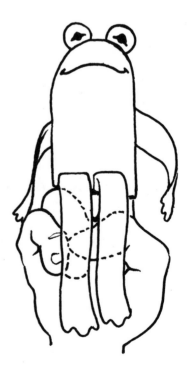

I'M TAGGARTY TOAD
by Peter Pavey (Puffin Books, 1980)

Story: The fearless Taggarty Toad brags about his daring exploits with giants, jungles, dragons, and witches, but the past catches up with him when the tiger pays a visit.

Materials: Taggarty Toad sign

Directions: Using poster paper and felt markers, make a sign similar to the one in the book. Include a picture of the toad, an arrow, and the words "Guest Speaker." Post the sign near your reading chair.

Point the sign out to the children. Explain that in the book that you are about to read, a sign just like this one leads the animals to the spot where Taggarty Toad gives a speech.

After you've read the story a few times, you might have a Taggarty Toad Speech Contest in which children can imitate the speech Taggarty Toad makes. Bring in a tape recorder and tape the contest. Afterward, let the children listen (and laugh).

FROG'S HOLIDAY
by Margaret Gordon (Viking, 1986)

Story: A group of frogs decide to leave their pond because of the many big fish and small boys. Their search for peace and quiet leads them to Mrs. Crumple's launderette.

Materials: small tub of water, wind-up frog (optional)

Directions: Use the tub to create the mood. If you can find a wind-up frog, place it in the water and let it swim around for a while. Tell the children they will have an opportunity to play with the frog later, but that now you want to read a story about some frogs who take a holiday away from their crowded pond.

IT'S MINE!
by Leo Lionni (Knopf, 1986)

Story: In this fable, three selfish frogs quarrel over the ownership of a pond until a storm makes them realize the advantages of sharing.

Materials: three frog stick puppets

Directions: Construct the frog stick puppets by copying the art from Lionni's book. Use green construction paper, then glue or tape the frogs onto Popsicle sticks. Draw on the features.

Introduce the frogs by name—Milton, Rupert, and Lydia. Ask three children to hold them as you explain that the frogs are always quarreling. The children can make the puppets quarrel by saying, "It's mine."

Act disgusted with the frogs because of their bickering. Have your puppeteers lay them down, and discuss with the children what might make the frogs learn to behave. Then tell them the story.

JUMP, FROG, JUMP
by Robert Kalan, il. by Byron Barton
(Greenwillow, 1981)

Story: This cumulative tale features a frog who tries to catch a fly without getting caught himself.

Materials: frog puppet

Directions: Before reading the story, ask the children how frogs get from one place to another. Using the puppet, illustrate how frogs jump. The children can pretend to be frogs and jump about for a while until they—or you—tire. Then they can jump to a lily pad and settle down to listen to the story. The lily pads could be a designated spot on the floor or on their magic carpets.

During the story, invite the children to join you with the refrain "Jump, Frog, Jump." They might even be able to recite the entire tale as the incidents are said over and over.

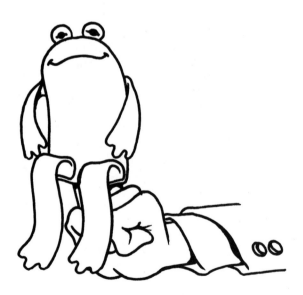

NEVER SNAP AT A BUBBLE

by Yvonne Winer, il. by Carol McLean-Carr
(Educational Insights, 1987)

Story: Mother and Father Frog warn their disobedient Baby Frog that he will float away if he doesn't stop snapping at bubbles.

Materials: bottle of bubble fluid

Directions: Set this beautifully illustrated 14 by 20 inch "Big Book" on an easel or chair.

Before opening the book, blow a few bubbles into the air. The children will enjoy trying to snare a few. Before complete bedlam develops, ask the children to sit so they can hear a story about a baby frog who snapped at too many bubbles.

THE OGRE AND THE FROG KING

by Gregoire Solotareff (Greenwillow, 1988)

Story: A clever frog becomes the king, and figures out how to stop a giant ogre from eating the forest animals.

Materials: frog puppet, King Frog crown (see Frog Crafts), crowns for children

Directions: Put the crown on the frog puppet and let the children guess why he's dressed that way. Set the Frog King on a chair which will serve as his throne.

Show the cover of the book and present the story. After you've read the story, give the children their crowns and ask each what he or she would do as King or Queen.

SEVEN FROGGIES WENT TO SCHOOL
by Kate Duke (Dutton, 1985)

Story: The frogs find adventures as they walk together to school. There they learn some important lessons from Master Bullfrog.

Materials: frog puppet, small book

Directions: Give the frog puppet a small book to carry. One of Mercer Mayer's wordless frog books would be a fine choice.

Dress the frog in a green jacket and white vest like the froggies in the story. Present the frog to the children and let them guess why he's carrying a book. Tell the children there are six other froggies just like him, and that they all are on the way to school. Ask the children what the frogs might learn in school.

TIDDALICK, THE FROG WHO CAUSED A FLOOD
by Robert Rosenfeldt (Penguin, 1986)

Story: A huge frog drank all the water in Australia. There wasn't any left for the other animals, who then had to come up with a plan to make the frog return the water.

Materials: large balloon frog (see Frog Crafts)

Directions: Introduce the balloon frog as Tiddalick, the frog who drank all the water in Australia. Explain that's the reason he's so huge.

After reading the story, ask the children to make funny faces as a way of getting the frog to laugh. Untie the balloon to let the air out, so that Tiddalick will become a normal-size frog again.

WHAT A CATASTROPHE!

by Wayne Campbell, il. by Eileen Christelow
(Bradbury Press, 1986)

Story: A green-spotted, mess-making frog hops about the breakfast table, in and out of bowls of porridge, and causes quite a catastrophe.

Materials: rubber or other pretend frog, bowl of dry cereal large enough for the frog to sit in

Directions: Hide the frog in the bowl. After you take him out, ask the children to suggest how the frog might have gotten into the bowl.

Tell the children that the frog has caused a "catastrophe." Let them say the word with you. Write the word "catastrophe" on the chalkboard. Explain that a catastrophe can be either a huge disaster or a "small disaster" that ruins someone's plans. Give an example of a small catastrophe that you experienced—preferably something you can now laugh about, for example, locking yourself out of your car or house.

Now read the book. Older children will delight in hearing the four possible endings and then discussing which one they like best. With younger children, it may be less confusing to present just one ending.

THE WIDE-MOUTHED FROG

by Rex Schneider (Stemmer House, 1980)

Story: A wide-mouthed frog thinks he is too grand to eat lowly bugs. Therefore, he searches through the swamp, asking the other animals what he should eat. Finally, he meets an alligator who eats the wide-mouthed frog.

Materials: swim fins, frog headband (see Frog Crafts)

Directions: Wear the swim fins and the frog headband while reading this story. For more fun, open your mouth very wide when speaking the frog's lines. Naturally, the children will giggle a lot.

If you depart from the actual text and use a single refrain—for example, "I'm a wide-mouthed frog in need of food grand enough for me"—the children will soon be able to repeat the line with you, with their mouths opened wide.

At the end, make your mouth very small when you reach the final page and say "Oh."

More Frog Stories

Bernstein, Joanne E. and Paul Cohen, il. by Alexander Wallner. **UN-FROG-GETTABLE RIDDLES** (Whitman, 1981)

This collection of frog riddles will delight frog lovers and eager readers.

Blake, Quentin. **THE STORY OF THE DANCING FROG** (Knopf, 1984)

George, the dancing frog, becomes famous when he travels about the world performing to enthusiastic crowds. On the journey, George is accompanied by Great Aunt Gertrude.

Cleveland, David, il. by Lisa Ernst. **THE FROG ON ROBERT'S HEAD** (Coward, McCann & Geoghegan, 1981)

Robert's sister assists in getting rid of a stubborn frog that has landed on his head.

Dauer, Rosamond, il. by Byron Barton. **BULLFROG AND GERTRUDE GO CAMPING** (Greenwillow, 1980)

When Bullfrog and Gertrude go camping, they find an unusual friend—a snake—who goes home with them.

Dauer, Rosamond, il. by Byron Barton. **BULLFROG BUILDS A HOUSE** (Greenwillow, 1977)

Bullfrog seeks Gertrude's assistance in building his house, and then discovers it's not a happy home without Gertrude there to share it with him.

Galdone, Paul. **THE FROG PRINCE** (McGraw-Hill, 1975)

In this retelling of the Brothers Grimm tale, after a princess throws an ugly frog against a wall, he turns into a handsome prince.

Hammond, Lucille. **WHAT'S THE MATTER, LITTLE FROG?** (Random House, 1987)

Little Frog is sad because he doesn't have a friend, but Duck is able to help him solve this problem.

Hawes, Judy, il. by Don Madden. **WHY FROGS ARE WET** (Harper & Row, 1968)

This amusing nonfiction book will tell children—and you—just about everything you ever needed to know about frogs.

Heller, Ruth. **HOW TO HIDE A GRAY TREE FROG AND OTHER AMPHIBIANS** (Grosset & Dunlap, 1986)

This nonfiction picture book illustrates how frogs and amphibians use natural camouflage to avoid their enemies.

Hoban, Russell, il. by Martin Baynton. **JIM FROG** (Holt, 1983)

Jim Frog is sad because there isn't any "hop" left in him. When night comes, he decides that the day really wasn't so terrible.

Kellogg, Steven. **THE MYSTERIOUS TADPOLE** (Dial, 1977)

Louis's Uncle McAllister sends him a pet tadpole from Scotland for his birthday, but it turns out to be a lovable—if hard to describe—creature.

Lionni, Leo. **FISH IS FISH** (Knopf, 1974)

A minnow and a tadpole become inseparable friends; however, their relationship is temporarily broken when the tadpole becomes a frog.

Lobel, Arnold. **FROG AND TOAD ALL YEAR** (Harper & Row, 1976)

One in a series of "I Can Read" books depicting the adventures of two amphibious friends. The frog tends to be adventurous, while the toad is more cautious. Other titles in the series include:

    DAYS WITH FROG AND TOAD
    FROG AND TOAD TOGETHER

Lucas, Barbara, il. by Stella Ormai. **SLEEPING OVER** (Macmillan, 1986)

Froggie Green spends the night with Bitty Bear, but sleeping in a bed is just too strange.

MacLachlan, Patricia, il. by Tomie de Paola. **MOON, STARS, FROGS, AND FRIENDS** (Pantheon, 1980)

Randall Frog longs for a friend; therefore, he's truly delighted when he becomes the pal of a frog who's actually a prince.

Maris, Ron. **BETTER MOVE ON, FROG** (Julia Macrae Books, 1982)

Looking for a home, Frog finds several holes that are already occupied, but he persists until he finds just the right place.

Mayer, Mercer. **A BOY, A DOG AND A FROG** (Dial, 1967)

The first of six wordless books about a frog who gets into lots of trouble. Other titles in the series from the same publisher are:

FROG, WHERE ARE YOU?
A BOY, A DOG, A FROG, AND A FRIEND
FROG ON HIS OWN
FROG GOES TO DINNER
ONE FROG TOO MANY

Pursell, Margaret. **SPRIG THE TREE FROG** (Carolrhoda, 1976)

Matthew raises tree frogs whose eggs he has found in a pond. Eventually, he returns the frogs to their natural environment.

Roy, Ron, il. by Victoria Chess. **THE GREAT FROG SWAP** (Pantheon, 1981)

Two boys devise a complex plan to guarantee themselves a win in the frog jumping contest.

Steig, William. **GORKY RISES** (Farrar, Straus & Giroux, 1980)

A young frog concocts a magic potion that allows him to fly.

Thaler, Mike, il. by Bruce Degen. **IN THE MIDDLE OF THE PUDDLE** (Harper & Row, 1988)

A frog named Fred and a turtle named Ted help each other survive the torrential rains that change their puddle into a pond.

Frog Poems

FIVE LITTLE FROGS

Before performing the poem, you might explain what a well is, especially for city children who may never have seen one. If you can find a picture in a book, so much the better.

The poem itself can be presented in several ways. One strategy is to make five frogs and a well from paper or felt to use on the flannel board when reciting the poem.

For more involvement, dramatize the poem by having five children play frogs while the others sit in a circle to make the well. Number the children so that each can fall into the center of the circle at the appropriate time. The five frogs can each yell out "Croak" on the final line.

Finally, you can adapt the poem as a finger play by extending the fingers on one hand and fold down a finger each time a frog falls into the well. Let everyone yell the five "Croaks" at the end of the poem.

Five Little Frogs

Five little frogs sitting on a well,
One jumped high
And in he fell.

Four little frogs sitting on a well,
One jumped a little
And in he fell.

Three little frogs sitting on a well,
One peeked in
And in he fell.

Two little frogs sitting on a well,
One jumped everywhere
And in he fell.

One little frog sitting on a well,
He fell asleep
And in he fell.

Along came the children
Who looked in the well.
Five little frogs were doing a yell
"Croak, croak, croak, croak, croak."

THE FROG SITTING ON A LOG

Present the next poem as a puppet show. Set a frog puppet on a real log or one made of rolled-up paper. Move a duck puppet past the frog. The duck quacks loudly at the frog who makes a series of jumps, the last of which lands him in the pond. Invite the children to join you in making the repeated sounds.

The Frog Sitting on a Log

Once there was a little green
Frog, frog, frog.
Who sat quietly upon a brown
Log, log, log.
A yellow duck came swimming by in the
Pond, pond, pond.
He looked at the frog and said,
Quack, quack, quack.
The frog was frightened and
Jumped, jumped, jumped.
And landed in the pond with a
Splash, splash, splash.
Gurgle, gurgle, gurgle.

More Frog Poems

"A Frog and a Flea" p. 4 in READ-ALOUD RHYMES FOR THE VERY YOUNG selected by Jack Prelutsky, il. by Marc Brown (Knopf, 1986).

"The Tree Frog" p. 82 in THE RANDOM HOUSE BOOK OF POETRY FOR CHILDREN selected by Jack Prelutsky, il. by Arnold Lobel (Random House, 1983).

"Bullfrogs" p. 44 in RIDE A PURPLE PELICAN by Jack Prelutsky, il. by Garth Williams (Greenwillow, 1986).

Frog Finger Plays and Songs

BULLFROG AND GERTRUDE

Bullfrog went for a hop,
   (Use fist as frog and hop it.)
And landed on a rock.
   (Stop hopping.)

Bullfrog went for a jog,
   (Make walking motion with fingers.)
And got lost in the fog.
   (Lift shoulders to show confusion.)

Gertrude came by with a jug,
   (Let fingers make walking motion.)
And Bullfrog gave her a hug.
   (Give hug with other hand.)

If I Were A Frog   by Maxine Riggers

If I were a frog I'd croak, croak, croak. If I were a frog I'd leap, leap, leap onto the lily pad.

More Frog Finger Plays

"A Friendly Frog," p. 8, "Junior the Frog," p. 9, "A Frog on a Log," p. 11, all in MOVE OVER, MOTHER GOOSE by Ruth I. Dowell, il. by Concetta Scott (Gryphon House, 1987)

"Bullfrog," p. 9, "Little Frog," p. 54, "Three Frogs," p. 93, "Three Little Leopard Frogs," p. 93, in RING A RING O'ROSES (Flint Public Library, 1988)

More Frog Songs

FROG WENT A-COURTING adapted by Nina Barbaresi (Scholastic, 1985)

   Before performing this song, explain that "courting" is what happens when a person (or an animal character who's acting like a person) wants to convince another person to marry him or her. Sing the song and have the children join in on the "uh hums." Invite the children to sing the whole song as you repeat it. Once the children are familiar with the words, have the girls sing the phrases only while the boys sing the "uh hums."

THE OGRE AND THE FROG KING by Gregoire Solotareff (see Read-Aloud Books)

"Little Green Frog," p. 15 in WEE SING

Frog Games

LEAP FROG

Children (in socks) squat in a line around the room. The child at the end of the line places hands on the back of the next child and leaps over the child. The leaping continues until the child reaches the beginning of the line. The new "frog" at end of the line does the same thing. The game ends when everyone has had a chance to leap.

FROG JUMPING CONTEST

Have all the frogs, played by children, stand behind a line. Take turns making one long leap and mark the distance the frog jumped. All frogs should receive a bag of flies (raisins).

JUMP, FROG, JUMP

The children pretend they're frogs by jumping about while croaking. Have a few spots on the floor designated as lily pads and let them jump from pad to pad.

FROGGIE IN THE PUDDLE

Teach the song "Froggie in the Puddle" to the children and then explain the rules of the game. One or more are chosen to be a frog who sits on a lily pad (a designated spot on the floor). Ask the children to pretend that the area around the pad is a pond. If the frog falls in, he will get wet. The others join hands and circle around the pond chanting the first verse of the following rhyme.

On the second verse, the froggie hops to the children with joined hands. On the final line, the children drop their joined hands and the frog hops out. Then another child is chosen to be a frog to repeat the game.

Froggie in the Puddle

Froggie in the puddle.
You can't get out.
Froggie in the puddle.
You can't get out.
You're covered with mud
And you can't get out.

Froggie hops to a friend who shouts,
"You can't get out."
Froggie hops to another who shouts,
"You can't get out."
Froggie hops to another who shouts,
"Now you can get out."

Frog Crafts

FROG PAPER BAG PUPPET

Materials: size 9 paper bag, green and pink construction paper, frog pattern, black felt marker, glue

Directions: Cut the frog head and body from green paper and the tongue from pink paper. Using the felt marker, draw on the eyes, nose, and spots. Glue the head onto the bottom of the sack—the folded section. Glue the body to the sack below the head. Open the folded part of the sack that is now the frog's mouth and glue on the tongue. Insert your hand into the sack and move the mouth up and down to make the puppet talk.

BALLOON FROG

Materials: 10 inch round green balloon, green construction paper, glue, black felt marker, pattern for frog parts

Directions: Inflate and tie balloon. Cut legs from green paper. Glue the frog parts onto the balloon (body) to resemble a frog. Use the felt marker to draw a wide mouth.

Tie a string to the balloon frog and bounce it around to use as the dancing frog in THE STORY OF THE DANCING FROG by Quentin Blake. You can also use the frog as the disobedient baby that floats away in NEVER SNAP AT A BUBBLE by Yvonne Winer.

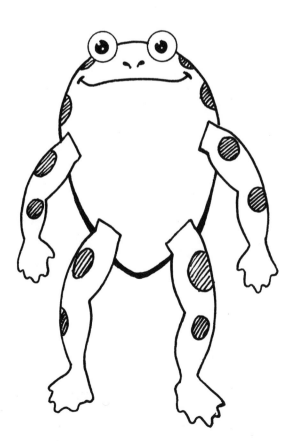

FROG KING CROWN

Materials: gold and red construction or tag paper, glue, stapler

Directions: Cut a three-pointed crown from gold paper approximately 20 by 5 inches. Cut three 1 inch circles from red paper and glue one to each point onto the crown. Staple together to fit the head. This craft can be used after reading THE OGRE AND THE FROG KING by Gregoire Solotareff. Make a smaller crown for the puppet.

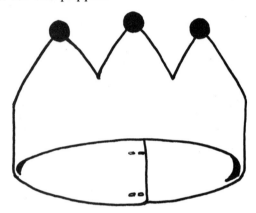

FROG HEADBAND

Materials: green and black construction paper, scissors, two 1½ inch Styrofoam balls, frog headband pattern, stapler, glue

Directions: Cut the frog headband pattern on the fold using green construction paper. Cut out the holes and insert the Styrofoam balls into the holes to make buggy-looking eyes. Cut small black circles for the inner eyes and glue to the Styrofoam balls. Staple the ends of the band together to fit your head. If the Styrofoam balls don't want to stay put, glue them in.

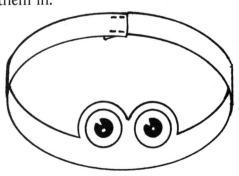

FROG AND TOAD PUPPETS

Materials: two shades of brown and green felt, black felt marker, white construction paper, sewing machine, Frog and Toad patterns

Directions: Cut Toad from the darker brown felt and the spots from the lighter brown. Cut Frog from the green felt in the same way. Make the eyes from white paper and color in with the felt marker. Sew the frog together on the stitching line, being sure to place the eyes and front legs in place to catch them in the seam as you're stitching. Turn right side out and glue the back legs across the front opening at the bottom. Glue the white eyes on top of the felt eyes, and glue the spots onto the puppets' backs. Insert the middle and index fingers to make the puppet come alive.

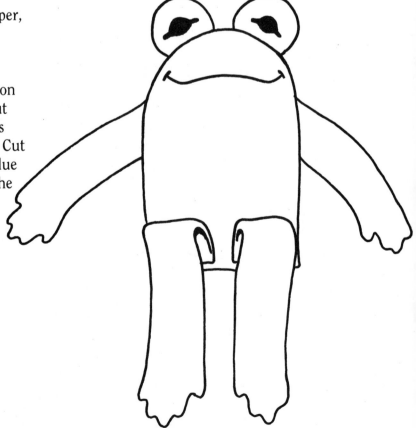

FROG AND TOAD PUPPET

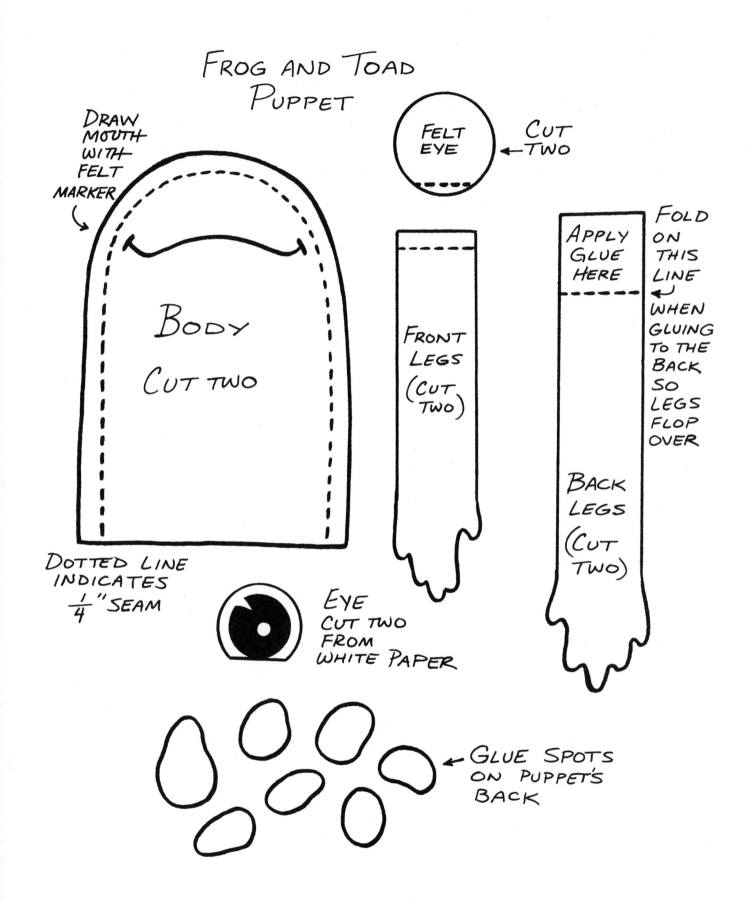

DRAW MOUTH WITH FELT MARKER

FELT EYE

CUT TWO

BODY
CUT TWO

DOTTED LINE INDICATES $\frac{1}{4}$" SEAM

FRONT LEGS (CUT TWO)

APPLY GLUE HERE

FOLD ON THIS LINE

WHEN GLUING TO THE BACK SO LEGS FLOP OVER

BACK LEGS (CUT TWO)

EYE CUT TWO FROM WHITE PAPER

GLUE SPOTS ON PUPPET'S BACK

FROG PAPER BAG PUPPET

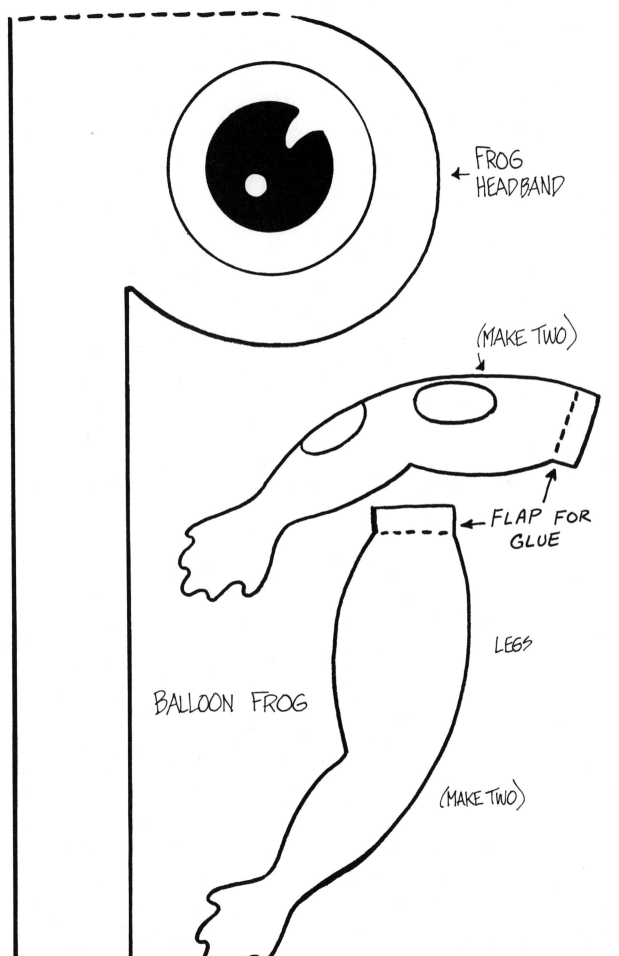

FROG HEADBAND

(MAKE TWO)

FLAP FOR GLUE

LEGS

BALLOON FROG

(MAKE TWO)

Frog Snacks

IMAGINARY FLIES

Serve individual boxes of raisins or make individual servings in sandwich bags. The children pretend they are frogs who are eating flies.

SHERBET FROG

Serve an ice cream scoop of lime sherbet in a bowl with raisins for eyes to make it look like a frog's head.

GREEN CUISINE

Serve anything green, for example, apples, grapes, or "Frog Jello."

Frog Jello

2 3-oz. boxes of lime jello
3 envelopes unflavored gelatin
1 cup cold water
2 cups boiling water

Soak unflavored gelatin in cold water for 5 minutes. Place lime jello in bowl. Pour unflavored jello into bowl with lime jello. Add boiling water. Stir until dissolved. Pour into 9 by 9 inch pan. Refrigerate.

MARVELOUS MICE

To introduce the mouse story hours, use Amanda, the story mouse. She lives in the library in her own little house and when she comes out of her mouse house, it's a signal that a story will be read. The children will watch for Amanda to come out and when they see her, they will be quiet and ready to listen to a story.

The first time the children meet Amanda, try saying something like this in your best mouse voice:

"Hello, I'm Amanda, the story mouse, and I live in this little house with my name on it. I moved here because there are many wonderful books in this place. I love stories! That's why they call me the story mouse. Is it okay with you children if I live here? I hope we can be good friends. Whenever _____ (name of the storyteller) reads a story, I'll come out of my house to listen because I don't want to miss a single tale. I want you children to watch for me and when I come out, you will know it's time to get ready to listen. Let's hear a story now."

Amanda's house can be made from a shoe box or any container with a hole for her doorway. Use colored poster paper to make a roof.

Purchase or make a small mouse that fits easily into the house. The children will fall in love with Amanda. You might want to use her for other story hours.

Setting the Stage

Wear Mickey Mouse ears or a Mickey Mouse T-shirt when you tell mouse stories. There are commercial patterns for mouse suits. You might even rent one from a costume shop.

There's an old saying: "Be as quiet as a mouse." The children can practice being quiet as mice by tiptoeing to and from the storytelling spot, trying not to make a single sound.

Create several bookmark mice following the directions in Mouse Crafts. Attach the bookmarks to walls, desks, chairs, and bookshelves. Put some mice behind the books so when the children pull out a book, they will find a mouse. You might want to slip some inside the books. With all these mice running around the room, it might be fun to place a stuffed cat somewhere to complete the picture.

Set a stuffed toy mouse on the shelf or table, and prop a mouse-size book in his hands, as if he's reading. Surround the mouse with other mice books. You'll have an attractive setting where the children can come to find mouse stories!

If you're using magic carpets to fly to Mouseville to hear mouse stories, you might stop by the moon to get some cheese, if you believe that's what the moon is made of . . . or even if you don't.

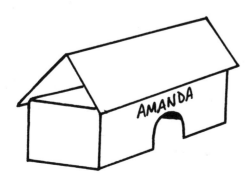

Bulletin Board Ideas

1. Use an opaque projector to enlarge and copy the "Sh! Mice Are Reading" illustration onto poster paper. Color and mat before pinning it to the board.

2. The poem "Mice," is a classic and all children should become familiar with it (see Mouse Poems). You might print the poem in large letters on poster paper. Make the title of the poem look like cheese lettering. Color it yellow and have a few mice nibbling on the letters as illustrated. The children should be able to see the words of the poem easily so they can read or recite the poem with you several times.

3. Use an opaque projector to enlarge and copy the cover of the book FREDERICK. Color and mat it. This makes a simple and effective display.

4. Enlarge Alexander and Willy from ALEXANDER AND THE WIND-UP MOUSE. Color and cut out each mouse. Pin the mice on the board along with this heading: "Alexander and Willy are Good Mouse Friends."

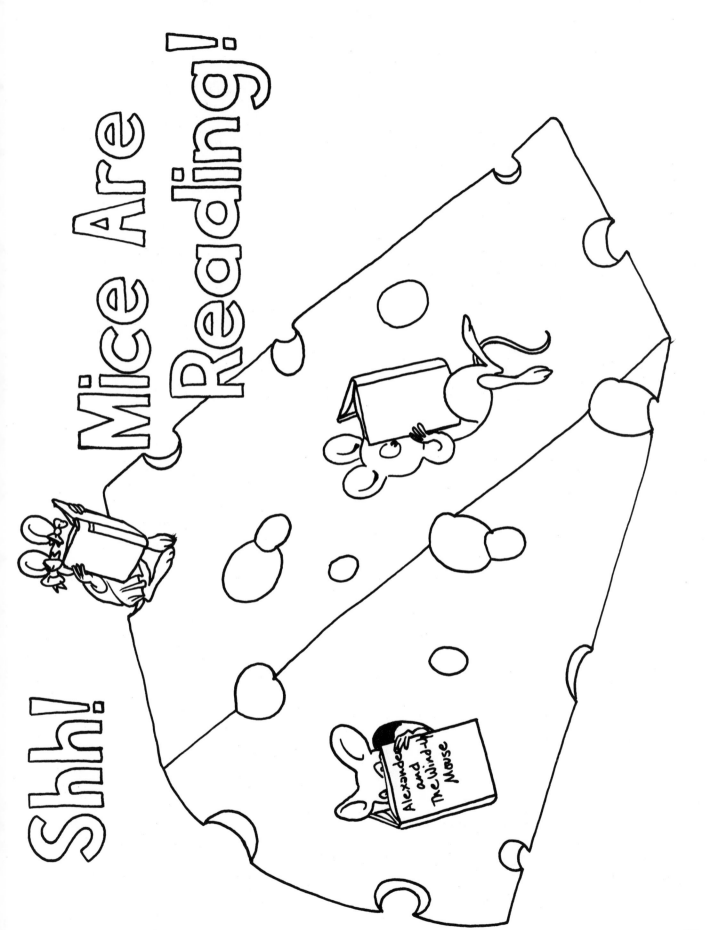

Read-Aloud Stories

ALEXANDER AND THE WIND-UP MOUSE
by Leo Lionni (Pantheon, 1969)

Story: Alexander, a real mouse, makes friends with Willy, a wind-up mouse. Alexander wants to be just like Willy until he discovers that Willy is going to be thrown away.

Materials: stuffed toy mouse, wind-up mouse, dance music

Directions: Introduce the stuffed mouse as Alexander and the wind-up mouse as Willy. Ask the children to pretend that Alexander is a real mouse. Wind Willy to demonstrate how he moves mechanically. Tell the children that these two characters become good friends in the story you're about to tell. Place the mice on the book shelf or table so that the mice and the children can listen to the story.

After reading the book, play some lively music for the children to dance to, as Alexander and Willy do in the story.

GERALDINE, THE MUSIC MOUSE
by Leo Lionni (Pantheon, 1979)

Story: Geraldine discovers a made-of-cheese mouse flutist in an enormous piece of cheese she is sharing with her friends. Her companions want to eat the cheese figure. Geraldine protests until she learns that she can play the flute music herself.

Materials: real flute or recording of flute music, mouse carved out of cheese

Directions: Because the story will be more meaningful if children are familiar with the sound of a flute, play a recording of some flute music. For more interest, blow a few notes yourself on a flute or invite a guest flutist to perform. The music can come before or during the reading.

Later, display the cheese mouse. The mouse will spark some lively discussion and also overcome some hunger pangs. Directions for carving the mouse will be found in Mouse Snacks.

IF YOU GIVE A MOUSE A COOKIE

by Laura Numeroff, il. by Felicia Bond (Harper & Row, 1985)

Story: A young boy is about to give a mouse a cookie. But the boy imagines how the mouse might next ask for milk, and then continue making one request after another.

Materials: cookies, milk, a stuffed toy mouse, a story scroll (see Mouse Crafts)

Directions: Give a cookie to a stuffed toy mouse as if you're feeding him. Tell the children that this mouse is different from most mice because he prefers cookies to cheese.

As you're reading the story, act tired and disgusted as each of the mouse's requests lead to another demand.

Make the story scroll as illustrated in Mouse Crafts. Then present the story again using the story scroll. Encourage the children to tell the story along with you. The children can later use the scroll to retell the story on their own.

Serve cookies and milk as a special treat!

THE LITTLE MOUSE, THE RED RIPE STRAWBERRY, AND THE BIG HUNGRY BEAR

by Don and Audrey Wood, il. by Don Wood (Child's Play, 1984)

Story: A little mouse picks a ripe strawberry, which he doesn't want the hungry bear to eat.

Materials: ripe strawberries, plastic knives, Groucho Marx-like eyeglasses (optional)

Directions: Hold up a big strawberry and say, "I know about a mouse who visited a strawberry patch to get one of these."

After reading the story, the children's mouths will be watering for red, ripe strawberries. Divide the group into pairs, and give each one berry and a plastic knife. Have the partners share their strawberry just like the mouse did in the story. If you have enough berries for seconds, the children will probably be eager to further practice the art of sharing.

For more fun, put on a pair of Groucho glasses like the ones worn as a disguise in the story. You might find a pair in a costume shop, or make your own. Ask the children if they can tell who you are. Then, let the children model the glasses in front of a mirror. Be prepared for lots of laughter.

THE MAID AND THE MOUSE AND THE ODD-SHAPED HOUSE
adapted by Paul Zelinsky (Dodd, Mead, 1981)

Story: This is a tell-and-draw story. A maid and a mouse live in an oddly-shaped house. When they add onto the house, it takes on the appearance of a cat who scares them away. In the end, they live in a regular-shaped house.

Materials: chalkboard and chalk or poster paper and felt marker

Directions: As you tell the story, draw each successive part of the picture as it's called for in the text. You will need to practice this to become familiar enough to tell the story and draw at the same time.

An alternative is to let a different child draw each part, directing him where to draw. If you are musical, sing this rhyming story to an original tune.

A MOUSE IN MY HOUSE
by John Houston, il. by Winnie Fitch (Addison-Wesley, 1972)

Story: A cat is brought into the house to chase out a mouse. Then a dog gets the job of getting rid of the cat. Next come a pig, a lion, and an elephant. Finally, the mouse returns.

Materials: flannel-board mouse, cat, dog, pig, lion, and elephant (see Mouse Crafts)

Directions: Display the animals in sequence as you tell or sing the story. Use the music in A MOUSE IN MY HOUSE or make up your own tune. Encourage the children to sing along with you.

After reading the story, choose six children to pantomime the actions of the six animals as you and the other children say or sing the words. Simple masks or costumes can add to the fun, but they aren't necessary. Repeat the story so that each child in the room has a chance to play an animal. If the group is large, two children can play a part at the same time.

THE MOUSE'S WEDDING
retold by Ruth Gross, il. by Susan Swan
(Scholastic, 1972)

Story: A mouse is looking for a wife. He wants her to be the daughter of the most powerful thing in the world. He visits the sun, the cloud, the wind, and the tower. But in the end he discovers that the mouse is the most powerful thing of all.

Materials: two toy mice—purchased or made (see Mouse Crafts)

Directions: Dress one mouse as a bride with a bouquet. Dress the second mouse as a groom.

It is better to tell this story in your own words. Use lots of dialogue and feel free to add details. Invite the children to join you with the refrain: "You can keep your daughter."

After telling the story, present the two mice that were "just married." Encourage the children to use the mice to retell the story.

NOISY NORA
by Rosemary Wells (Dial, 1973)

Story: Nora doesn't get any attention from her family. She makes a lot of noise, but when that doesn't get their attention, she runs away from home. Everyone misses her and is glad when she returns.

Materials: five mouse finger puppets representing Nora and her mouse family (see Mouse Crafts)

Directions: After reading the story, show the puppets to the children. Retell the story as five children present the action using the puppets. As you read, encourage the children to join you in the refrain: "Nora had to wait." Add to the fun by making sound effects such as a crashing sound when the chairs fall.

Later, have other groups of five children tell the story with the help of the puppets.

TWO TERRIBLE FRIGHTS
by Jim Aylesworth, il. by Eileen Christelow (Atheneum, 1987)

Story: A little girl and a little mouse are each told they can have a bedtime snack if they get it themselves. When they meet in the kitchen they frighten each other, but later their encounter turns out positive for both.

Materials: a walnut-shell bed, a small toy mouse or mouse-shaped button

Directions: Make a walnut-shell bed for the baby mouse. Use scraps of fabric and batting for blankets and a pillow. Put the small mouse in the bed.

When reading the story, use a squeaky voice for the mouse's dialogue. Pretend you're scared when the girl and the mouse first meet in the kitchen. Use a soothing voice when their mothers comfort them. Sing a lullaby as the mouse and the girl are tucked into bed.

As a follow-up, have each child make a walnut-shell bed. This activity will help the children remember the story forever.

WHERE ARE YOU GOING, LITTLE MOUSE?
by Robert Kraus, il. by Jose Aruego and Ariane Dewey (Greenwillow, 1986)

Story: Little Mouse runs away from home because he believes nobody loves him. But when it begins to get dark, he decides that home isn't such a bad place after all.

Materials: hobo's stick with a bag tied on the end, as illustrated in the story

Directions: Put the stick with the bag over your shoulder. Tell the children that you know a story about a mouse who put his things into a bag because he wants to run away.

At the appropriate points in the story, signal the children to say the refrain: "Have you found them?" At the conclusion of the story, have the children hug each other as the mouse family does.

Divide older children who can read into two groups. One group reads the black lettered words and the other group reads the red. Children will enjoy this question-and-answer interaction.

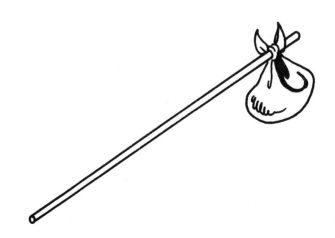

More Mouse Stories

Aesop, il. by Bob Dole. **THE LION AND THE MOUSE** (Troll Associations, 1981)

A lion captures a little mouse who promises the lion he will do him a favor if the lion will let him loose. The lion does. When the lion is captured, the mouse gnaws a hole in the net to set him free. The moral is: Anyone might need help sometime.

Brown, Marcia. **ONCE A MOUSE . . .** (Scribner's, 1961)

This fable from ancient India tells of a hermit who rescues a mouse from a crow. The hermit's magical powers turn the mouse into a cat, then into a dog, and finally into a tiger. When the tiger is ungrateful, the hermit turns him back into a mouse.

Bunting, Eve, il. by Jan Brett. **THE MOTHER'S DAY MICE** (Houghton Mifflin, 1986)

Three mouse brothers search for a present for their mother. The littlest mouse surprises everyone when he sings a song to their mother as his gift to her.

Chorao, Kay. **CATHEDRAL MOUSE** (Dutton, 1988)

A little mouse runs away from the pet shop and ends up living in a cathedral. A stone carver carves the mouse in stone and they become the best of friends.

Ernst, Lisa. **THE RESCUE OF AUNT PANSY** (Viking, 1987)

Russell the cat has a toy mouse which Joanne, a curious mouse, mistakes for her Aunt Pansy. When Joanne tries to rescue the toy, a game of hide-and-seek results.

Felix, Monique. **THE STORY OF A LITTLE MOUSE TRAPPED IN A BOOK** (Green Tiger Press, 1980)

A mouse is caught between the pages of this wordless book. He keeps turning the pages but can't get out until he uses one of the pages to make an airplane.

Freeman, Don. **THE GUARD MOUSE** (Viking, 1967)

The guard mouse takes his visiting cousins on a mouse's-eye sightseeing tour of London. When they return to the castle, they discover the guard mouse's royal hat is missing. Fortunately, the hat is found in time for the changing of the guard.

Freeman, Don. **NORMAN THE DOORMAN** (Viking, 1959)

Norman is a doorman for a mouse hole in an art museum, where he acts as a guide to other mice. When Norman secretly enters his mouse sculpture in a contest at the museum, he wins the grand prize.

Freeman, Lydia and Don Freeman. **PET OF THE MET** (Penguin, 1988)

Maestro Petrini is a musical mouse who loves his work at the Opera House. But he doesn't like the pesky cat Mefisto. The performance of "The Magic Flute" brings a change and the two become friends.

Gackenbach, Dick. **THE PERFECT MOUSE** (Macmillan, 1984)

In this retold classic tale, Molly Margaret is such a perfect mouse her parents want her to marry the sun, a cloud, the wind, or a stone wall. She says no to each of them, instead choosing a mouse for her mate.

Henkes, Kevin. **CHESTER'S WAY** (Greenwillow, 1988)

Chester and Wilson are mouse friends who always do things the same way. Then Lilly moves into the neighborhood. She shows them that there are different ways to do the same activity.

Henkes, Kevin. **SHEILA RAE, THE BRAVE** (Greenwillow, 1987)

Sheila Rae, who thinks of herself as a very brave mouse, looks after her little sister, Louise. But when Sheila Rae becomes lost and then frightened, Louise goes to her rescue and discovers her own courageousness.

Henkes, Kevin. **A WEEKEND WITH WENDELL** (Greenwillow, 1986)

Wendell is spending the weekend with Sophie and her family. Sophie doesn't like to play with the rambunctious Wendell until she learns to assert herself.

Hoff, Syd. **MRS. BRICE'S MICE** (Harper & Row, 1988)

Mrs. Brice cares for her 25 mice, giving them the best cheese and always keeping them clean. But one mouse, who refuses to conform, causes plenty of trouble for Mrs. Brice. However, this nonconformist mouse proves his worth by rescuing the mice when the cat appears.

Holabird, Katharine, il. by Helen Craig. **ANGELINA BALLERINA** (Clarkson N. Potter, 1983)

Angelina mouse desperately wants to become a real ballerina. She works diligently until her dream comes true. Other stories about Angelina include:

> **ANGELINA'S CHRISTMAS**
> **ANGELINA AT THE FAIR**

Hurlimann, Ruth. **THE CAT AND MOUSE WHO SHARED A HOUSE** (Walck, 1973)

This Grimm fairy tale features a cat and a mouse who share a house and a pot of butter meant to last them through the winter. The cat eats all the butter herself, and when the mouse complains, the cat eats the mouse, too.

Ivimey, John, il. by Paul Galdone. **THREE BLIND MICE** (Clarion, 1987)

In this rhyming story, three small mice looking for fun are bold, cold, hungry, glad, scared, sad, sick, and—finally—happy when their eyesight is restored.

Kraus, Robert, il. by Jose Aruego and Ariane Dewey. **ANOTHER MOUSE TO FEED** (Prentice-Hall, 1980)

Mr. and Mrs. Mouse are exhausted because they have too many children to care for. They work at several jobs to support their family. Finally, the little mice decide to take over and Mr. and Mrs. Mouse are able to get some rest.

Kraus, Robert, il. by Jose Aruego and Ariane Dewey. **COME OUT AND PLAY, LITTLE MOUSE** (Greenwillow, 1987)

Every day the cat asks the mouse to come out and play, but the mouse is always too busy. Then one day the mouse's little brother decides he'll play with the cat. A rescue is called for, and that's just what the older mouse accomplishes.

Kraus, Robert, il. by Hilary Knight. **THE GOOD MOUSEKEEPER** (Dutton, 1977)

A loving mother cat cares for her active mice—as many as 32 on some days. She works diligently and is tired by the end of the day, but her heart is filled with sweet contentment.

Kraus, Robert, il. by Jose Aruego. **WHOSE MOUSE ARE YOU?** (Macmillan, 1970)

The mouse describes the disastrous things that have happened to his family. He then rescues his family from a trap and is pleasantly surprised when he gets a new baby brother.

Leonard, Marcia, il. by Karen Schmidt. **LITTLE MOUSE MAKES A MESS** (Bantam, 1985)

Little Mouse wants to help prepare the house for his grandparents' visit. Unfortunately, he's not too successful in his efforts to assist.

Lionni, Leo. **FREDERICK** (Pantheon, 1967)

The mice accuse Frederick of not helping to gather and store the winter food supply. Frederick replies that he's gathering rays of sunshine. The mice are surprised when he really does provide the warmth of the sun. The story shows that there is more than one way to help.

Lionni, Leo. THE GREENTAIL MOUSE (Pantheon, 1973)

During their Mardi Gras celebration, the gentle field mice wear big, scary animal masks. For a while, the mice forget who they are and fall into the roles of the ferocious animals they are pretending to be. Then they remove their masks and return to being gentle mice.

Lionni, Leo. NICOLAS, WHERE HAVE YOU BEEN? (Knopf, 1987)

Nicolas sets out in search of ripe, red berries, but a bird picks him up and carries him into her nest. The bird then brings him the berries he was searching for, and the two become friends.

Lionni, Leo. TILLIE AND THE WALL (Knopf, 1989)

Tillie the mouse longs to discover the unknown on the other side of the wall. Because none of the other mice is as curious as she is, she goes over the wall by herself.

Lobel, Arnold. MOUSE TALES (Harper & Row, 1972)

Papa mouse will tell these seven mouse tales to his seven sons, one for each son, if they will promise to go to sleep when he has finished all the tales.

Majewski, Joe, il. by Marcia Majewski. A FRIEND FOR OSCAR MOUSE (Dial, 1988)

Oscar, a house mouse, creeps through a hole in the garden where he meets a field mouse who becomes a good friend.

Martin, Jacqueline, il. by Stella Ormai. BIZZY BONES AND THE LOST QUILT (Lothrop, 1988)

Bizzy is a small mouse who is attached to his quilt. When Bizzy's quilt is left behind on a harvesting expedition, the trouble begins.

Martin, Jacqueline, il. by Stella Ormai. BIZZY BONES AND UNCLE EZRA (Lothrop, 1984)

Bizzy, who is living in an old shoe, is afraid that the shoe will blow away in the wind. His Uncle Ezra helps Bizzy overcome his fear by building a merry-go-round propelled by wind.

McCully, Emily. PICNIC (Harper & Row, 1984)

This wordless book tells the story of a little mouse who gets lost during a family picnic. All the other mice search until she is found.

Miller, Edna. MOUSEKIN'S THANKSGIVING (Prentice-Hall, 1985)

Someone has taken the winter food supply of Mousekin and his forest friends. Mousekin discovers a wild turkey took the food, not realizing it belonged to someone else. When the turkey returns the food, the feast begins.

Muntean, Michaela, il. by Christopher Santaro. A GARDEN FOR MISS MOUSE (Parents Magazine Press, 1982)

Miss Mouse plans a huge garden, but the vegetables are too abundant. Something has to be done quickly because they are growing out of bounds.

Oakley, Graham. THE CHURCH MICE AT BAY (Atheneum, 1978)

When the vicar goes on vacation, a new curate comes to the church to take over for a few weeks. He doesn't get along too well with the mice who finally chase him away. Then the old vicar returns to the delight of the mice. Other enchanting books in this series include:

> THE CHURCH MOUSE
> THE CHURCH CAT ABROAD
> THE CHURCH MICE AND THE MOON
> THE CHURCH MICE SPREAD THEIR
>   WINGS
> THE CHURCH MICE ADRIFT
> THE CHURCH MICE AT CHRISTMAS

Potter, Beatrix. THE TALE OF TWO BAD MICE (Frederick Warne, 1985)

Tom Thumb and Hunca Munca play in the doll's house when the nursery is empty. They are naughty and wreck the playhouse, but Tom Thumb finds a sixpence and pays for the damage.

Pryor, Bonnie, il. by Maryjane Begin. **THE PORCUPINE MOUSE** (Morrow, 1988)

Mouse brothers Louie and Dan leave their mother's home to find a place of their own. They quarrel and find it difficult to live together peacefully until Louie tricks a cat to save Dan's life.

Quackenbush, Robert. **MOUSE FEATHERS** (Clarion, 1988)

Maxine Mouse is babysitting when her nephews have a pillow fight. The feathers fly onto the fresh paint, into the bread dough, and all over a freshly iced cake.

Quackenbush, Robert. **NO MOUSE FOR ME** (Franklin Watts, 1981)

Having a pet mouse might be trouble because a cat could come to chase the mouse and then a dog might come to chase the cat and on and on until the entire house would be destroyed. Therefore, a pet snake might be better than a pet mouse.

Roche, P. K. **GOOD-BYE ARNOLD!** (Dial, 1979)

Webster is happy when his brother, Arnold, goes to visit their grandmother. Then he discovers that he misses his brother after all.

Roche, P. K. **WEBSTER AND ARNOLD GO CAMPING** (Viking, 1988)

Two mouse brothers enjoy a real adventure as they hold their first camp-out in their own backyard.

Steig, William. **DOCTOR DESOTO** (Scholastic, 1982)

Doctor DeSoto is a mouse dentist who rarely accepts dangerous animals for clients. He makes an exception for a fox with a terrible toothache. When the fox tries to devour the dentist, Doctor DeSoto outfoxes him.

Steptoe, John. **THE STORY OF JUMPING MOUSE** (Lothrop, 1984)

This native American legend tells of a humble mouse who journeys into the world to find new challenges. The mouse's compassion for others is rewarded, and when the mouse jumps high into the sky, he becomes an eagle. Now he can fly to the far-off land he longs to see.

Vincent, Gabrielle. **FEEL BETTER, ERNEST!** (Greenwillow, 1988)

Celestine, a delicate mouse, nurses her lumbering bear friend, Ernest, back to health in a most caring way.

Vincent, Gabrielle. **WHERE ARE YOU, ERNEST AND CELESTINE?** (Greenwillow, 1986)

Ernest and Celestine are best friends. When they are separated during a visit to a museum, there are some anxious moments. Other mouse books in the series include:
> ERNEST AND CELESTINE
> BRAVO, ERNEST AND CELESTINE
> SMILE, ERNEST AND CELESTINE
> ERNEST AND CELESTINE'S PICNIC
> MERRY CHRISTMAS, ERNEST AND
> CELESTINE

Wells, Rosemary. **STANLEY AND RHODA** (Dial, 1978)

Stanley and Rhoda are brother and sister. In this series of three separate adventures, Stanley is always trying to convince Rhoda to act right.

Ziefert, Harriet, il. by David Prebenna. **A CLEAN HOUSE FOR MOLE AND MOUSE** (Viking, 1988)

Mole and Mouse clean house, but once it's clean, Mouse doesn't want Mole to do anything for fear he'll make a mess.

Ziefert, Harriet, il. by David Prebenna. **A NEW HOUSE FOR MOLE AND MOUSE** (Viking, 1987)

Mole and Mouse try out everything in their new home. All goes well until they receive a bouquet of balloons that lifts Mouse to the ceiling.

Mouse Poems and Finger Plays

PUSSY CAT

Pussy cat, pussy cat,
Where have you been?
I've been to London
To look at the Queen.
Pussy cat, pussy cat,
What did you do there?
I frightened a little mouse
Under her chair.
—Mother Goose

SIX LITTLE MICE

Six little mice sat down to spin;
Pussy passed by and she peeped in.
What are you doing, my little men?
Weaving coats for gentlemen.
Shall I come in and cut off your threads?
No, no, Mistress Pussy, you'd bite off our heads.
Oh, no, I'll not, I'll help you to spin.
That may be so, but don't you come in.
—Mother Goose

THREE BLIND MICE

Three blind mice.
Three blind mice.
See how they run.
See how they run.
They all ran after the farmer's wife.
Who cut off their tails with a carving knife.
Did you ever see such a thing in your life
As three blind mice?
—Mother Goose

HICKORY, DICKORY, DOCK

Hickory, dickory, dock
　(Raise right arm.)
The mouse ran up the clock.
　(With the fingers of the left hand, run up
　the right arm.)
The clock struck one.
　(On "one," clap hands.)
And down he ran.
　(Run fingers back down again.)
Hickory, dickory, dock.
—Mother Goose

More Mice Poems

"Naughty Little Brown Mouse" p. 30 in RIDE A PURPLE PELICAN by Jack Prelutsky, il. by Garth Williams (Greenwillow, 1986)

"Mice" p. 30 and "Field Mouse to Kitchen Mouse" p. 10 in POEMS TO READ TO THE VERY YOUNG selected by Josette Frank, il. by Eloise Wilkin (Random House, 1982)

"The Mouse House" p. 24 and "The Snail and the Mouse" p. 4 in READ-ALOUD RHYMES FOR THE VERY YOUNG selected by Jack Prelutsky, il. by Marc Brown (Knopf, 1986)

More Finger Plays

"Five Little Mice," p. 30, "Little Mice," p. 55, "Where Are the Baby Mice?" p. 104 in RING A RING O' ROSES (Flint Public Library)

"A Mouse Chased a Pussy Cat," p. 23, "Said Father Mouse," p. 25 in MOVE OVER, MOTHER GOOSE! by Ruth Dowell, il. by Concetta Scott (Gryphon House, 1987)

Mouse Songs

THREE BLIND MICE

After reading the picture book, THREE BLIND MICE, sing the song. The music is included in the book. Create additional verses by substituting the following words for "blind" in the original: *bold, cold, hungry, glad, scared, sad, sick,* and *happy.* The children should dramatize each feeling. For example, they can stick out their chests to signify boldness, shiver for coldness, and hold their stomachs for hunger. Naturally, it's best to let the children create their own gestures.

THE MOUSE'S WEDDING

After reading THE MOUSE'S WEDDING, teach the following song to the children. It's about a mouse seeking the most powerful thing to be his wife.

The Mouse Wants a Wife
(Tune: "Farmer in the Dell")

A wife it is I want.
A wife it is I want.
Tra-la-tee-boom-dee-aye,
A wife it is I want.

I shall ask the sun.
I shall ask the sun.
Tra-la-tee-boom-dee-aye,
I shall ask the sun.

I shall ask the cloud.
I shall ask the cloud.
Tra-la-tee-boom-dee-aye,
I shall ask the cloud.

I shall ask the wind.
I shall ask the wind.
Tra-la-tee-boom-dee-aye,
I shall ask the wind.

I shall ask the tower.
I shall ask the tower.
Tra-la-tee-boom-dee-aye,
I shall ask the tower.

I shall ask the mouse.
I shall ask the mouse.
Tra-la-tee-boom-dee-aye,
I shall ask the mouse.

How happy we will be.
How happy we will be.
Tra-la-tee-boom-dee-aye,
How happy we will be.
—Melodee Riggers

Mouse Games

GRAB A MOUSE TAIL

Every child needs a mouse tail, which can be a handkerchief or a scrap of cloth stuck into a back pocket or waistband. Or make mice tails from gray fabric following the directions for making monkey tails (see Monkey Crafts).

The children should scatter about in a designated area. When the signal to go is given, everyone tries to grab as many mice tails as possible. Children can continue to play even if their tails have been grabbed. This game only lasts for a few seconds, so you may want to play it several times.

CAT AND MOUSE

Children join hands to make a circle. One child is the mouse who stands in the center of the circle. Another child is the cat who is on the outside of the circle. The cat then tries to catch the mouse as both dart in and out of the circle. The children in the circle can assist the cat or mouse by raising their arms to let either player in or out. When the cat catches the mouse, two more children are chosen until all have had a chance to play.

Mouse Crafts

MOUSE BOOKMARK

Materials: gray and pink construction paper, felt marker, glue, scissors, pink yarn, mouse patterns

Directions: Cut the body from the gray paper and the ears from the pink paper. Draw the nose and eyes with the felt marker. Glue the ears onto the head as illustrated. Glue a six inch piece of pink yarn onto the underside of the body for the tail.

    This mouse can save your place by hanging his tail out of the book.

A MOUSE IN MY HOUSE FLANNEL BOARD CHARACTERS

Materials: gray, pink, brown, yellow, and black construction paper, felt markers, scissors, carbon paper, scraps of flannel, rubber cement

Directions: Use gray paper for the mouse and elephant, pink for the pig, yellow for the lion, brown for the dog, and black for the cat. Photocopy the animals from A MOUSE IN MY HOUSE. Then cut them out and trace them onto the construction paper. Add the features with felt markers. Use rubber cement to glue a piece of flannel onto the backs of the animals, so they will adhere to the flannel board as you tell the story.

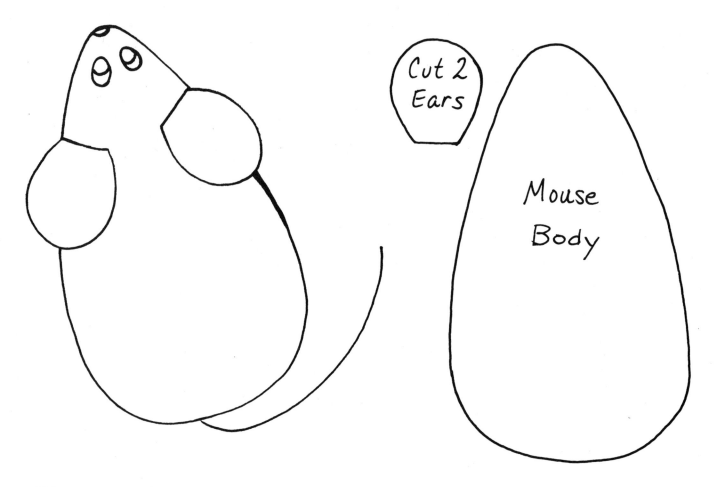

NOISY NORA FINGER PUPPET

Materials: gray, black, and white felt, glue, gray or black yarn, patterns, sewing machine, scissors

Directions: Use the patterns to cut the body and ears from the gray felt. Cut small circles from the black and white felt for the eyes. Use black felt for the nose and mouth. Cut a four inch piece of yarn for the tail.

Position the ears at the top between the two body pieces so the straight edges will be caught in the seam as you sew the bodies together, taking an ⅛ inch seam. Turn inside out. Glue the eyes, nose, and mouth onto the body as illustrated. Stitch the tail into place on the back side.

IF YOU GIVE A MOUSE A COOKIE STORY SCROLL

Materials: two 6 inch dowels, a 4 x 36 inch piece of white, lightweight paper, glue, tape, felt markers, patterns

Directions: Copy the patterns for the 15 items the mouse might request on the 4 x 36 inch paper. Tape the ends to the dowels (pencils will work) and roll the paper around the sticks to make a scroll.

Use the scroll when retelling the story, letting the children say it with you the second time. The older children will delight in making their own story scrolls.

As a group project, make a larger scroll which all the children can help illustrate. They can then use the scroll when presenting the story to another group.

STUFFED TOY MOUSE

Materials: soft gray fabric, black or gray felt and yarn, glue, mouse patterns, sewing supplies, sewing machine, heavy thread, scissors

Directions: Cut the body pieces from the gray fabric and the ears from the black or gray felt. Cut a six inch piece of gray or black yarn for the tail. Cut the eyes and nose from black felt. Sew the upper body pieces together on the curved edge. Stitch the upper body to the bottom leaving an opening for turning at the back of the mouse. Turn and stuff with batting. Insert tail and stitch the opening closed. Glue or stitch the ears, eyes, and nose to the body. Stitch heavy thread through the nose to make three whiskers on each side.

This mouse can be used for Amanda, the story mouse, or other mice as described in the read-aloud section.

MOUSE EARS

Materials: gray and pink construction paper, glue, scissors, stapler, patterns

Directions: Cut the ears and a 1½ x 23 inch headband from gray paper. Cut the ear centers from pink paper. Glue the centers onto the ears. Staple the headband together to fit the child. Staple the ears onto the headband as illustrated.

The children can wear their ears while listening to or reading mouse stories.

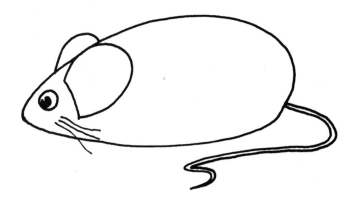

Stuffed Toy Mouse

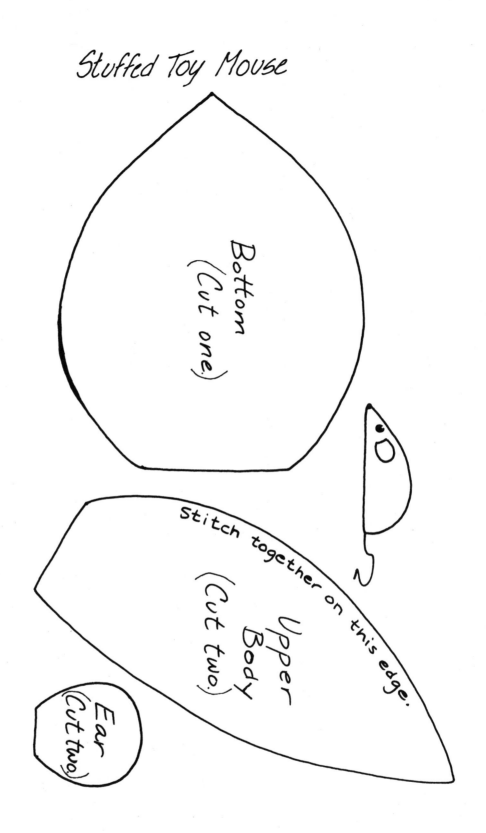

Bottom
(Cut one.)

Stitch together on this edge.

Upper
Body
(Cut two.)

Ear
(Cut two.)

Mouse Ear Patterns

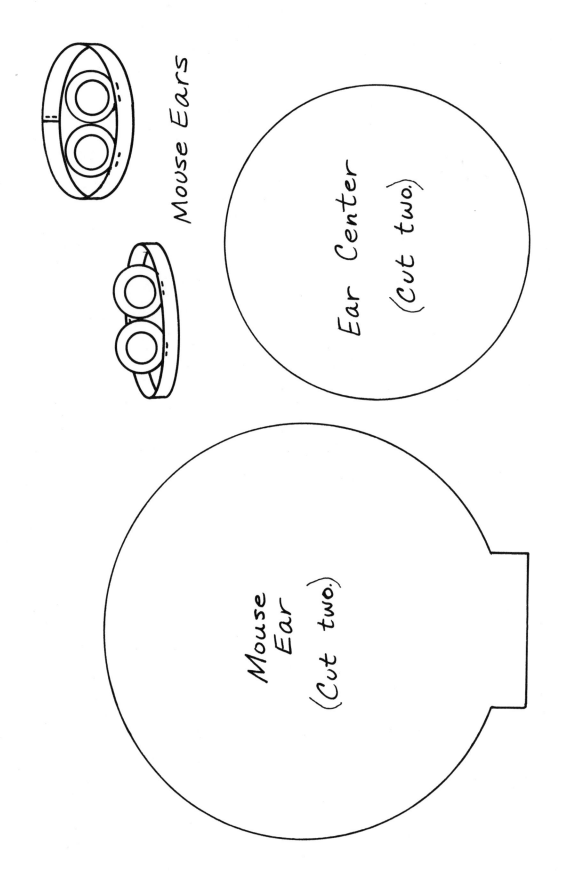

Mouse Ears

Ear Center
(Cut two.)

Mouse Ear
(Cut two.)

Story Scroll Patterns

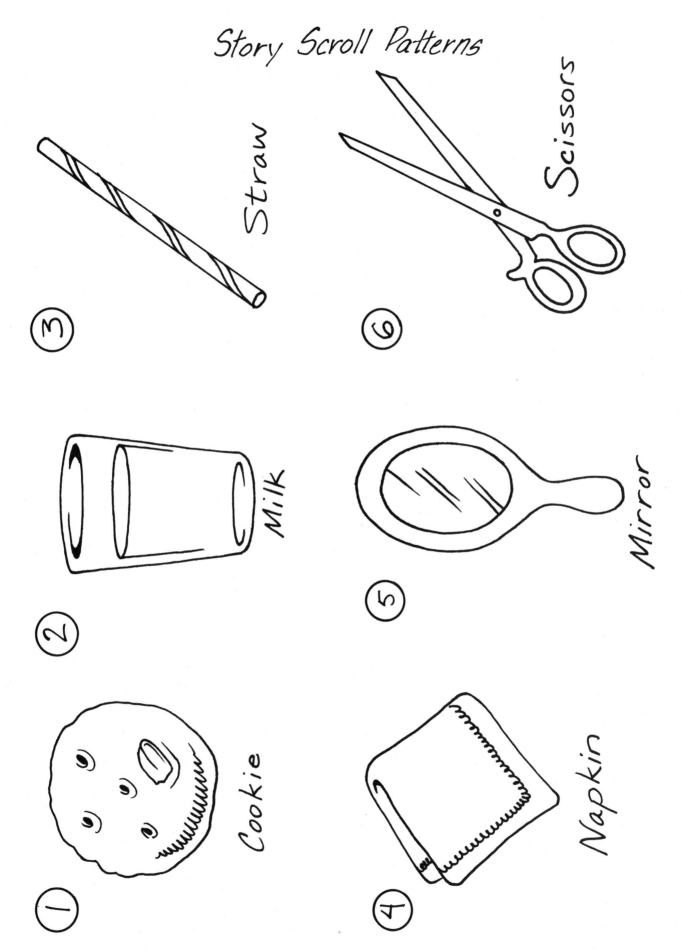

Straw

Scissors

Milk

Mirror

Cookie

Napkin

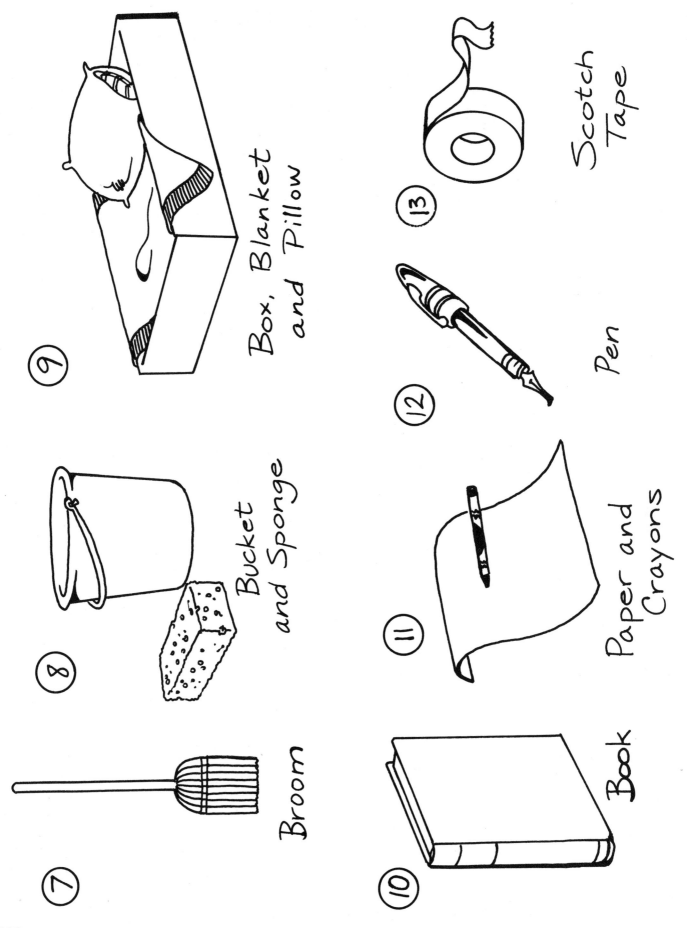

7 Broom

8 Bucket and Sponge

9 Box, Blanket and Pillow

10 Book

11 Paper and Crayons

12 Pen

13 Scotch Tape

Mouse Snacks

SWISS CHEESE SNACKS

Serve "mouse cheese" and crackers. The traditional choice is Swiss cheese, with holes that might have been made by nibbling mice.

CHEESE FLUTIST

After reading GERALDINE, THE MUSIC MOUSE, carve a mouse flutist out of cheese. A soft cheese such as mozzarella works well. Begin by tracing an outline of the mouse with a knife. After cutting the figure, use your fingers to shape and smooth the mouse. Don't worry if it's not perfect; children are forgiving. Serve the mouse and scraps left from the carving.

BANANA MOUSE

Cut a two inch piece from both ends of a small banana. Use the ends because of the points. If you're not going to eat the mouse right away, brush the banana with lemon or orange juice to keep it from turning brown. Press two sliced almonds into the top of the banana for the ears, two raisins for the eyes, and a round candy for the nose. Cut black string licorice into six small pieces and push into the banana around the nose for the whiskers. Cut a longer piece of licorice and push into the back to make a mouse's tail.

It's best to bring all the ingredients and let the children make their own. They'll love it and it gives them a chance to be creative.

MOUSE CAKE

Make a cake by following the directions on a packaged cake mix and bake in two 8 or 9 inch round cake pans. Remove from the pans when cool. Make the frosting by following the directions on a white cream frosting mix and add gray food coloring. Frost the layers together and frost the entire cake. Use two 4 inch round cookies for ears, round candies for eyes and nose, and black string licorice for whiskers and mouth. You may frost the cookies if you like. The children will delight in seeing a mouse cake and will especially enjoy eating it.

MISCHIEVOUS MONKEYS

There's a lot of monkey business involved in monkey story hours because these mischievous characters are always involved in amusing antics that children love.

Because Curious George and Arthur are extra popular, you might consider devoting special days to each of their books, many of which are discussed in this chapter.

You can purchase a Curious George doll at many book stores. Or you can order one by mail from A Child's Collection (see Resources).

Monkey stories are fun to read any time, but the stories will be even more meaningful following a trip to the zoo.

Have fun monkeying around with some entertaining monkey books!

Setting the Stage

To make a pretend monkey cage from a large cardboard carton, begin by cutting out "bars" on one side. Then cut away the opposite side of the carton so that the children can get inside the cage. Attach a sign saying: "Reserved for anyone reading monkey books. Do not feed."

Construct the hanging monkeys. (See Monkey Crafts). Hang them around the room to create a room full of monkeys. The children will enjoy making the monkeys to help decorate the room.

Bulletin Board Ideas

1. Use an opaque projector to enlarge the "Monkey Around with Books" illustration. Color and mat.

2. Draw or trace a Curious George illustration from one of his books. Color and cut it out. Tack the drawing to a bulletin board and surround it with Curious George book jackets. If you don't have the book jackets, make copies of the book covers and have the children color them before putting them on the board.

119

Read-Aloud Stories

CAPS FOR SALE
by Esphyr Slobodkina (Harper & Row, 1968)

Story: A peddler walks up and down the streets. While balancing a huge stack of caps on his head, he calls out "Caps for sale." When he stops to rest under a tree, the monkeys take his caps for themselves.

Materials: caps made of gray, brown, blue, and red paper; one checkered cap (see Monkey Crafts)

Directions: Wear the checkered cap which can be purchased at a costume shop, and explain that you know of a peddler who sells gray caps, brown caps, blue caps, and red caps. As you mention each color, model the appropriate cap on your own head. Then present the story.

Tell—rather than read—this tale so you can dramatize the actions by moving about the room. If the weather's nice, you might perform it on a grassy area out of doors. In your role of the peddler, perform the actions of sitting under a tree, falling asleep, and so on. The children will want to join in when the monkeys say, "Tsz, tsz, tsz."

CURIOUS GEORGE
by Margaret and H. A. Rey (Houghton Mifflin, 1941)

Story: George is fascinated by the circus and inadvertently becomes a star when he gets in the way of the performing acrobats.

Materials: Curious George doll, a stuffed toy elephant

Directions: Dress the elephant to look like a circus elephant and set Curious George on top of the elephant.

Before reading the book, introduce Curious George as a monkey who wanted to know what was going on at the circus. Explain what the word *curious* means. Ask the children to tell what things they might be curious about at a circus. Then read the story.

THE MONKEY AND THE CROCODILE
by Paul Galdone (Seabury, 1969)

Story: The hungry crocodile wants a monkey for dinner, so he offers a frisky one a ride across the river, supposedly to get fruit. The monkey escapes by convincing the crocodile not to eat him until the monkey can retrieve his heart which, he says, he left on the other side of the river.

Materials: stuffed toy monkey, crocodile puppet, cutout paper or felt heart

Directions: Set the monkey on the crocodile's back. Explain that the crocodile has promised to take the monkey across a river to get some delicious fresh fruit. Ask the children if they think the crocodile is just being helpful. Why else might the crocodile offer a ride?

After reading the story, show the children the cutout heart and ask them whose heart it might be. Of course, it's the monkey's heart which he left on the shore.

FIVE LITTLE MONKEYS JUMPING ON THE BED
by Eileen Christelow (Clarion Books, 1989)

Story: In this classic counting rhyme, the little monkeys jump onto the bed only to fall off and bump their heads. Each time Mamma calls the doctor.

Materials: five monkey finger puppets (see Monkey Crafts)

Directions: Read the story to the children, showing the illustrations. Then put five monkey puppets on the fingers of one hand. While you reread the story, wiggle and then lower a finger each time a monkey falls. The children can recite the rhyme with you, using their fingers, with or without the puppets.

THE MONKEYS AND THE PEDLAR
by Susanne Suba (Viking, 1970)

Story: When the peddler stops to rest near the woods, a group of monkeys open his pack to play with the contents. However, they put everything back into the pack before the peddler wakes from his nap.

Materials: a peddler's pack

Directions: Fill a bag with some of the items that the monkeys find in the peddler's pack (hat, shoes, teddy bear, mirror, spectacles) or other things that children might like to play with.

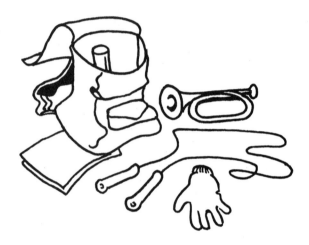

Begin by explaining that long ago peddlers were people who would go from place to place selling things they carried.

Put the pack on your back and pretend to be a peddler. Walk around for a while telling the children that you are a peddler. Wipe your brow and say that you're so hot and tired, you're going to set your pack down and rest.

Sit down and read the story. Later, allow time for the children to get into the pack to play with the contents.

MOONKEY
by Mike Thaler, il. by Giulio Maestro (Harper & Row, 1981)

Story: Monkey is in love with the moon, but he can't reach the moon until his animal friends build an animal ladder for him to climb on.

Materials: stuffed toy monkey, a paper moon, party hats, monkey cake decorated like the one in the story

Directions: Attach the paper moon to a wall or hang it from the ceiling. Put on a party hat similar to the one in the story. Tell the children that they're all invited to a party outside in the moonlight. Explain that you know about a monkey who wouldn't come to the party because he was in love with the moon.

Read the story. Then have a party. Place a party hat on the monkey and give each child one. Serve the monkey cake with "Moonkey" printed on it.

MORE SPAGHETTI, I SAY

by Rita Golden Gelman, il. by Jack Kent
(Scholastic, 1977)

Story: Minnie the monkey doesn't have time to play with Freddy the monkey because Minnie's always eating spaghetti. But when Minnie is finally full of spaghetti and wants to play, Freddy decides he also likes eating spaghetti and doesn't have time to play with Minnie.

Materials: bowl full of cooked spaghetti, fork, spoon

Directions: Show the children a big bowl of spaghetti. Demonstrate how to eat spaghetti by wrapping it around a fork held against a spoon.

Read the story using two different voices for the monkeys. Then, if you're courageous, throw a spaghetti party. Provide the children with forks and spoons so that they can practice the skill of eating spaghetti the elegant way.

A WISE MONKEY TALE

by Betsy and Giulio Maestro (Crown, 1975)

Story: Monkey is eating a piece of banana cake. Because she isn't paying any attention to where she is going, she falls into a big hole. When she can't get out by herself, the clever monkey tricks the lion, the snake, the zebra, and the elephant into helping her climb out of the hole.

Materials: banana leaf (real or made of green paper), banana cake (see Monkey Snacks)

Directions: Wrap a piece of banana cake in a banana leaf. Take a nibble from the cake and explain that one day a monkey was eating a banana cake wrapped in a banana leaf. Put the cake aside and read the story, sharing the wonderful illustrations.

When the story is finished, serve the cake. If you want to make a cake from scratch, you'll find a recipe included in the monkey snacks section of this chapter. You or the children can cut paper banana leaf place mats.

More Monkey Books

Asch, Frank. **MONKEY FACE** (Parents Magazine Press, 1977)

One day in school, Monkey paints a picture of his mother. On the way home, he shows it to his friends who suggest changes. When he finally gets home, the picture looks nothing like his mother, but she likes it just the same.

Brown, Marc. **THE TRUE FRANCINE** (Little, Brown, 1981)

Francine and Muffy are good friends until Muffy cheats on a test and lets Francine take the blame. The teacher punishes Francine, but when Muffy admits her guilt, the two become friends again.

Browne, Anthony. **WILLY THE WIMP** (Knopf, 1984)

A young chimpanzee named Willie is tired of being bullied by the suburban gorilla gang. He builds up his muscles, rescues Millie from the gang, and is proud he's no longer a wimp.

Another book by the same author is **WILLY THE CHIMP**.

Bunting, Eve, il. by Lynn Munsinger. **MONKEY IN THE MIDDLE** (Harcourt, 1984)

Two coconut pickers, Hashim and Mohammed, are good friends until they quarrel over a bicycle. Mohammed's clever monkey finds a way to make peace.

Galdone, Paul. **THE TURTLE AND THE MONKEY** (Clarion Books, 1983)

Turtle asks a greedy monkey to help her plant a banana tree. In return, Turtle will share the bananas with Monkey. When Monkey doesn't share the bananas, Turtle outwits Monkey and then escapes.

Goodall, John. **JACKO** (Harcourt, 1971)

This wordless book features Jacko, a delightful monkey who escapes from his organ-grinder master and stows away on a sailing ship. Jacko eventually arrives at his homeland where he is reunited with his monkey family.

Hoban, Lillian. **ARTHUR'S HALLOWEEN COSTUME** (Harper & Row, 1984)

Arthur worries that his costume for Halloween won't be scary enough, but he's pleased when he ends up winning a prize for the most original costume in school.

Hoban, Lillian. **ARTHUR'S HONEY BEAR** (Harper & Row, 1974)

Arthur and his sister Violet decide to sell some of their old toys. They put price tags on the toys, but when it comes to selling his favorite possession, a teddy named Honey Bear, Arthur changes his mind.

Hoban, Lillian. **ARTHUR'S LOOSE TOOTH** (Harper & Row, 1985)

Arthur brags that he's going to be the bravest chimp in the world when he grows up. But he's not very brave when his tooth becomes loose. After his lovable sister teaches him a lesson in courage, he pulls out his tooth by himself.

Hoban, Lillian. **ARTHUR'S PEN PAL** (Harper & Row, 1976)

Arthur thinks his pen pal, Sandy, would be more fun to play with than his sister, Violet, because all Violet wants to do is skip rope. But Arthur soon discovers that his sister can be a terrific playmate.

Howe, James, il. by Lillian Hoban. **THE DAY THE TEACHER WENT BANANAS** (Dutton, 1984)

There's a big mix-up when a gorilla is sent to the school to be the teacher and the teacher is sent to the zoo. The children love having a gorilla for a teacher because they get to do lots of fun things.

Kazuo, Iwamura. **TAN TAN'S HAT** (Bradbury Press, 1983)

Tan Tan the little monkey can do nearly everything with his hat. He can toss it, spin it, and make it do tricks.

Kazuo, Iwamura. **TAN TAN'S SUSPENDERS** (Bradbury Press, 1978)

Tan Tan's suspenders do much more than hold up his pants. They give him rides, work as a swing, serve as a parachute, and offer more fun than most monkeys can think of.

McKissack, Patricia, il. by Paul Meisel. **MONKEY-MONKEY'S TRICK** (Random House, 1988)

In this African folk tale, the mean, greedy hyena plays tricks on Monkey-Monkey. However, the tricks eventually backfire and the hyena finds out how it feels to be deceived.

Myers, Walter, il. by Leslie Morril. **MR. MONKEY AND THE GOTCHA BIRD** (Delacorte, 1984)

Monkey walks around with his nose in the air, thinking he's invincible, until Gotcha Bird captures him for dinner. Monkey must use his creativity to keep from being eaten.

Oechsli, Kelly. **TOO MANY MONKEYS** (Golden Press, 1980)

This one-to-ten counting book illustrates numbers with some very funny antics performed by a troop of delightful monkeys.

Perkins, Al, il. by Philip Wende. **TRAVELS OF DOCTOR DOLITTLE** (Random House, 1967)

Dr. Dolittle, a friend to all animals, is invited to Africa to cure the monkeys who have a terrible disease. After the long and dangerous trip, Dr. Dolittle arrives safely and is able to bring the monkeys back to health.

Pursell, Margaret. **MANDY THE MONKEY** (Carolrhoda Books, 1977)

Mandy the monkey lives in a zoo. When she becomes ill one day, the new zoo keeper takes her to his home to nurse her back to health. The zoo keeper's wife and children make her feel like a member of the household.

Rey, H. A. **CECILY G. AND THE 9 MONKEYS** (Houghton Mifflin, 1969)

A lonely giraffe teams up with nine playful monkeys who need a place to live. They have so much fun together playing games that they decide to stay together forever.

Rey, H. A. **CURIOUS GEORGE GETS A MEDAL** (Houghton Mifflin, 1957)

George's curiosity gets him into lots of trouble until he's offered a chance to fly in a space ship. When he successfully parachutes to earth, he receives a medal.

Rey, H. A. **CURIOUS GEORGE RIDES A BIKE** (Houghton Mifflin, 1952)

The man in the yellow hat gives George a bicycle. One day, when George is riding his bike, he is captured and forced to work in the circus. George is eventually rescued by his friend and brought safely back home.

Rey, Margaret, and H. A. Rey. **CURIOUS GEORGE GOES TO THE HOSPITAL** (Houghton Mifflin, 1966)

Curious George becomes ill after swallowing a jigsaw puzzle piece. He goes to the hospital where the children love his antics.

Rey, Margaret, and H. A. Rey. **CURIOUS GEORGE LEARNS THE ALPHABET** (Houghton Mifflin, 1963)

When Curious George shows interest in reading books, his friend, the man in the yellow hat, uses a drawing pad to illustrate the letters of the alphabet.

Weil, Lisl. **MONKEY TROUBLE** (Scholastic, 1971)

Dudley, a very kind but clumsy elephant, steps on a monkey's toes. The monkey takes advantage of Dudley's kindness and stays in bed while Dudley caters to his every whim. Dudley eventually tires of caring for the monkey who then decides he will care for the elephant.

Monkey Finger Plays and Action Verse

I SEE THE MONKEYS

Divide the children into two groups facing each other. Each group will do the appropriate actions while reciting the action verse. One group always recites the first line of each verse and the other recites the second line.

I See the Monkeys, Do You?

Do you see the monkeys scratch, scratch, scratch?
Yes, I see the monkeys scratch, scratch, scratch.
Do you see the monkeys swing, swing, swing?
Yes, I see the monkeys swing, swing, swing.
Do you see the monkeys jump, jump, jump?
Yes, I see the monkeys jump, jump, jump.
Do you see the monkeys stomp, stomp, stomp?
Yes, I see the monkeys stomp, stomp, stomp.
Do you see the monkeys twirl, twirl, twirl?
Yes, I see the monkeys twirl, twirl, twirl.
Do you see the monkeys hug, hug, hug?
Yes, I see the monkeys hug, hug, hug.
Do you see the monkeys fall asleep?
Yes, I see the monkeys fall asleep.

FIVE LITTLE MONKEYS

Extend the fingers of one hand and lower a finger each time a monkey leaves. Or you can use the monkey finger puppets and pull off a puppet each time one leaves.

Five Little Monkeys Sitting on a Door

Five little monkeys
Sitting on a door,
One fell off
And then there were four.

Four little monkeys
Sitting in a tree,
One fell out
And then there were three.

Three little monkeys
Going to the zoo,
One got lost
And then there were two.

Two little monkeys
Were having fun,
One ran away
And then there was one.

One little monkey
Sitting in the sun,
He ran away
And then there was none.

Monkey Songs

WHERE IS MONKEY?

Make two monkey finger puppets for each child (see Monkey Crafts). The older children will be able to make their own. Put a puppet on each index finger and hide your hands behind your back. Bring them out when reciting the second line of the song. The monkeys nod at each other on lines three and four. On the last line, put the monkeys behind your back again.

Where Is Monkey?
(Tune: "Are You Sleeping?")

Where is Monkey? Where is Monkey?
Here I am. Here I am.
How are you today, sir?
Very well, I thank you.
Run away. Run away.

POP! GOES THE WEASEL

The song is found on page 41 in WEE SING by Pamela Conn Beall and Susan Hagen Nipp. Show a picture of a weasel and talk about it before learning the song. Children join hands to make a circle. Walk around in a circle while singing the song. On "Pop!" clap your hands and fall down.

WHERE HAS MY MONKEY GONE?

When the children aren't in the room, hide a toy monkey. Teach the song to the children, then sing it together while the children are looking for the hidden monkey.

Where Has My Monkey Gone?
(Tune: "Oh, Where Has My Little Dog Gone?")

Oh where, oh where, has my monkey gone?
Oh where, oh where, can he be?
With his ears so big,
And his tail so long,
Oh where, oh where can he be?

SWING YOUR TAIL

When singing the following song, wear a monkey tail (see Monkey Crafts). Use the tail to act out the lyrics.

Swing Your Tail
(Tune: "Camptown Ladies")

Swing your tail into the air,
Oo-oo, ee-ee.
Shake it, shake it while it's there,
Oo-oo, ee-ee-ee.
Twirl it to the left.
Twirl it to the right.
Twirl it all around and then
Twirl it out of sight.
—Melodee Riggers

Monkey Games

CAPS FOR SALE

Make eight peddler caps using four different colors (see Monkey Crafts). You will need nine children, one to be the peddler and eight to be the monkeys. The peddler wears a checkered cap and then stacks the other eight caps on top of it in the correct order. (If the caps won't balance, use a shorter stack.)

The storyteller tells the story while the children do the acting. Encourage the child who is the peddler to say the peddler's dialogue himself, perhaps with some prompting by you. The monkeys, of course, will delight in saying, "Tsz, tsz, tsz" at the appropriate times.

The children catch on very quickly and will want to play it over again and again, giving many of them a chance to play the peddler.

JUST LIKE ME

Have children perform this silly poem with a partner.

Voice 1: I went up one pair of stairs.
Voice 2: Just like me.

Voice 1: I went up two pairs of stairs.
Voice 2: Just like me.

Voice 1: I went into a room.
Voice 2: Just like me.

Voice 1: I looked out of a window.
Voice 2: Just like me.

Voice 1: And there I saw a monkey.
Voice 2: Just like me.
—Anonymous

GRAB THE MONKEY'S TAIL

Because this game requires a lot of room, you might wish to move to the gym or outdoors. The children form a line, each holding the waist of the child in front. Pin a monkey's tail (see Monkey Crafts) on the last child in line.

When you say "Go!", the leader of the line circles around and tries to grab the monkey's tail that's pinned on the last child in line. As the line moves, the children delight in trying to hold on while the leader is trying to grab the monkey's tail. Play again until the children tire. Each time you play, choose different children for each end of the line. This game is a good tension releaser!

More Monkey Poems

"When You Talk to a Monkey" and "Before the Monkey's Cage" p. 22 in READ-ALOUD RHYMES FOR THE VERY YOUNG selected by Jack Prelutsky, il. by Marc Brown (Knopf, 1986)

"Tails" p. 70 in SING A SONG OF POPCORN (Scholastic, 1988)

Monkey Crafts

PEDDLER'S CAPS

Materials: gray, brown, blue, and red construction paper, scissors, tape, stapler; cap pattern—a circle traced around a cake pan

Directions: You will need one sheet of 9 x 12 inch colored construction paper for each cap. Draw a cake pan-sized circle to use as a cap pattern. Make the band by cutting two 1¼ x 9 inch strips from the remainder of the sheet of paper. Staple the bands together by overlapping the ends about ¼ inch. Tape the band onto the circle as illustrated. Your cap is now ready for peddling!

MONKEY FINGER PUPPETS

Materials: crayons or felt markers, puppet pattern, scissors, stapler

Directions: Copy several of the patterns onto an 8½ x 11 inch sheet of paper. Duplicate the sheet until you have as many puppets as needed. Color and cut out. Staple together to fit around a finger as illustrated.

Use the puppets when singing "Where Is Monkey?" (see Monkey Songs) and when reciting "Five Little Monkeys" (see Read-Aloud Stories).

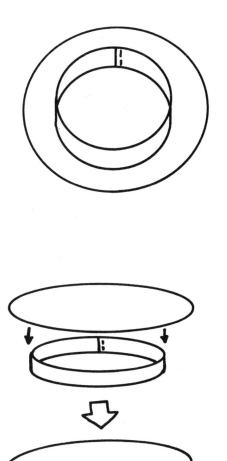

HANGING MONKEY

Materials: brown and tan construction paper, scissors, felt marker, glue, pattern

Directions: Copy the hanging monkey pattern onto brown construction paper and cut it out. Use tan paper to make the monkey's face and stomach. Cut out and glue onto the monkey. Draw the features using the felt marker. To make bigger monkeys, enlarge the pattern with an opaque projector. Hang the monkeys by their tails on a rod or pencil. They will swing back and forth when touched lightly.

MONKEY TAILS

Materials: ½ yard of 60 inch brown single knit fabric, scissors, safety pins

Directions: Cut twelve 1½ inch strips from the length of the fabric. Cut each strip into thirds, making three tails about 20 inches long. No sewing is necessary. Stretch each strip by pulling on both ends at the same time; the fabric will roll together to look like a tail. Pin the tail at the child's waist in the back with a safety pin. Fold the fabric over the pin so the pin won't show. This is enough fabric to make 30 tails.

Use the tail in playing the Grab the Monkey's Tail game (see Monkey Games). Also, use the tail when singing "Swing Your Tail" (see Monkey Songs).

Hanging Monkey
Pattern

131

Monkey Snacks

BANANAS

Hang a bunch of bananas on a hook and let the children pick them as if they were picking bananas from a tree. Dried banana chips also make an appropriate snack.

MONKEY FACE COOKIES

Make the recipe for alligator cookies (see Alligator Snacks). Roll the dough ⅛ inch thick and cut a number of three-inch circles. In half of them, cut out eyes and mouths. Bake as directed. When cool, spread jelly on the solid cookies and place the cookies with the cutout eyes and mouths on top. The jelly will show through to make a monkey face.

MONKEY BANANA CAKE

¼ cup softened butter
1⅓ cups sugar
1½ tsp vanilla
3 eggs
2 cups flour
1 tsp. baking soda
1 tsp baking powder
1 tsp salt
1 8 oz. carton of sour cream
1 cup ripe mashed bananas
1 cup chopped walnuts, if desired

Preheat oven to 350 degrees. Grease and flour a 9 x 12 inch pan. In a large bowl, cream butter and sugar together. Add eggs and vanilla and blend thoroughly. Mix flour, baking powder, baking soda, and salt, and add to creamed mixture alternately with the sour cream. Stir in bananas and walnuts. Spread batter evenly into the prepared pan. Bake 25 to 30 minutes. Serves 16.

MANGO TREAT

After reading THE MONKEY AND THE CROCODILE, the children will want to eat a piece of mango to be like the monkey sitting in the mango tree.

MAGNIFICENT MONSTERS

All children think and dream about monsters. All of the magnificent monsters in this chapter are happy, friendly, and adorable. There's nothing frightening about any of them. In fact, monsters have never been so much fun!

Use the happy monster puppet (see Monster Crafts) or a Cookie Monster puppet to introduce the monster story hours. In a monstrous voice—slow and soft—explain to the children that monsters are only pretend and that their antics actually teach all sorts of interesting things. Encourage the children to ask the monster questions.

Inexpensive monster puppets (see Monster Crafts) can enable children to act out many of the stories that you read. With theatrical make-up, help the children become youthful monsters.

Setting the Stage

Draw chalk monster tracks on the sidewalk if you have an outside entrance to the room—a dramatic way to invite the children in.

But don't stop at the doorway. Use black paper to cut 12 by 18 inch monster footprints. Starting at the doorway, tape the tracks up the wall, across the ceiling.

When the children ask where the monsters are, explain that they're hiding in the books that you're about to share with them.

Set Cookie Monster, Herry Monster (characters from Sesame Street), and any other stuffed monsters on a shelf or table with monster books to create interest in reading the monster stories.

Make a monster library by attaching a cave made from gray paper onto a large box. Cut an opening for the doorway large enough to allow the children to crawl in. Leave the top open for light and cut windows to make more light if needed. Put a few monster books at a time in the monster library for the children to read. Change the books regularly.

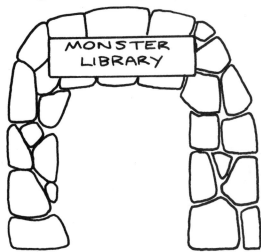

Bulletin Board Ideas

1. Enlarge the "Monsters Devour Books" illustration. Color and mat.

2. Have the children draw or paint their own monsters. Display them on the board with the heading, "We Love Our Monsters."

3. Draw and cut a closet door about 1½ by 3 feet. Cut the door on three sides and crease the fourth side so that it will open easily. Make a nightmare similar to the one in THERE'S A NIGHTMARE IN MY CLOSET. Pin the nightmare and the door on the board so when the door's opened, the nightmare will be visible. Make another nightmare a little smaller than the first to pin behind the first nightmare. When it comes out of the closet, there will be another nightmare there. You can make as many nightmares as you like. Encourage the children to tell a story as each nightmare leaves the closet. Why are they leaving? Where are they going? What are they going to do? Pin the nightmares back in place for the next child to use.

4. Use CLYDE MONSTER as a guideline to make Clyde and his cave from paper. Pin to the board. Cover the cave entrance with a separate paper "rock" that is pinned over the entrance and can be moved over when Clyde comes out to play. When Clyde goes to bed, put him back into the cave. Pin the rock back in place leaving a small opening so Clyde won't be scared. Put this display at an appropriate height to allow the children to move Clyde and the rock about.

5. Cut out several monster bodies, heads, ears, eyes, noses, mouths, feet, legs, arms, and hands. Make a monster by pinning the various parts onto the bulletin board. Change the parts to make a different monster. It's fun to see what can be created.

6. You can buy a WHERE THE WILD THINGS ARE poster from book stores or from The Peaceable Kingdom Press (see Resources).

7. Make a "Have You Hugged Your Monster Today?" banner. Use a computer, if available.

Read-Aloud Stories

THE BUNYIP OF BERKELEY'S CREEK

by Jenny Wagner, il. by Ron Brooks (Penguin, 1987)

Story: In this Australian tale, a creature appears out of the muddy river bottom, scrapes the mud off, and wanders around asking what he looks like. A platypus tells the creature that he's a "bunyip." The bunyip discovers what he looks like when another bunyip appears out of the muddy billabong.

Materials: hand mirror and comb in hobo-type bag on a stick, small bucket (known in Australia as a "billy")

Directions: Use a low, raspy voice for the bunyip's dialogue and say the "What am I?" refrain slowly and deliberately. Pretend to scrape mud off yourself. If you like, use the props to help dramatize the action.

　　After telling the story, show the book to the children to interest them in reading it themselves.

CLYDE MONSTER

by Robert Crowe, il. by Kay Chorao (Dutton, 1976)

Story: Clyde Monster is afraid to go into his dark cave because inside might be people who will jump out and get him. His mother convinces him that people are scared of him. He goes into his cave, but he wants the rock door left open just a little.

Materials: Clyde, Clyde's cave

Directions: See the Bulletin Board section of this chapter for tips on making Clyde and Clyde's cave.

　　Explain that monsters enjoy being ugly, the uglier the better. No one likes a pretty monster. Ask the children if they believe monsters are afraid of people. If so, why would that be?

　　As you read the book, use a soft, frightened voice for Clyde's dialogue and a comforting voice for his mother and father.

DO NOT OPEN
by Brinton Turkle (Dutton, 1981)

Story: Miss Molly collects treasures left on the beach after a storm. She's collected a banjo clock that doesn't work and some colored bottles. One day she finds a purple bottle labelled "Do Not Open." When she opens it and a monster appears, Molly tricks the monster and her wish comes true—her banjo clock begins to work.

Materials: tin cookie box, purple bottle with the inscription "Do Not Open," a red rug or a piece of cloth, a loudly-ticking clock

Directions: Before reading the story, place the clock in an inconspicuous place where the children will not be able to see it. As you read this story, show the tin cookie box, the red rug, and the purple bottle as Miss Molly finds them. At the conclusion of the story, ask the children to be very quiet so that they can hear the ticking clock.

Leave the items in the room so that the children may use them to retell the story themselves.

THE GUNNIWOLF
retold by Wilhelmina Harper, il. by William Wiesner (Dutton, 1967)

Story: Little Girl's mother cautions her to never go near the jungle. One day, however, she accidentally wanders into the jungle while picking flowers. Though Little Girl meets up with the gunniwolf, she's able to fool him and escape to her home.

Materials: none

Directions: This is a fine participation story. Sing along with Little Girl when she sings, "Khi-wa, kum, kwa." Ask the children to join in. Tap your feet on the "pit-pats" and slap your legs on the "hunker-chas." The children will soon be joining in. Everyone will want to boom out the refrains: "Little Girl, why for you move?" and "I no move."

THE MONSTER AT THE END OF THIS BOOK
by Jon Stone, il. by Mike Smollin (Western, 1971)

Story: Sesame Street's Grover warns the reader not to turn the pages of this book because there's a scary monster on the last page. The monster turns out to be Grover.

Materials: Grover puppet

Directions: Introduce Grover to the children. Using Grover's gravelly voice say, "Hello, everybodeee. I'm the lovable, furry old Grover you see on Sesame Street." Invite the children to ask Grover questions about what it's like to live on Sesame Street. Think ahead so that you'll be able to answer the questions.

Set Grover in a listening position, so that he can enjoy the story along with the children. Hint: This is a good book for opening a story hour because most of the children will be familiar with Grover.

THE MONSTER BED
by Jeanne Willis, il. by Susan Varley (Lothrop, 1986)

Story: There's a monster named Dennis who lives in a gloomy cave. Dennis sleeps under the bed because he's afraid scary humans will hide under his bed to get him. A boy sleeps on top of Dennis' bed and they're both in for a surprise.

Materials: stuffed toy monster, cave made from a box

Directions: Use a dragon-like stuffed toy for Dennis. Make a cave from a box by covering it with gray paper made to look like rocks. Cut a hole for the entrance.

Introduce Dennis to the children and explain that he lives in a cave with his mother. Explain that Dennis is afraid that humans will get him and he does not want to go to bed, but mother insists that the humans will not harm him. Dennis reluctantly goes to bed. Put Dennis in the cave and read the story. Because the text is in rhyme, read every word as written. At the end of the story bring Dennis out of the cave as he runs away from the boy.

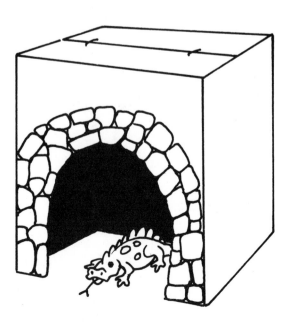

MONSTER TRACKS
by A. Delaney (Harper & Row, 1981)

Story: A little boy named Harry wonders if those huge, gallumphing tracks in the snow really belong to a monster. He follows the tracks until they end, then turns to run away because he's afraid the tracks were made by a monster. In fact, they were made by his big, lovable dog.

Materials: stocking cap, mittens

Directions: As you put on the cap and mittens, talk to the children about dressing warmly when going out in the snow. (If the temperature is in the 90s, pick another story.)

Ask children what kind of tracks might be found in the snow. Tell them you have a book about a young boy who finds some very odd tracks. Invite the children to guess what kind of tracks they might be. Don't show the cover until you're finished, or you'll give away the surprise.

Later, you might share with the class a nature guide that shows what different animals' tracks look like in the snow.

SIMON'S BOOK
by Drescher Henrik (Lothrop, 1983)

Story: A young boy draws a story about Simon and the scary monster. While the boy sleeps, his characters become alive and finish the story book.

Materials: sketch pad, bottle of ink, stick pen

Directions: Ahead of time, draw or trace Simon and monster in the middle of the sketch pad.

Introduce the story by showing the artist's sketch pad. Thumb through it until you come to the page where you've drawn Simon and the monster.

Show the children the ink bottle and stick pen. Most children will not be familiar with these items. Explain that your drawing is the beginning of a book about Simon and a scary monster. Set the artist pad up so that it will be visible while reading the story. After reading the story, talk briefly about how the children can make their own books. A simple book can be bound by using a stapler or a hole punch and yarn.

THERE'S A MONSTER UNDER MY BED

by James Howe, il. by David Rose (Macmillan, 1986)

Story: Simon imagines there are different monsters under his bed. He uses a flashlight to investigate, but finds his brother there instead. They sleep together to build their courage.

Materials: flashlight

Directions: Begin by asking the children if they've ever suspected monsters lurking under their beds. Tell them you know about a young boy who used a flashlight to go hunting for monsters. Demonstrate your flashlight and flick it on at crucial points in the story.

This book lends itself to many dramatic actions. For example, breathe loudly when the boy hears what he thinks is the monster breathing. Invite the children to join you in making breathing noises.

THERE'S A NIGHTMARE IN MY CLOSET

by Mercer Mayer (Dial, 1968)

Story: A young boy decides to get rid of the nightmare in his closet. But the nightmare ends up sharing the boy's cozy bed.

Materials: black box, nightmare puppet, real key

Directions: Make a nightmare puppet by tracing the monster from the book onto flesh-colored paper. Color and cut out. Attach the figure to a dowel. Place it in a box painted black or covered with black paper. Draw two keyholes.

Introduce the story by reciting the poem below:

In the dark, dark night
Where there wasn't any light.
I found a strange little box
With two, strong, strong locks.
The locks opened with this key.
And what strange thing did I see?
A nightmare monster looking at me.
And now...he's looking at you!

Explain that the nightmare is glad to get out of the box because he wants to go home, which happens to be a closet.

WHERE THE WILD THINGS ARE
by Maurice Sendak (Harper & Row, 1984)

Story: After Max makes mischief around the house, he is sent to his room without his supper. He imagines a voyage across the sea to "where the Wild Things are." Because he tames them, the Wild Things make Max their king. Eventually, Max tires of the Wild Things' antics and longs for home and the love he's known there.

Materials: Max stuffed doll, box

Directions: Set the book on top of a box containing the Max doll. Open the book a little and say, as if someone in the book is talking, "Help, let me out of here. It's too dark in here." Take the Max doll out of the box (as if from the book). Talk to Max about what he's been doing in the book. Show the children his wolf costume.

Place the doll on the shelf with his legs crossed. Suggest that the children sit that way too.

When the story is over, Max's legs will still be crossed. It's fun to see how many children have kept their legs crossed.

Refer to the Monster Games section of this chapter for games that relate to this story.

THE WIZARD, THE FAIRY, AND THE MAGIC CHICKEN
by Helen Lester, il. by Lynn Munsinger (Houghton Mifflin, 1983)

Story: Three boastful magicians—a wizard, a fairy, and a chicken—try to outdo one another. When their magic creates three angry monsters, the magicians learn to work together to solve the problem of getting rid of the monsters.

Materials: three magicians' wands—the first with a paper star attached, the second with a paper moon, and the third with a real pickle

Directions: Use dowels for the wand handles. Cut the star from white paper. Cover it with glue and sprinkle on some sparkles. Then staple or tape it to a dowel. Cut the moon from yellow paper and attach it to a dowel. Stick a real pickle onto a dowel for the third wand. Use heavy tape on both ends to keep it in place.

Show the wands as you introduce the magicians. Sing when the frog sings. As a follow-up, help the children make wands to use as props when they retell the story.

More Monster Stories

Alexander, Martha. MAYBE A MONSTER (Dial, 1968)

A young boy builds an enormous cage to hold a monster. Failing to catch one, he captures a rabbit instead. The rabbit becomes the boy's playmate, and they have great fun together.

Appleby, Ellen. THE THREE BILLY GOATS GRUFF (Scholastic, 1984)

Colorful illustrations breathe new excitement into this familiar story of a family of goats who triumph over a scary troll.

Babbitt, Natalie. THE SOMETHING (Farrar, Straus, & Giroux, 1970)

At night Mylo is afraid that "Something" might come through his window. But after he makes a clay model and dreams about the Something, he overcomes his fear.

Cameron, Ann, il. by Jeanette Winter. HARRY—THE MONSTER (Pantheon Books, 1980)

Harry—a monster with purple hair, big orange ears, and a green tongue—lives alone in a cave. He's afraid people will come into his cave at night. He then discovers that people are even more afraid of him.

Chevalier, Christa. SPENCE AND THE SLEEPYTIME MONSTER (Whitman, 1984)

Spence goes to bed, sure that a monster wants to get him. After the lights are out, the monster attacks! Spence captures it in his sheets, but when his mother comes to see it, the monster turns out to be the family cat.

Christian, Mary Blount, il. by Marc Brown. GO WEST, SWAMP MONSTERS (Dial, 1985)

The delightful swamp monsters misbehave while visiting their cousins. When their uncle yells at them, they decide to play with a group of human children. Soon they return to play with their cousins.

Cole, Joanna. MOVIE MONSTER (Scholastic, 1987)

Rosie and Prunella want to earn money so they can see a new movie in town. They try a variety of schemes such as selling freshly squeezed bug juice, washing windows, and putting on a play.

Cumings, Art. THERE'S A MONSTER EATING MY HOUSE (Parents Magazine Press, 1981)

Machinsaurus—half animal and half machine—is eating everyone's trees and houses. Something must be done! Sir William solves the problem by feeding Mrs. Walter's delicious pies to the monster.

Delaney, M. C., il. by Ned Delaney. THE MARIGOLD MONSTER (Dutton, 1983)

Audrey wants to sell marigold seeds. The neighborhood monster promises to buy all of them if Audrey will keep telling him jokes.

Demarest, Chris. MORTON AND SIDNEY (Macmillan, 1987)

Morton's shy friendly monster, Sidney, is kicked out of the closet by the other monsters. When poor Sidney can't find anywhere to go, Morton helps him regain his place in the closet.

Dian, Carolyn. THE LUNCH BOX MONSTER (Faber & Faber, 1983)

A boy keeps his lunch in one lunch pail, and his helpful monster in another. It's hard work caring for the monster, but the effort is justified because the monster takes the blame for the boy's misdeeds.

Flora, James. THE GREAT GREEN TURKEY CREEK MONSTER (Atheneum, 1976)

A great green hooligan vine grows and grows until it takes over the town of Turkey Creek. It's a monstrous nuisance. Fortunately, the town's people learn how to use trombone music to shrink the vine.

Freedman, Sally, il. by Diane Dawson. **MONSTER BIRTHDAY PARTY** (Whitman, 1983)

A rich boy named Peter is bored spending his birthday with his sedate uncles and aunts. With a wave of his hand, the kindly butler invites several merry monsters to enliven the party.

Gackenbach, Dick. **HARRY AND THE TERRIBLE WHATZIT** (Seabury, 1977)

When Harry's mother doesn't return from the cellar, he goes to investigate and discovers a terrible, two-headed monster, the Whatzit. After the Whatzit shrinks away to nothing, Harry finds his mother in the garden.

Galdone, Paul. **THE MONSTER AND THE TAILOR** (Clarion Books, 1982)

The Grand Duke promises to give the tailor a bag of gold if the tailor will stitch a pair of lucky trousers in the graveyard at night. A horrible creature appears, but the tailor overcomes his fear and finishes the trousers in time.

Goode, Diane. **I HEAR A NOISE** (Dutton, 1988)

A young monster snatches a small boy and his mother, but the monster's mother insists he take them right back home.

Graham, Richard, il. by Susan Varley. **JACK AND THE MONSTER** (Houghton Mifflin, 1989)

Jack thinks of his new baby brother as a monster. However, after Jack's father reads "The Frog Prince," Jack decides to kiss his brother who turns out to be a nice ordinary baby.

Hutchins, Pat. **THE VERY WORST MONSTER** (Greenwillow, 1985)

Bill Monster's parents think he will grow up to be the worst monster in the world. His sister Hazel disagrees. She thinks *she* is the worst monster in the world, and she proves it.

Hutchins, Pat. **WHERE'S THE BABY?** (Greenwillow, 1988)

Grandma, Ma, and Hazel Monster attempt to find Baby Monster by following the messy trail that goes from room to room. He spills paint, writes on the wall, and overflows the tub. When Baby Monster is found, he's fast asleep in his tidy room.

Kellogg, Steven. **THE ISLAND OF THE SKOG** (Dial, 1973)

A group of adventurous mice sail to an island to make a new home. When they find huge footprints in the sand, they decide they must catch the monster who turns out to be a tiny skog. The skog and the mice live happily together.

Mayer, Mercer. **TERRIBLE TROLL** (Dial, 1968)

The imaginary adventures of a small boy take him through medieval times as he fights dragons, rescues fair ladies, and saves the kingdom from a terrible giant troll.

Mayer, Mercer. **THERE'S SOMETHING IN MY ATTIC** (Dial, 1988)

A little girl is awakened at night by the creaking sound of the nightmare who lives in her attic. She uses her lasso to capture the nightmare. But when she takes it to show her parents, the nightmare escapes to the attic. Other monster books by Mercer Mayer include:
> **APPLELARD AND LIVERWURST**
> **LITTLE MONSTER AT HOME**
> **LITTLE MONSTER AT SCHOOL**
> **LITTLE MONSTER AT WORK**
> **LITTLE MONSTER'S ALPHABET**
> **LITTLE MONSTER IS BACK**
> **LITTLE MONSTER'S COUNTING BOOK**
> **LITTLE MONSTER'S NEIGHBORHOOD**
> **LIVERWURST IS MISSING**

McKee, David. **TWO MONSTERS** (Bradbury, 1985)

Two delightful monsters who live on opposite sides of a mountain argue about whether the day is departing or the night arriving. Because of their battle, the mountain is destroyed. They discover each is right.

McQueen, John, il. by Marc Brown. **A WORLD FULL OF MONSTERS** (Crowell, 1986)

A long time ago the world was full of monsters. They ran the farms, served as police, carried garbage to the dump, played baseball, and danced in the ballet. No one was afraid of monsters then. And no one should be afraid of them today, either.

Meddaugh, Susan. **BEAST** (Houghton Mifflin, 1981)

Anna's family wants to destroy a big, furry beast that comes to their house from the forest. Anna likes the beast, who turns out to be friendly. She turns him loose so that he can return to his home.

Meddaugh, Susan. **TOO MANY MONSTERS** (Houghton Mifflin, 1982)

Howard, along with 99 other monsters, lives in the center of a dark forest. The monsters love to frighten and tease Howard. When a tree falls and sunlight shines in the forest, all the other monsters leave, much to Howard's delight.

Morgan, Michaela, il. by Sue Porter. **THE MONSTER IS COMING!** (Harper & Row, 1987)

A little girl hides from a large, hairy, blue monster while the monster hunts for her in a game of hide-and-seek. Then the monster hides while the girl hunts for him. Throughout the book, the reader participates in the game by lifting flaps and looking for the girl.

Mueller, Virginia, il. by Lynn Munsinger. **MONSTER CAN'T SLEEP** (Whitman, 1986)

Monster's mother reads him a bedtime story, and his father brings him warm milk, but Monster still can't sleep. When Monster puts his pet spider to sleep, he, too, falls asleep.

O'Keefe, Susan, il. by Lynn Munsinger. **ONE HUNGRY MONSTER** (Little, Brown, 1989)

A young boy first finds a hungry monster under his bed. Soon there are ten monsters, all demanding more and more food. The boy tells the monsters to leave, and they do go away because they can find nothing else to eat. Once they are gone, the boy eats a single apple muffin that he had hidden from the monsters.

Paige, Rob, il. by Paul Yalowitz. **SOME OF MY BEST FRIENDS ARE MONSTERS** (Bradbury, 1988)

A young boy's best friends are monsters who help him move the refrigerator, tie his shoes, and scare a barking dog away. He especially likes the monsters when they keep him company in the dark.

Parish, Peggy, il. by Marc Simont. **NO MORE MONSTERS FOR ME** (Harper & Row, 1981)

Minn's mother won't allow her to keep any pets, but she's determined to have one anyway. She finds a baby monster and keeps it in the basement. However, when it gets huge and causes too much trouble, she returns it to its home in the forest.

Parish, Peggy, il. by Paul Galdone. **ZED AND THE MONSTERS** (Doubleday, 1979)

Zed cleverly tricks four monsters who have been pestering the governor. After the monsters leave, the governor pays Zed well for the work he has done.

Ross, Tony. **I'M COMING TO GET YOU** (Dial, 1984)

After gobbling up several planets, a hairy, howling bully of a monster heads for earth. He's coming to get little Tommy Brown who doesn't want anything to do with monsters. When the monster arrives at Tommy's door, Tommy doesn't see him because the monster is really very tiny.

Sendak, Maurice. **SEVEN LITTLE MONSTERS** (Harper & Row, 1977)

In this very short book, seven monsters make different kinds of trouble. Then they line up and leave.

Sharmat, Marjorie, il. by Dennis Kendrick. **SCARLET MONSTER LIVES HERE** (Harper & Row, 1979)

Scarlet Monster is new in the neighborhood. She bakes brownies, fixes pickled beets, leaves her door open, but no one comes to visit. She's too busy to realize that her guests are waiting for her to invite them in.

Slater, Teddy, il. by Mary Morgan. **MOLLY'S MONSTERS** (Platt and Munk, 1988)

While Molly is trying to sleep, monsters come to call on her. There's one gruesome glog, two toothsome trogs, and more. Molly turns on the light and the monsters disappear, except for one who wants to be Molly's friend.

Steptoe, John. **MY DADDY IS A MONSTER . . . SOMETIMES** (Lippincott, 1980)

Two children think their daddy is nice. But sometimes, when he's angry, he has a way of turning into a scary monster in their imagination.

Stevens, Kathleen, il. by Ray Bowler. **THE BEAST IN THE BATHTUB** (Harper & Row, 1985)

Lewis takes a bath with a huge, green beast. Later, they play together, pretending that they are cattle rustlers and have a pillow fight. Lewis' parents come looking for the beast, but they don't find him because now he's hiding under the bed.

Stevenson, James. **WHAT'S UNDER MY BED?** (Greenwillow, 1983)

Louis and Mary Ann complain to Grandpa that there's something scary under their beds. In a reassuring manner, Grandpa explains that he was scared in the same way when he was young, and that his grandpa had given him ice cream to comfort him. The children feel better. In fact, they are now ready for bowls of ice cream.

Ungerer, Tomi. **THE BEAST OF MONSIEUR RACINE** (Farrar, Straus, and Giroux, 1971)

A beast takes Monsieur Racine's wonderful pears. However, the two become good friends and enjoy wonderful times together. In the end, the beast turns out to be two children in a costume.

Viorst, Judith, il. by Kay Chorao. **MY MAMMA SAYS THERE AREN'T ANY ZOMBIES, GHOSTS, VAMPIRES, CREATURES, DEMONS, MONSTERS, FIENDS, GOBLINS OR THINGS** (Atheneum, 1973)

A young boy sees zombies, ghosts, and other bedtime fiends, but his mama insists that they do not exist. Sometimes even mamas make mistakes. But it's not a mistake when mama cuddles the little boy.

Willoughby, Elaine, il. by Lynn Munsinger. **BORIS AND THE MONSTERS** (Houghton Mifflin, 1980)

Boris is afraid of the night monsters who keep pestering him. Boris' dad gives him a watchdog to scare the monsters away. When the dog becomes frightened, Boris comforts him and, in the process, overcomes his own fears.

Winthrop, Elizabeth, il. by Tomie de Paola. **MAGGIE AND THE MONSTER** (Holiday House, 1987)

At first Maggie doesn't know how to get rid of the monster that visits her room every night. But when Maggie discovers the monster is looking for its mother, she helps reunite the two, and all is well again.

Wylie, Joanne and David Wylie. **THE GUMDROP MONSTER** (Childrens Press, 1984)

A young boy and his dog follow a trail of gumdrops. They encounter all sorts of colorful creatures as they continue their search for the gumdrop monster.

Yolen, Jane, il. by Bruce Degen. **COMMANDER TOAD IN SPACE** (Coward, McCann, & Geoghegan, 1980)

Commander Toad is in charge of the space ship "Star Warts" that lands on a water-covered planet inhabited by a monster, Deep Wader. The crew uses their ingenuity to escape from the horrible, hungry monster.

Monster Poems

WHAT THE MONSTER REALLY WANTS

I'm a monster
Through and through.
But please don't scream.
I won't hurt you.

I do not want
To make you cry.
That's the truth.
And I never lie.

I won't give you
A nasty stare.
Or wake you with
A strange nightmare.

So why am I here
This very day?
The answer is easy.
I just want to play.
—Murray Suid

WHO'S AFRAID?

Do monsters and goblins
And ghosts frighten you?
I'll tell you a secret.
I'm sometimes scared, too.

But here's a hint
About what to do.
When awful things come close
Scare them back with a "Boooooo."

Of course, if a monster
Seems to be really tame.
Then give it a smile
And offer to play a game.
—Murray Suid

More Monster Poems

"Ah! A Monster's Lot is Merry" p. 34 and "There is a Thing" p. 119 in THE NEW KID ON THE BLOCK by Jack Prelutsky, il. by James Stevenson (Greenwillow Books, 1984)

"Monsters I've Met" p. 23 and "The Creature in the Classroom" p. 212 in A LIGHT IN THE ATTIC by Shel Silverstein (Harper & Row, 1981)

"Fun" p. 47 and "Five Little Monsters" p. 50 in READ-ALOUD RHYMES FOR THE VERY YOUNG selected by Jack Prelutsky, il. by Marc Brown (Knopf, 1986)

"Monsters Everywhere" and "The Bogeyman" p. 109, "Midnight" and "The Grebs" p. 110 in CELEBRATIONS by Caroline Bauer (H.W.Wilson, 1985)

Monster Poem Books

MONSTER POEMS by Daisy Wallace, il. by Kay Chorao (Holiday, 1976)

THE SNOPP ON THE SIDEWALK AND OTHER POEMS by Jack Prelutsky, il. by Bryon Barton (Greenwillow, 1977)

NIGHTMARES by Jack Prelutsky, il. by Arnold Lobel (Greenwillow, 1976)

Monster Action Verse

MONSTERS GALORE

The children pretend to be monsters. The storyteller repeats the following verse to the children as they follow the suggested actions.

Monsters galore,
Can you roar?
   (Roar.)

Monsters galore,
Can you soar?
   (Make a flying motion.)

Monsters galore,
Please shut the door!
   (Pretend to shut the door.)

Monsters galore,
Fall on the floor!
   (Fall down.)

SEVEN LITTLE MONSTERS

Begin with one child who follows the suggested action for one monster. Ask another child to join the first and they follow the action for two monsters. Continue on in this manner. Repeat the verse until all the children have had a turn.

One little monster is very tall.
   (Reach toward ceiling, standing on toes.)

Two little monsters are very small.
   (Squat.)

Three little monsters like to creep.
   (Creep on the floor.)

Four little monsters like to leap.
   (Leap into the air.)

Five little monsters dance on the rug.
   (Dance.)

Six little monsters like to hug.
   (Hug each other.)

Seven little monsters in a row.
   (Line up.)

All bend down to touch a toe.
   (Touch a toe.)

WHAT DO MONSTERS DO?

The children pretend they're monsters who don't know what to do. They repeat the first refrain to the leader who tells them what to do. The children follow the suggested actions.

What do monsters do?
They stretch and touch their toes.

What do monsters do?
They comb their purple hair.

What do monsters do?
They stick out their green tongues.

What do monsters do?
They brush their teeth with a broom.

What do monsters do?
They rub their yellow eyes.

What do monsters do?
They wiggle their orange ears.

Boy, am I glad I'm not a monster!

Monster Songs

TEN LITTLE MONSTERS

Sing the following song through once. Arrange ten children in a circle. They should wear their monster masks (see Monster Crafts). Number the children one through ten. The children squat or sit when their number is mentioned in the song. Sing again in the reverse order, each standing when their number is sung. Play until every child has had a chance.

Ten Little Monsters
(Tune: "Ten Little Indians")

One little, two little, three little monsters,
Four little, five little, six little monsters,
Seven little, eight little, nine little monsters,
Ten little happy monsters.

YOU ARE MY MONSTER

Sing the following song after making clay monsters or other monster projects (see Monster Crafts).

You Are My Monster
(Tune: "You Are My Sunshine")

You are my monster,
My only monster.
You make me happy,
When I am sad.
You never know dear,
How much I love you.
Please don't take
My monster away!

Monster Games

WHERE THE WILD THINGS ARE CIRCLE

The children form a circle. A child playing Max stands in the middle of the circle. The other children play "Wild Things" who walk around the circle dancing and chanting "Wild Thing, Wild Thing, Max is a Wild Thing." Max may join in. Let the children create their own dance. The monsters may wear the paper bag masks to help them get into their parts, and Max may wear the crown (see Monster Crafts).

An alternative is to play the recorded music that accompanies the book. The children pretend they're "Wild Things" having a party. Before beginning the music, suggest that the children do the following actions: stomp feet, wave arms, turn around, make faces, wiggle fingers, hop on one foot, jump up and down and leap. The children will probably be able to invent other appropriate actions as well.

MONSTER EXERCISES

Pretend you are monsters wanting to get fit. You'll exercise to the following song. If necessary, before singing explain the meaning of words such as "fangs." You can do this by demonstrating the exercise: touch your "horns," your "fangs," and so on as each part is mentioned in the song. When the children join in, start slowly and then repeat, going faster and faster each time.

Horns and Fangs
(Tune: "Head and Shoulders")

Horns and fangs,
   knees and claws,
   knees and claws.
Horns and fangs,
   knees and claws,
   knees and claws.
Eyes and ears and tail and paws,
Horns and fangs,
   knees and claws,
   knees and claws.

Monster Crafts

SINGING MONSTER PUPPET

Materials: six inch paper plate, scraps of construction paper (different colors), tape, glue, crayons or felt markers, scissors, patterns

Directions: Use the patterns to cut out the monster legs, arms, and eyes from any color of paper. Or each child may want to cut patterns from scratch. Color the plate if desired. Fold the plate in half. Tape or glue the monster parts onto the paper plate as illustrated. Tape a five inch strip of paper to the plate. (The hand will be inserted under the strip.) Open and close the monster's mouth for singing monster songs. (Monsters are good singers, you know.)

WHERE THE WILD THINGS ARE MASKS

Materials: paper sack, construction paper (many colors), glue, scissors, patterns

Directions: Cut off the open end of the paper sack so that the remainder is 12 inches long. Cut out the pattern pieces using various colors. (This is a good project for using up paper scraps.) Glue on the eyes five inches from the top. Glue the other features in place. For the hair, cut a 4 x 8 inch strip of paper. Fringe the paper and curl by wrapping around a pencil. Glue to the top of the sack. Cut out the eyes and it's ready to wear in conjunction with WHERE THE WILD THINGS ARE activities found in Monster Action Verse and Monster Games.

CLAY MONSTER

Materials: ingredients for clay recipe (see Bear Crafts), food coloring, white and black pieces of felt or felt-tipped markers, glue, scissors

Directions: Make the clay recipe adding green food coloring. When the monsters are dry, glue on felt eyes or draw the eyes with a felt marker. The children will enjoy working with the clay. The project gives them an opportunity to let their imaginations go because a monster can look like almost anything. Display the finished crafts on a shelf where passers-by can be delighted, scared, or both.

HAPPY MONSTER PUPPET

Materials: blue furry cloth; red, pink, yellow, green, and tan felt; curling ribbon (many colors); batting; sewing supplies; scissors; monster patterns

Directions: Follow the directions for cutting the happy monster puppet pattern pieces. Stitch and stuff the horns. Pin to the right side of the fabric on the puppet's head. Pin the claws in place. Pin twelve 4 inch pieces of curling ribbon between the horns. Place the right sides together and stitch around the puppet, catching the horns, ribbons, and claws in the seam. Turn right side out. Stitch the eyes, mouth, and tongue in place. Curl the ribbon with the scissors edge and your happy monster is complete. Insert your three middle fingers into the head and your thumb and little finger into the hands to make the puppet perform.

This puppet can be used by the storyteller with many different books. And, of course, children can use it also for retelling the stories they hear.

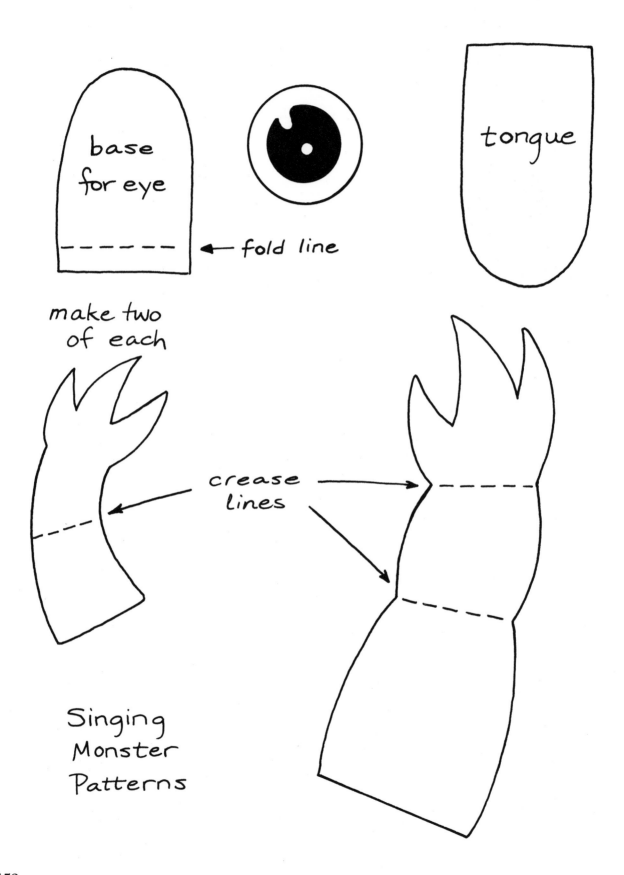

base
for eye

tongue

← fold line

make two
of each

crease
lines

Singing
Monster
Patterns

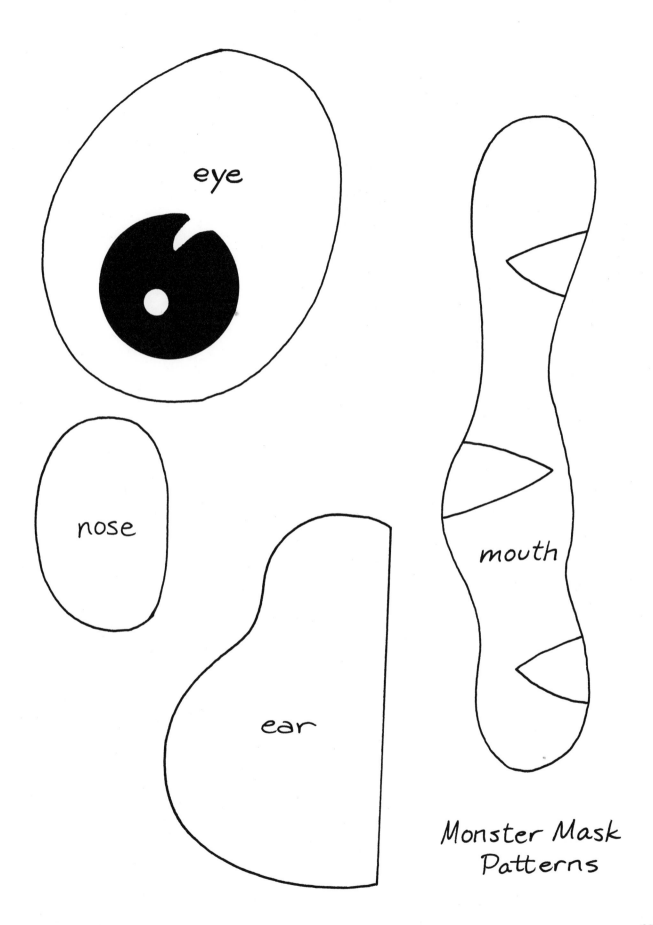

eye

nose

ear

mouth

Monster Mask
Patterns

Happy Monster Patterns

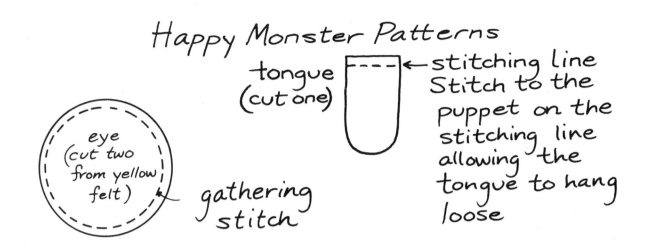

tongue
(cut one)

← stitching line
Stitch to the puppet on the stitching line allowing the tongue to hang loose

eye
(cut two from yellow felt)

gathering stitch

Eye: Gather circle using a hand basting stitch. Stuff with batting and stitch to puppet. Glue a small circle cut from green felt onto the eye.

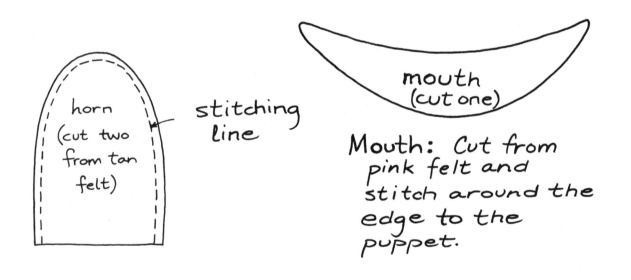

horn
(cut two from tan felt)

stitching line

mouth
(cut one)

Mouth: Cut from pink felt and stitch around the edge to the puppet.

Horns: Stitch on stitching line, turn and stuff with batting. Place on the puppet's head to catch in the seam as the puppet is sewn together.

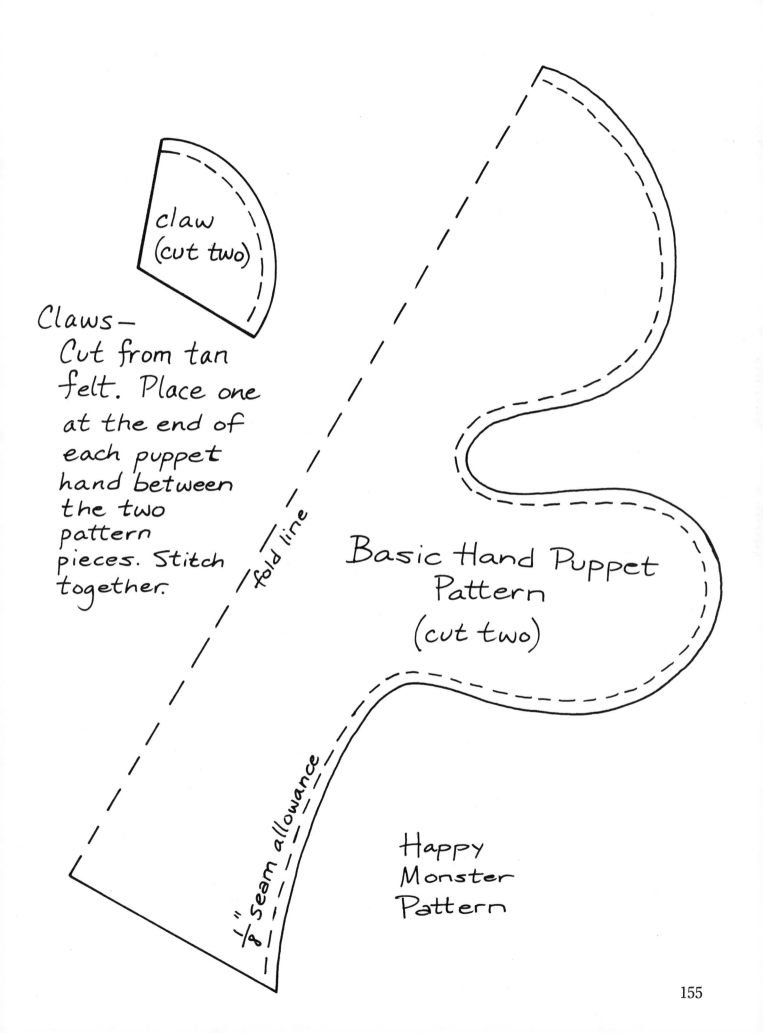

claw
(cut two)

Claws—
Cut from tan
felt. Place one
at the end of
each puppet
hand between
the two
pattern
pieces. Stitch
together.

fold line

Basic Hand Puppet
Pattern
(cut two)

$\frac{1}{8}$" seam allowance

Happy
Monster
Pattern

Monster Snacks

PEANUT BUTTER MONSTERS

Cut a three inch circle from whole wheat bread. Spread with peanut butter. Cut fangs from a cheese slice. The eyes are olive slices; the nose, a green grape; and the ears, carrot slices.

If you prepare the pieces ahead of time, the children can help you assemble this healthy snack.

BANANA MONSTER

Cut a banana in half. Spread peanut butter on the cut side of the banana. Stick it onto a graham cracker. Coat with multi-colored sprinkles and use two candies for eyes. It's a little messy, but great fun.

COOKIE MONSTER TREE

Prepare your favorite cookie recipe. (Rolled sugar cookies work well.) Before baking, stick a short piece of straw or an uncooked spaghetti noodle into each cookie to make a hole. After the cookies are baked, thread the hole with a piece of ribbon or yarn. Hang the cookies from a "tree" made from a branch stuck into modeling clay or nestled in a vase.

MONSTER SANDWICH

Slice a large round loaf of bread in half or thirds lengthwise. Fill with your favorite meats and cheese, or whatever else you like in a monstrous sandwich. If a real monster doesn't appear at your story hour, cut the humongous sandwich into child-size portions.

MONSTER GLOBS

(also known as "Slime Cookies")
Make green gelatin. Before it completely sets, spoon globs of the gelatin onto sugar cookies or graham crackers. Refrigerate until eating time.

MONSTER PIZZA

Follow the directions given in Alligator Snacks for making individual pizzas. Make a monster face on each pizza by using pineapple for teeth, olive rings for eyes, pepperoni slices for ears, and green pepper for the nose.

PRETTY PIGS

All of us have been told—at least once—"Don't make a pig of yourself!" Well, now's your chance to indulge yourself with some wonderful pig stories and activities. Before beginning the story hours, you might want to read about pigs in an animal encyclopedia or other source. The word "pig" really refers only to the baby hog, whose parents are boar (male) and sow (female). Hogs are quite intelligent, clean when given the chance, and not really lazy, considering that most of them have been hired, so to speak, to lie around and get fat.

Setting the Stage

When reading a pig story, wear a pig's nose. Later, the children can wear it when pretending to be a pig or when talking about pigs.

If you're using magic carpets, travel to Pigtown to hear all about pigs. You'll know you've reach your destination when you can hear the "oinks" of the pigs.

Encourage the children to bring stuffed pigs or any pigs they might have to arrange on a shelf with the pig books for a "pretty pigs" display.

Bulletin Board Ideas

1. The Adventures of Pig Pig—Use the opaque projector to enlarge and copy the Pig Pigs onto poster paper. Color and cut out. Use all four Pig Pigs from the four Pig Pig books. Arrange the Pig Pigs on the bulletin board with the title "The Adventures of Pig Pig."

2. Pig Poems—Chose some of your favorite pig poems to display on the bulletin board. The children can add their favorites, also.

3. Enlarge the illustration "Pig Out on Good Books" included in this section, color it, and display it on the board. The children could do the coloring. Also, this could be copied as is and each child can have his own copy.

4. Enlarge and copy any of the book covers to make a poster. HAMILTON by Robert Peck would be a good choice.

PIG OUT ON GOOD BOOKS

Read-Aloud Stories

THE AMAZING PIG

retold and il. by Paul Galdone (Houghton Mifflin, 1981)

Story: A peasant's son tells the king some unusual tales about his amazing pig in an attempt to win the beautiful princess for his wife.

Materials: hat; red, green, and white ribbon and flowers

Directions: Decorate a hat similar to the hat that the peasant boy wears and then wear it while reading this old Hungarian tale. Invite the children to repeat " 'I believe you,' said the king," as you're reading to them.

GERALDINE'S BLANKET

by Holly Keller (Greenwillow, 1984)

Story: Because Geraldine doesn't want to give up her baby blanket, she devises a way to keep it.

Materials: small piece of patched pink fabric, gift-wrapped box, Geraldine and doll stick puppets (see Pig Crafts), scissors

Directions: Gift wrap the "blanket" (piece of pink fabric) in the box. Attach a tag saying "To Geraldine, From Aunt Bessie." Choose a child to open the gift. Then introduce the Geraldine stick puppet. Explain that the pink fabric is Geraldine's blanket and that her parents think she should give it up. You might ask the class how Geraldine might feel about having to give up her blanket.

You could also relate a story about a favorite bit of clothing you refused to give up. You might ask if the children want to share their stories about favorite blankets. Then read the story.

Later, introduce the doll stick puppet and cut a dress for the puppet from the fabric to dress the puppet. You may want to have the pattern drawn on the back side of the fabric ahead of time. This story is a good lesson in sharing.

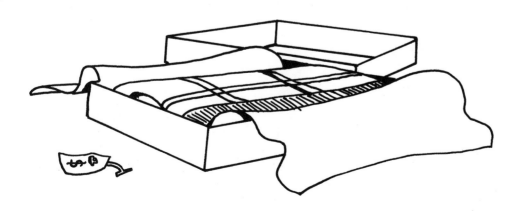

HAMILTON

by Robert Newton Peck, il. by Laura Lydecker
(Little, Brown, 1976)

Story: Hamilton has a huge appetite. The other farm animals are disgusted with him because he eats everything in sight. One night a wolf invades the barnyard. Hamilton becomes the hero when, mistaking the wolf's tail for a carrot, he bites it and scares the wolf away.

Materials: stuffed pig or a pig stick puppet, blue and orange felt or paper

Directions: Turn your pig into Hamilton by dressing him in a pair of blue overalls with a big orange "H" on the back pocket. Make the overalls out of paper or—if you have a stuffed pig and feel ambitious—denim. The pants don't need to be fancy.

Hide Hamilton among some food, such as your lunch. Now, tell your class you've brought someone for them to meet, but you can't find him! Describe him and have the children help in the search. After someone finds him, say, "Of course! All Hamilton really cares about is food!" Then have the children introduce themselves to Hamilton, but instead of using their names, they should use their favorite food.

HUMPHREY THE DANCING PIG

by Arthur Gets (Dial, 1980)

Story: Humphrey, a pretty pink pig, decides to lose weight by dancing the pounds away.

Materials: cassette tape with dancing music, cassette player

Directions: Make a tape with about 15 to 20 seconds of appropriate music for each of the following dances: skipping, kicking, Indian dancing, rock 'n roll, ballet, hula, and whirling. There should be a short pause between the music for each dance. The tape should not be too long because the children will tire.

After reading the story, the children form one or two circles to perform the dances. As the music plays, someone leads the dances and the children follow the leader. If you can't find the appropriate music, ask the music teacher to help you.

Make the tape available to the children so they can do this activity on their own during free time.

THE PIGS' PICNIC
by Keiko Kasza (Putnam, 1988)

Story: On his way to ask Miss Pig to join him on a picnic, Mr. Pig meets his friends and each persuades him to don a portion of their bodies.

Materials: picnic basket, magazines, scissors

Directions: Place the empty picnic basket (or cooler or paper bag) in front of the class. Explain that Mr. Pig wants to take Miss Pig on a picnic, but that he needs their help in deciding which foods to bring. Divide them into small groups and distribute the magazines and safety scissors. Tell them to look through the magazines. When they find a picture of a food that would be good on the picnic, they should cut it out and put it in the picnic basket.

You may use pretend food and make the picnic basket available for the children to dramatize the story as a directed activity or during their free time.

THE OLD WOMAN AND HER PIG
retold and il. by W. T. Mars (Whitman, 1964)

Story: The old woman's pig refuses to jump over the stile on the stone wall. She seeks the help of a dog, a stick, a fire, a waterfall, an ox, a butcher, and a rope, but none will help her. Finally, a little mouse gnaws on the rope and starts a sequence of events which forces the pig over the stile.

Materials: bonnet, shiny sixpence (any coin)

Directions: Wear a bonnet to tell this story. "One day I was sweeping the floor and I found this shiny sixpence." (Show the coin to the children.) "I was very excited because now I could buy a nice fat pig. So off to the market I went." Finish telling the story in the first person as though you were the old woman.

After telling the story, the children will love to dramatize it. Suggestions for dramatizing are given in the Pig Games section of this chapter.

A TREEFUL OF PIGS

by Arnold Lobel, il. by Anita Lobel (Greenwillow, 1979)

Story: The farmer's wife uses her ingenuity to get her lazy husband to help with the care of the pigs.

Materials: 12 cutout pigs, string or yarn, small tree branch, modeling clay or Styrofoam

Directions: To build a treeful of pigs, begin by cutting 12 pigs from pink paper (see below). Next, stand the tree branch in a base of modeling clay or Styrofoam. Tie the pigs on the branch.

Before reading the story, show the children the treeful of pigs. Ask them why they think the pigs are in the tree. Expect some interesting explanations!

Leave the tree on display as a remembrance of how the wife tricked her husband into helping care for the pigs.

WIGGLES THE LITTLE WISHING PIG

by Pauline Watson, il. by Paul Galdone (Random House, 1978)

Story: Wiggles' wishes come true, and he becomes a very scary monster.

Materials: a copy of the folded note found in the story

Directions: Before reading the story, unfold the note you've copied, and read it to the children. The children will love to say "Minou! Minou! Tee-Bay-Bay!" along with you as you're reading. Be dreamy when the pig is saying the wishes, and don't forget to shout and squeal. The children can wish for wings and then repeat "Minou! Minou! Tee-Bay-Bay!" to see if their wish comes true. When it doesn't, it's probably because they're not near the tree. Post the note on the bulletin board as a reminder of the story.

This is a fun book to read because there's so much interaction between the pigs.

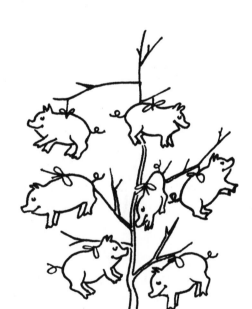

THE WONDERFUL PIGS OF JILLIAN JIGGS

by Phoebe Gilman (Scholastic, 1988)

Story: Jillian Jiggs makes wonderful pigs from old stockings. She gives them button noses and dresses them in fancy clothes. Jillian wants to sell her pigs and become a billionaire, but she discovers she can't part with them.

Materials: one or several of Jillian Jiggs' pigs

Directions: Follow the directions in the book to make one or several of Jillian Jiggs' pigs. Briefly explain to the children how they are made and that they were made by a girl named Jillian Jiggs. Before reading the story, sing "Jillian, Jillian, Jillian Jiggs, Maker of wonderful, marvelous pigs!" Encourage the children to sing along with you.

The older children will enjoy making their own Jillian Jiggs pig with some adult supervision. Get volunteers to make the pigs for the younger children. They'll all love them.

YUMMERS!

by James Marshall (Houghton Mifflin, 1972)

Story: Emily decides to go walking for the exercise and to lose weight; however, she's tempted by the yummy food she finds along the way.

Materials: pig dressed as Emily, small purse

Directions: Ahead of time dress a pig (stuffed or cut from poster paper) in a blue and white checkered skirt. Put a small purse on the pig's arm, and your pig is Emily.

Introduce Emily to the children. Explain that because she feels she's overweight, she decides to get exercise by walking. As you're reading, the children will want to join in with you every time you say "Yummers."

More Pig Stories

Athea. **PETER PIG** (Rourke Enterprises, 1981)

Peter is a lovable saddleback pig (a pig with black and white marks that resemble a saddle). He shows his appreciation to Rose Pig by bringing her a special present.

Bishop, Claire, il. by Kurt Wiese. **THE TRUFFLE PIG** (Coward, McCann & Geoghegan, 1971)

Pierre and his pig Marcel become good friends, and they won't have to be lonely any more.

Bloom, Suzanne. **WE KEEP A PIG IN THE PARLOR** (Clarkson N. Potter, 1988)

A disgruntled pig lives in a barn, sleeps on straw, and eats unpopped corn. He dislikes living like a pig. The farmer finds a new home for the pig in the parlor where the pig sleeps on the settee, watches TV, and eats popped popcorn.

Bond, Felicia. **POINSETTIA AND HER FAMILY** (Crowell, 1981)

Poinsettia thinks her six brothers are always in her way until she learns how lonesome she is without them.

Bond, Felicia. **POINSETTIA AND THE FIREFIGHTERS** (Crowell, 1984)

Poinsettia the pig is too lonely and scared to sleep on her first night alone in her new bedroom. However, after she learns about the firefighters who stay awake at night to protect everyone, she sleeps comfortably.

Boynton, Sandra. **HESTER IN THE WILD** (Harper & Row, 1979)

Hester the pig encounters some difficulties on a camping trip.

Brown, Marc and Stephen Krensky. **PERFECT PIGS** (Little, Brown, 1983)

Delightful pigs demonstrate proper etiquette in a book that delightfully teaches children the importance of good manners.

Carlson, Nancy. **LOUANNE PIG IN THE PERFECT FAMILY** (Carolrhoda Books, 1985)

After Louanne spends a weekend with her friend George, five sisters and four brothers, she decides she doesn't want to be a part of a large family.

Coxe, Molly. **LOUELLA AND THE YELLOW BALLOON** (Crowell, 1988)

After Louella drops her yellow balloon into the circus ring, the fun begins as she becomes part of the circus act while trying to retrieve the balloon.

Dubanevich, Arlene. **PIGS IN HIDING** (Four Winds Press, 1983)

Pigs play hide-and-seek as the reader hunts for the pigs in their hiding places. Other books by the same author include:
   PIGS AT CHRISTMAS
   PIG WILLIAM
   THE PIGGEST SHOW ON EARTH.

Dunn, Judy, photographs by Phoebe Dunn. **THE LITTLE PIG** (Random House, 1987)

Michael's little piglet, Lucy, has a mind of her own and leads him on some wild adventures.

Gackenbach, Dick. **HARVEY, THE FOOLISH PIG** (Clarion, 1988)

Harvey, a very poor, foolish pig, goes to visit the Great King to ask for wealth, failing to recognize the riches offered to him on his journey.

Gackenbach, Dick. **THE PIG WHO SAW EVERYTHING** (Seabury Press, 1978)

Piglet Henry ventures through the barnyard and sees the other animals. He believes the barnyard is the entire world and that he has seen everything there is to see.

Hale, Irina. **CHOCOLATE MOUSE AND SUGAR PIG** (Atheneum, 1978)

The mouse and pig run away to escape being eaten.

Hofstrand, Mary. **BY THE SEA** (Atheneum, 1989)

When a happy pig family takes a vacation, they indulge in activities they are too busy to do at home. During the day, they chase waves and make sand castles. At night they stay up late to dance and watch rockets.

Jeschke, Susan. **PERFECT THE PIG** (Holt, 1981)

A small pig who wishes for wings and gets them is thrilled with flight until he becomes lost in the fog.

Johnston, Tony, il. by Megan Lloyd. **FARMER MACK MEASURES HIS PIG** (Harper & Row, 1986)

When Farmer Mack attempts to measure his very fat pig, there's chaos on his farm.

Keller, Holly. **GERALDINE'S BIG SNOW** (Greenwillow, 1988)

Geraldine Pig is quite impatient as she waits for the first big snowfall so she can go sledding.

Lamont, Priscilla. **THE TROUBLESOME PIG** (Crown, 1985)

In this retelling of the old folk tale, an old woman tries to get her newly purchased pig over the stile on their way home.

Lobel, Arnold. **SMALL PIG** (Reader's Digest, 1973)

Small Pig decides to run away when the farmer's wife makes the barnyard too neat and shiny.

Marshall, James. **THE THREE LITTLE PIGS** (Dial, 1989)

In this witty version of the traditional story, the three little pigs seek their fortune. The wolf rides a bicycle and wears a sports jacket, but he still huffs and puffs and pig is still his favorite food. "Capital idea," "colossal," and "Oh, pooh," are some of the words used to create this modern classic.

Marshall, James. **YUMMERS TOO, THE SECOND COURSE** (Houghton Mifflin, 1986)

Emily Pig attempts to earn money to pay off the debts created by her love of food. She's not successful because her large appetite hinders her. Another delightful James Marshall book is:
PORTLY MCSWINE

McPhail, David. **PIG PIG AND THE MAGIC PHOTO ALBUM** (Dutton, 1986)

Pig Pig looks at a magic photo album while waiting for the photographer to take his picture. Each time Pig Pig says cheese he magically appears in the photo he's looking at. After several adventures, he decides he wants his photo taken without saying "Cheese."

McPhail, David. **PIG PIG GOES TO CAMP** (Dutton, 1983)

Pig Pig goes to summer camp where he enjoys swimming, boating, learning first aid, and cooking over a campfire. But what he loves most about camp are the frogs. When he gathers too many frog friends, he is sent home with the frogs, much to his mother's surprise.

McPhail, David. **PIG PIG GROWS UP** (Dutton, 1980)

Pig Pig wants to remain a baby. He sleeps in a crib that is too little, he wears baby clothes and makes his mother push him in the stroller. One day when Pig Pig saves a baby from being hurt, he decides he has grown up and he pushes his mother in the stroller.

McPhail, David. **PIG PIG RIDES** (Dutton, 1982)

Pig Pig tells his mother about all the amazing feats he plans to accomplish, including jumping over 500 elephants on his motorcycle.

Munsch, Robert, il. by Michael Martchenko. **PIGS** (Annick Press, 1989)

After leaving the gate open because she believes the pigs are too dumb to get out, Megan discovers that these creatures are smarter than she gave them credit for.

Rayner, Mary. **GARTH PIG AND THE ICE CREAM LADY** (Atheneum, 1977)

The big bad wolf dresses up as the Ice Cream lady, but he doesn't outfox the piglets.

Rayner, Mary. **MR. AND MRS. PIG'S EVENING OUT** (Atheneum, 1976)

Mr. and Mrs. Pig's new babysitter is really the wolf in disguise, but the ten piglets have fun handling the situation.

Rayner, Mary. **MRS. PIG'S BULK BUY** (Atheneum, 1981)

After Mrs. Pig serves a dinner of ketchup to her piglets, they decide ketchup isn't so great after all.

Rayner, Mary. **MRS. PIG GETS CROSS AND OTHER STORIES** (Dutton, 1987)

In this busy pig household, Father, Mother, and their ten children have a party, try to deal with bad moods, and crowd together in the same bed.

Scarry, Richard. **RICHARD SCARRY'S POSTMAN PIG AND HIS BUSY NEIGHBORS** (Random House, 1978)

The reader and Postman Pig meet his neighbors as he delivers mail in Busyville.

Schwartz, Mary, il. by Lynn Munsinger. **SPIFFEN: A TALE OF TIDY PIG** (Whitman, 1988)

In a Renaissance setting lives a pig named Spiffen who is clean and tidy. He's different from the other pigs who are dirty and messy, and he likes it that way.

Scieszka, Joe, il. by Lane Smith. **THE TRUE STORY OF THE 3 LITTLE PIGS** (Viking, 1989)

In this wolf's version of the old classic, the traditional villain explains that he was framed. His tale starts when he visits the first little pig to borrow some sugar for making his granny a birthday cake. Suffering from a bad cold, the wolf just happens to sneeze and blow the pig's house down. This begins a most unfortunate chain of events.

Stevens, Carla, il. by Rainey Bennett. **HOORAY FOR PIG!** (Seabury, 1974)

Pig's friends won't play with him until he learns how to swim.

Stevens, Carla, il. by Rainey Bennett. **PIG AND THE BLUE FLAG** (SEABURY PRESS, 1977)

Non-athletic Pig dislikes gym at school until he learns to play capture the flag.

Stolz, Mary. **EMMETT'S PIG** (Harper & Row, 1959)

Emmett wants a pig for a pet more than anything else in the world.

Van Leeuwen, Jean, il. by Arnold Lobel. **TALES OF OLIVER PIG** (Dial, 1979)

Five tales feature Oliver, his little sister Amanda, who is just learning to talk, and their loving parents. Other books about Oliver and Amanda include:
  MORE TALES OF OLIVER PIG
  TALES OF AMANDA PIG
  MORE TALES OF AMANDA PIG
  OLIVER AND AMANDA'S CHRISTMAS

Wilhelm, Hans. **OH, WHAT A MESS** (Crown, 1988)

Franklin Pig wins a contest with his picture of a rainbow. He inspires his family to clean up their home because his picture deserves a nice setting.

Wheeler, Cindy. **ROSE** (Knopf, 1985)

It's a hot day and Rose Pig searches for a way to cool off.

Winthrop, Elizabeth, il. by Anne Burgess. **SLOPPY KISSES** (Macmillan, 1984)

Emmy Lou's family loves to kiss each other a lot, but she's not sure she likes all those sloppy kisses.

Yolen, Jane, il. by Jane Dyer. **PIGGINS** (Harcourt, 1987)

After the lights go out at a dinner party, Mrs. Reynard's beautiful diamond necklace is stolen. Piggins, the dignified butler, identifies the real thief.

Pig Poems

THE BRAND-NEW TAIL
I had a little pig,
I fed him in a trough.
He got so fat
His tail dropped off.
So I got me a hammer,
And I got me a nail,
And I made my little pig
A brand-new tail.
—Mother Goose

DICKERY, DICKERY, DARE
Dickery, dickery, dare
The pig flew up in the air;
The man in brown
Soon brought him down,
Dickery, dickery, dare.
—Mother Goose

BARBER, BARBER
Barber, barber, shave a pig,
How many hairs will make a wig?
Four and twenty, that's enough.
Give the barber a pinch of snuff.
—Mother Goose

More Pig Poems

"The Pigs," "Mary Middling," "There Was a Small Pig Who Wept Tears" p. 36 in READ-ALOUD RHYMES FOR THE VERY YOUNG selected by Jack Prelutsky, il. by Marc Brown (Knopf, 1986)

"Pink Pig" p. 24 in PURPLE PELICAN by Jack Prelutsky, il. by Garth Williams (Greenwillow, 1986)

"Flying Pigs," "Pig," and "The Pig" p. 155 in CELEBRATIONS by Caroline Feller Bauer (H. W. Wilson, 1985)

Pig Poem Books

THIS LITTLE PIG-A-WIG AND OTHER RHYMES ABOUT PIGS chosen by Lenore Blegvad, il. by Erik Blegvad (Atheneum, 1978)

THE BOOK OF PIGERICKS by Arnold Lobel (Harper & Row, 1983)

PADDY PIG'S POEMS by Donald Charles (Simon & Schuster, 1989)

Pig Finger Plays and Action Verse

IF YOU MEET A PIG

If you should meet a pig
  (Point finger.)
Doing a jig,
  (Dance a jig.)
Or if you meet a hog,
  (Point finger.)
Out for a jog,
  (Jog in place.)
You best get out of the way,
  (Move to the side.)
And let them pass, I say.
  (Point to self.)

THIS LITTLE PIG

Use a fine felt marker to draw a pig's nose on each fingernail of one hand. Then, as you recite "This Little Pig," slightly fist your hand and, beginning with the small finger, extend one finger each time a pig is mentioned. Wiggle your thumb on the last line. Encourage the children to make up their own verse. They can try this in groups or as individuals.

This little pig went to the library.
This little pig stayed home.
This little pig read books.
This little pig read none.
And this little pig went
Oink, oink, oink
All the way to the library.

This little pig went to school.
This little pig stayed home.
This little pig learned to read.
This little pig was bored.
And this little pig went
Grunt, grunt, grunt
All the way to school.

This little pig went to (your home town).
This little pig stayed in bed.
This little pig had ice cream.
This little pig had popcorn.
And this little pig went
Slurp, slurp, slurp
All the way to (your home town).

More Finger Plays

"Five Little Pigs" p. 31 in RING A RING O' ROSES (Flint Public Library, 1988)

"Can a Pig Dance a Jig?" p. 108 in MOVE OVER MOTHER GOOSE! by Ruth Dowell, il. by Concetta Scott (Gryphon House, 1987)

Pig Songs

OINK, OINK, OINK, OINK, LITTLE PIG
(Tune: "Twinkle, Twinkle, Little Star")

Oink, oink, oink, oink, little pig,
Can you do a little jig?
In the bright light of the sun,
Are you having lots of fun?
Oink, oink, oink, oink, little pig,
I think that you will grow big.

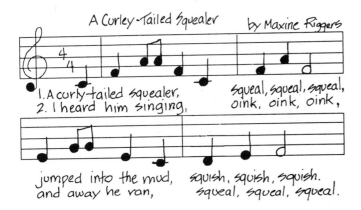

A Curley-Tailed Squealer   by Maxine Riggers

1. A curly-tailed squealer,
2. I heard him singing,
jumped into the mud,
and away he ran,
squeal, squeal, squeal,
oink, oink, oink,
squish, squish, squish.
squeal, squeal, squeal.

THE TAIL OF A PIG
(Tune: "The Wheels of a Bus")

The tail of a pig curls round and round,
Round and round, round and round.
The tail of a pig curls round and round,
All through the mud.

The mouth of a pig goes oink, oink, oink,
Oink, oink, oink, oink, oink oink.
The mouth of a pig goes oink, oink, oink,
All day long.

The snout of a pig goes root, root, root,
Root, root, root, root, root, root.
The snout of a pig goes root, root, root,
All day long.

The hooves of a pig go run, run, run,
Run, run, run, run, run, run.
The hooves of a pig go run, run, run,
All day long.

The ears of a pig go twitch, twitch, twitch,
Twitch, twitch, twitch, twitch, twitch, twitch,
The ears of a pig go twitch, twitch, twitch,
All day long.

Pig Games

THE OLD WOMAN AND THE PIG

You will need 11 children to dramatize this story. If there are extra children who want to participate, two may play the same role together, or you may need to put on the play twice. The storyteller reads or tells the story while the children pantomime their parts.

The old woman wears a bonnet and the pig wears a paper bag pig mask (see Pig Crafts). One child lies on his or her side to make the stile. Select eight children to hold the following items: a rope, a cardboard butcher's knife, a stick, a dog (drawing), a fire (drawing), a waterfall (drawing), an ox (drawing), and a mouse (drawing).

Arrange the children in proper order and begin. If props are unavailable, name tags or sign-necklaces (signs hung with yarn from the neck) can be effective substitutes.

The children may want to do the drama several times and play different parts.

HIDE AND SEEK

Play this game after reading PIGS IN HIDING.

CAPTURE THE FLAG

Play this game after reading PIG AND THE BLUE FLAG.

THE THREE LITTLE PIGS PLAY

Tell the story as the children perform the actions and say the dialogue. While props are not necessary, you might add to the fun by making available pig noses, a wolf puppet, masks and houses (see Pig Crafts).

Pig Crafts

PIG BOOKMARK

Materials: pig stickers or pattern of a pig, colored paper

Directions: Divide an 8½ x 11 inch sheet of paper into four equal horizontal parts. On each part print the words "Pig Out on Good Books." If you don't have pig stickers, draw a picture of a pig on each master bookmark. Using a copy machine, copy as many bookmarks as needed onto colored paper. Cut each sheet to make four bookmarks. If you're using pig stickers, each child can choose a sticker for the book mark.

GERALDINE'S BLANKET STICK PUPPETS

Materials: pink construction paper or tag board, scissors, Popsicle sticks, glue or tape, felt markers

Directions: Cut a pig and a pig doll from pink paper. Draw on Geraldine's and the doll's features. Draw on Geraldine's dress. Glue or tape the figures to Popsicle sticks. With these easy-to-make puppets, the children will bring the story of Geraldine to life.

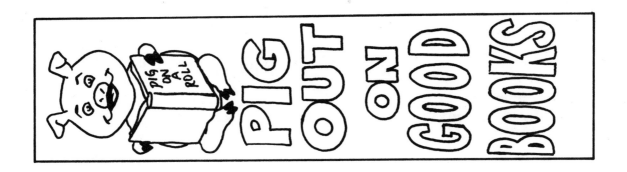

PIG AND WOLF PAPER BAG MASKS

Materials: Paper bags about 8 inches wide, colored construction paper (pink, brown, red, and tan), black felt marker, glue, scissors, pig and wolf patterns

Directions: For the pig, cut the pig patterns from pink paper. Mark and cut out the eyes. With the felt marker, outline the ears, eyes, and nose. Draw on the eyebrows and nose. Glue the ears and nose in place. Trim the bag so that it is only about 12 inches deep. Glue the pig face to the bag as illustrated. Cut out the eyes from the paper bag. Slip it on and you're ready to be a pig!

For the wolf, follow the above directions using brown paper for the face and ears, tan for the inside ears, and red for the tongue. Follow the illustration for the placement of the features, and you're ready to become the big bad wolf!

Kids can take these masks home to retell the classic story for their parents, or they can use them in school to tell the story to each other or to other classes.

THE THREE LITTLE PIGS' HOUSES

Materials: 2 cardboard boxes, straw, sticks, large cardboard toy blocks, felt markers, glue, scissors

Directions: Cut up the boxes leaving 3 sides as illustrated. Draw a door with a window on the middle section. Glue straw on one house and sticks on the other. These will fall flat when the wolf huffs and puffs. Build the brick house by stacking toy blocks. Leave an opening for the door. These blocks should not tumble down when the wolf comes by.

The children will be huffing and puffing as they dramatize this popular story for their own enjoyment or for others.

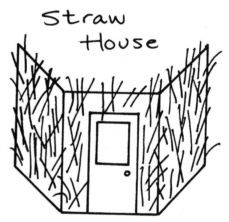

Straw House

Stick House

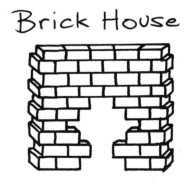

Brick House

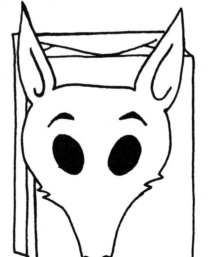

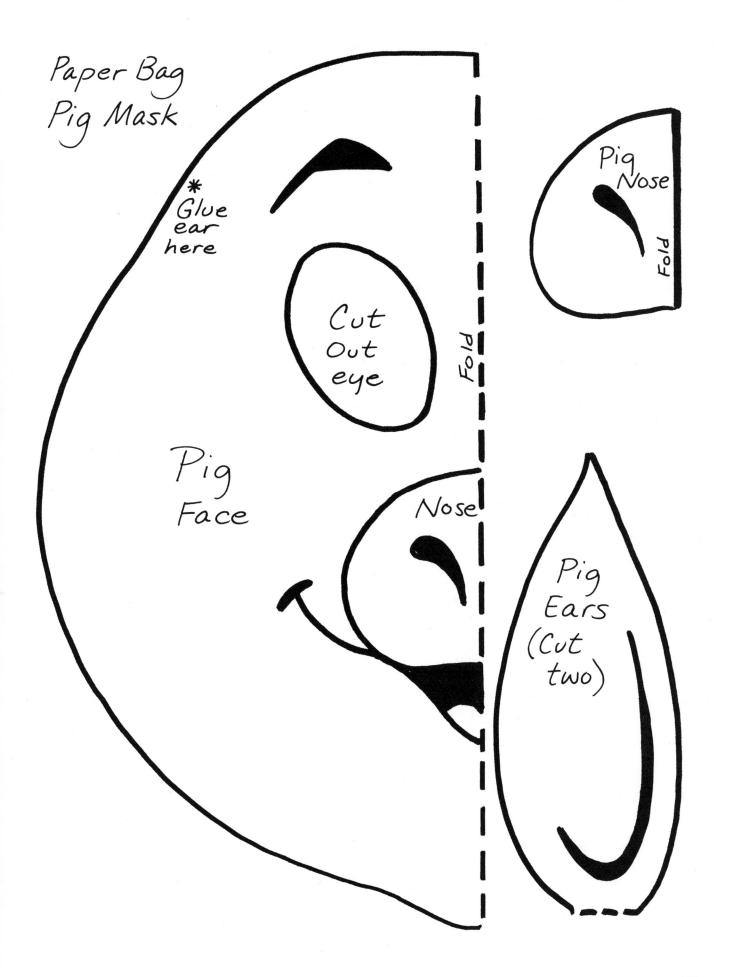

Paper Bag Pig Mask

*
Glue ear here

Cut Out eye

Pig Face

Nose

Fold

Pig Nose

Fold

Pig Ears (Cut two)

173

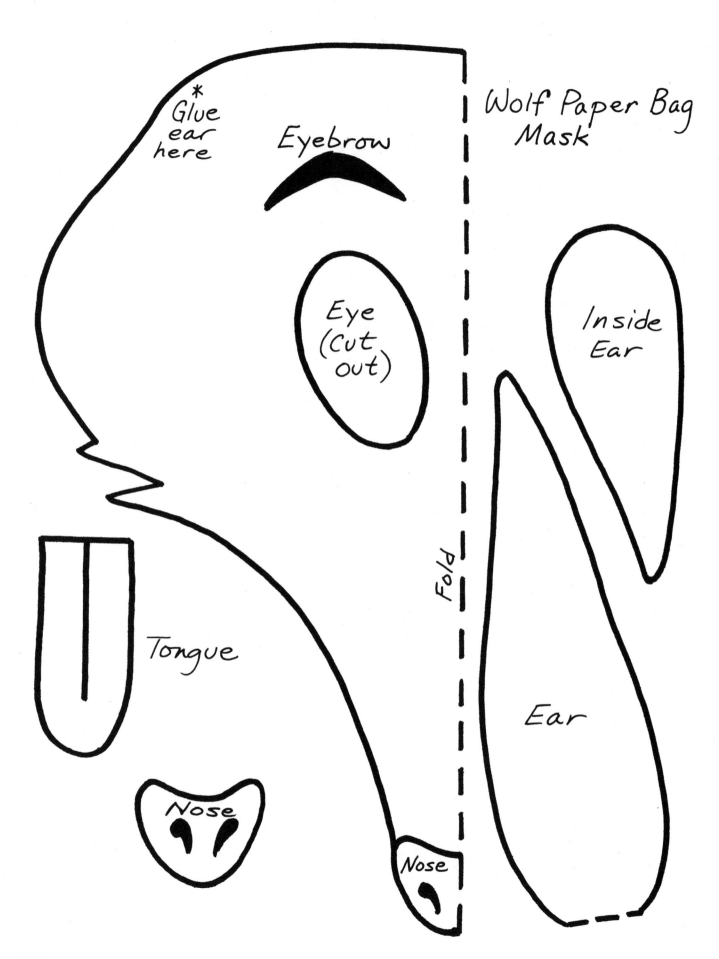

Glue ear here *

Eyebrow

Wolf Paper Bag Mask

Eye (Cut out)

Inside Ear

Fold

Tongue

Ear

Nose

Nose

Pig Snacks

PIG COOKIES
(perfect for pigging out)

¾ cup shortening	1½ tsp. vanilla
¾ cup butter	5 cups flour
2 cups sugar	2 tsp. baking powder
4 eggs	1½ tsp. salt

Mix shortening, butter, sugar, eggs, and vanilla thoroughly. Stir flour, baking powder, and salt together; blend with the shortening mixture. Chill at least two hours.

Heat oven to 400 degrees. Roll dough about ¼ inch thick on lightly floured board. Cut with round 3 inch cookie cutter. Place on ungreased baking sheet. Bake 6 to 8 minutes. Makes about 4 dozen.

"Make up" for pig face

1 package frosting mix
pink food coloring
raisins
marshmallows
tiny round candies

Prepare the frosting mix according to directions on the box. Add pink food coloring. Cut a large marshmallow in half for the nose and attach to the cookie with frosting. Attach two small raisins to the nose by pushing them into the marshmallow. Frost the cookie and add two round candies for the eyes.

CORN ON THE COB
While eating, explain that corn is a favorite food of pigs, though they don't eat it boiled and buttered.

ICE CREAM
Serve your favorite flavors after reading GARTH PIG AND THE ICE CREAM LADY.

PICNIC
Before reading THE PIG'S PICNIC, prepare a picnic lunch—sandwiches, carrot strips, cookies, and juice.

REMARKABLE RABBITS

Children love everything about rabbits—their cuddly fur, twitching noses, and bright eyes. No wonder bunny books multiply as fast as . . . bunnies.

When reading rabbit stories, remember to be "rabbity"—wrinkle your nose, blink your eyes, and hop when you want to go from here to there.

Teach the children the sign language symbol for rabbit. Encourage them to share it with their friends and family.

If funds allow, purchase one or two stuffed rabbit characters. Peter Rabbit, Max, and the Velveteen Rabbit can be found in many stores, and they can also be ordered by mail from A Child's Collection (see Resources).

Consider wearing a rabbit costume during your story hours. Rent one from a costume shop, or make your own. A costume helps set the mood for the stories. But remember that the costume should not distract from the books.

Setting the Stage

Since many people keep rabbits as pets, you might try to borrow one for your room. Establish clear guidelines about the handling of these—and all other—pets. Children need to learn that animals are not toys.

If you are ambitious, you might arrange for a long-term rabbit stay, during which the children might learn a lot about caring for these appealing creatures.

Whether or not you have real rabbits in the room, you might construct a make-believe rabbit house for the children to enter while reading rabbit stories. Make a tree from green and brown poster paper. Staple the tree onto a large cardboard box. Keep the top of the box open for light. Cut a hole for the door large enough for children to crawl through. Cut a window on one side. To give the interior a homey feel, hang bunny pictures, put a ruffled curtain on the window, and throw a braided rug on the floor. Keep a couple of rabbit ears handy for the children to wear when reading in the rabbit house. For the sake of comfort and order, limit occupancy to one or two bunnies—kids—at a time.

Bulletin Board Ideas

1. After reading LET'S MAKE RABBITS, have the children draw their own rabbits. Display their artwork on the bulletin board under the heading, "Let's Make Rabbits."

2. Use an opaque projector or a photocopy machine to enlarge some of the classic rabbit drawings from your favorite books. Display the pictures under the title "Famous Rabbits."

3. Enlarge the "Hopping to the Library for a Good Book" illustration. Color it using markers or crayons. Mat and pin to the bulletin board.

Read-Aloud Stories

FOOLISH RABBIT'S BIG MISTAKE
by Rafe Martin, il. by Ed Young (Putnam, 1985)

Story: A foolish rabbit believes a loud crash is the sound of the earth breaking up. He hurries off in a panic to warn two other rabbits, two bears, an elephant, and the snakes. A lion finally brings the frightened animals to their senses.

Materials: rabbit, bear, elephant and lion masks; snake puppets, apples

Directions: This action-filled story gives the storyteller a chance to read with gusto. If possible, have a hidden helper use pie tins or other objects to make the loud crash heard early in the story. When introducing the lion, give a big roar of the sort that might get you a job as the voice of the MGM lion.

This story lends itself to dramatization. Refer to Rabbit Dramatic Play and Rabbit Crafts for ideas.

Since an apple plays an important part in the story, you might end with an apple snack.

IT'S NOT EASY BEING A BUNNY
by Marilyn Sadler, il. by Roger Bollen (Random House, 1983)

Story: When P. J. Funnybunny becomes dissatisfied with being a bunny, he tries being a bear, a bird, a beaver, a pig, a moose, a possum, and a skunk. In the end, he discovers that he's happiest just being a bunny.

Materials: P. J. Funnybunny stick puppet

Directions: Use an opaque projector to enlarge a picture of P. J. from the book onto poster paper. Color and cut out. Attach a flat stick to complete your extra-large puppet. Introduce P. J. to the children, explaining that he is tired of eating carrots, doesn't like his long ears, and just plain hates being a bunny. Ask what they think he might do about it.

Develop a voice you can use for P. J. while reading the story. Do a very loud moose call for the moose, and a little "mooo" for P. J.'s attempt to respond. Later, let the children make their own moose calls. Kids enjoy participating by echoing the refrain: "I want to be a..."

LET'S MAKE RABBITS
by Leo Lionni (Pantheon, 1982)

Story: Two make-believe rabbits—one a drawing, the other a cutout—are friends. Upon eating a real carrot, they become real rabbits. They know they're real because they can see their shadows.

Materials: pencil, scissors, paper, two toy stuffed rabbits, carrot

Directions: Begin by taking the pencil in one hand and the scissors in the other. Have these items act out the story as if they were puppets. At the appropriate moment, use the scissors to cut out a rabbit and use the pencil to sketch a rabbit. (If you prefer, you could make these props ahead of time.)

When you reach the point about the two rabbits becoming real, bring out the stuffed toy rabbits and a real carrot, and show how they cast shadows. If you present the story on a sunny day, you might lead the children outside to look for their own shadows.

Another option is to use flannel board characters to tell the story (see Rabbit Crafts).

LITTLE RABBIT'S LOOSE TOOTH
by Lucy Bate, il. by Diane de Groat (Crown, 1975)

Story: When Little Rabbit loses a tooth in his chocolate ice cream, he can't decide what to do with it. He considers several options, but finally follows his mother's suggestion and puts the tooth under his pillow.

Materials: a square mint meant to serve as a tooth, pillow, toy rabbit, "tooth" envelope (see Rabbit Crafts)

Directions: Children from five to seven will especially identify with the rabbit's feelings. With very young children, you may need to simplify some of the dialogue.

At the appropriate point in the story, put the tooth (mint) into the "tooth" envelope. Place the tooth under the pillow and the rabbit on the pillow as if he's going to bed.

As a special treat, give each child chocolate ice cream with a "tooth" in it.

MR. RABBIT AND THE LOVELY PRESENT
by Charlotte Zolotow, il. by Maurice Sendak
(Harper & Row, 1982)

Story: A little girl asks Mr. Rabbit to help her choose a colorful birthday gift for her mother. After reviewing all sorts of colorful things, they decide on a basket filled with red, yellow, green, and purple fruit.

Materials: rabbit ears and girl's hat (see Rabbit Crafts); real apples, bananas, pears, grapes, and a basket

Directions: For a dramatic effect, find a second adult to help you tell this story as a conversation between the girl and the rabbit. No need to memorize the lines of the book. Just become familiar with the sequence of ideas. Then improvise.

Before starting, put on the hat and the ears. During the dialogue, place each type of fruit into the basket at the right moment. As the story ends, the two characters walk away, with the girl carrying the basket. A moment later, the girl returns and explains that her mother wants her to share the fruit with the audience. Cut up the fruit for everyone to enjoy.

THE RUNAWAY BUNNY
by Margaret Wise Brown, il. by Clement Hurd
(Harper & Row, 1972)

Story: In an imaginary game of hide and seek, a little bunny repeatedly runs away from his loving mother who finds him wherever he goes.

Materials: carrots, toy white bunny

Directions: Introduce the soft white bunny and let the children pet it in your lap. This is better than passing the bunny around, which can take too much time or even lead to squabbles.

Explain that one day this bunny decides to run away from his mother. Ask the children what they think the mother should do.

During the reading, use a loving voice for the mother's dialogue. At the end of the story say to the children, "Have a carrot." Then give each child a carrot, with the green end on if possible.

THE TALE OF PETER RABBIT
by Beatrix Potter (Frederick Warne, 1902)

Story: This classic tale features the daredevil adventures of Peter Rabbit who sneaks into Mr. McGregor's garden.

Materials: Peter Rabbit, flower pot

Directions: Purchase a toy Peter Rabbit. (See A Child's Collection in Resources.) Or dress any plump rabbit toy you already own to look like Peter by pinning on a blue felt jacket with gold buttons.

Hide the rabbit in a flower pot—or something of that shape. Before reading the story, ask the children if they have seen a rabbit in a blue jacket. Explain that you saw him earlier.

Encourage the children to look around for the rabbit. If necessary, give them little hints. When they find the rabbit, have them bring him to you to act as a puppet. Tell the rabbit that you heard he had an exciting adventure and that you think the children would like to hear all about it. Then read the story.

Afterwards, you might try one of the Peter Rabbit activities described in the Rabbit Games section of this chapter.

THE TORTOISE AND THE HARE
adapted by Janet Stevens (Holiday House, 1984)

Story: The boastful hare challenges the tortoise to a race. The hare zooms into the lead and is so confident of victory he stops to nap. Meanwhile, the tortoise plods on to the finish line.

Materials: banner reading "Don't quit."

Directions: Hang the banner—printed by hand or by a computer—while you're talking to the children about the meaning of persistence. Ask the children to give examples of when they have stayed with a job until the end.

Explain that you know a story about a tortoise who was persistent. While reading, let the tone of your voice indicate how boastful and arrogant the hare is. The children can also act out the story (see Rabbit Dramatic Play).

TWO HUNDRED RABBITS

by Lonzo Anderson, il. by Adrienne Adams
(Viking, 1958)

Story: A young boy would like to attend Festival Day at the castle. He tries several ways to get in, but without success. He finally succeeds by using a magic whistle to lead 200 marching rabbits into the celebration.

Materials: toy whistle, rabbit ears (see Rabbit Crafts), tubes from paper towels or toilet paper

Directions: For a dramatic effect, tell the story from the point of view of the narrator, using "I." Blow a toy whistle—a tonette is especially good—at the point in the story when the boy assembles the rabbits. Since, as the narrator, you play the 200th rabbit, wear rabbit ears. At the end of the story, pretend you're marching with the other rabbits.

Refer to Rabbit Games for an activity related to this story.

THE VELVETEEN RABBIT

by Margery Williams, il. by Florence Graham
(Knopf, 1985)

Story: The Boy and his toy velveteen rabbit become good friends as they play together. Because the rabbit is loved by the Boy, the rabbit becomes alive and joins the real rabbits in the forest.

Materials: Velveteen Rabbit (see A Child's Collection in Resources) or a scrap of velveteen fabric

Directions: Show the Velveteen Rabbit to the children, explaining that a young boy received it as a present. If you are unable to get the rabbit, pass around a piece of velveteen so the children will know what the rabbit feels like to the boy.

Because the text is rather long, you may wish to shorten the story by retelling it in your own words. In this case, read the story ahead of time to become familiar with it, and let the pictures be cues as you tell it.

More Rabbit Stories

Aardema, Verna, il. by Jerry Pinkney. **RABBIT MAKES A MONKEY OUT OF LION** (Dial, 1989)

Rabbit craves a taste of honey and tries to outsmart Lion who has no intention of sharing. Another delightful Verna Aardema book is:
   WHO'S IN RABBIT'S HOUSE

Balian, Lorna. **HUMBUG RABBIT** (Abingdon, 1974)

Father Rabbit says "Humbug" to the idea that he's the real Easter Bunny although his children believe he is. But Easter isn't spoiled for his children thanks to Granny.

Becker, John, il. by Barbara Cooney. **SEVEN LITTLE RABBITS** (Scholastic, 1973)

In this rhyming story, seven little rabbits walk down the road to call on their old friend, Toad. One by one the rabbits find a mole hole where they stay until there are no rabbits left.

Billiam, Rosemary, il. by Vanessa Julian-Otter. **FUZZY RABBIT IN THE SKY** (Random House, 1986)

Ellen's toy rabbit, Fuzzy, goes through some scary adventures when he's lost in the park. Cinnamon, a dog, finds Fuzzy and returns him to Ellen, who makes the rabbit feel comfortable and safe again.

Boujon, Claude. **THE CROSS-EYED RABBIT** (Macmillan, 1988)

The cross-eyed rabbit saves his two brothers from a hungry fox when he mistakes the fox's tail for a carrot.

Brown, Marc and Laurene Krasny Brown. **THE BIONIC BUNNY SHOW** (Little, Brown, 1984)

In real life, Wilbur is an ordinary father rabbit; but when he goes to work at the TV station, he becomes the superhero Bionic Bunny. Along the way, the reader gets a behind-the-scenes view of television production.

Caldwell, Mary, il. by Ann Schweninger. **MORNING, RABBIT, MORNING** (Harper & Row, 1982)

In the early morning, a rabbit visits a beautiful meadow and playfully stretches, scratches, hops, sniffs, nibbles, pounces, and jumps before returning home.

Carlson, Nancy. **BUNNIES AND THEIR SPORTS** (Viking, 1987)

Different bunnies like different sports such as jogging, swimming, acrobatics, skiing, hiking, and playing ball. They enjoy sports because it makes them feel good. A related book is:
   BUNNIES AND THEIR HOBBIES

Carlson, Nancy. **LOUDMOUTH GEORGE AND THE SIXTH-GRADE BULLY** (Carolrhoda Books, 1983)

On his way to school, George's lunch is stolen by a bully. When George becomes hungry, his friend Harriet finds a way to trick the bully. Other titles in this series include:
   LOUDMOUTH GEORGE AND THE BIG RACE
   LOUDMOUTH GEORGE AND THE CORNET
   LOUDMOUTH GEORGE AND THE FISHING TRIP
   LOUDMOUTH GEORGE AND THE NEW NEIGHBORS

Christelow, Eileen. **HENRY AND THE RED STRIPES** (Clarion Books, 1982)

Henry, a small brown rabbit who tries to disguise himself by painting red stripes on his back, is easily caught by the fox who plans to eat him for dinner. Luckily for Henry, Mrs. Fox won't cook him because she believes the stripes indicate he has a disease.

Cleveland, David, il. by Nurit Karlin. **THE APRIL RABBITS** (Coward, McCann & Geoghegan, 1978)

On April 1, a single rabbit appears. On April 2, another rabbit appears. So it goes through the month until on April 29, there are 29 rabbits. On the last day of the month, all the rabbits disappear.

Delton, Judy, il. by Lisa McCue. **HIRED HELP FOR RABBIT** (Macmillan, 1988)

Tired from working in his garden, Rabbit hires some animals to do the housework. Soon he has a house full of animals that he's waiting on. At that point Rabbit realizes he would do better without "help."

Delton, Judy, il. by Joe Lasker. **RABBIT FINDS A WAY** (Crown, 1975)

Rabbit wakes up in the morning, excited because this is the day Bear "always" makes carrot cake. On his way to Bear's house, Rabbit turns down food his other friends offer so as not to ruin his appetite. Unfortunately, this particular day Bear didn't bake a cake. Another delightful book in this series is:

RABBIT GOES TO NIGHT SCHOOL

Dunn, Judy, photos by Phoebe Dunn. **THE LITTLE RABBIT** (Random House, 1980)

Sarah loves the rabbit she received as an Easter gift. She and the rabbit soon become good friends. When the rabbit gives birth to seven bunnies, Sarah finds a home for each of them.

Eagle, Mike. **THE MARATHON RABBIT** (Holt, 1985)

A rabbit is allowed to race against people in a marathon. When the rabbit wins the race, the people say they'll be glad when the race returns to normal. But then a moose decides to enter next year's competition.

Feczko, Kathy, il. by John Jones. **THE GREAT BUNNY RACE** (Troll Associates, 1985)

Toby, a rabbit, is reluctant to enter the annual rabbit race, because Boomer Bunny always wins. Darby Duck convinces Toby to enter the race, and with encouragement from Darby Duck, Toby wins.

Gackenbach, Dick. **HATTIE RABBIT** (Harper & Row, 1976)

In the first of this book's two stories, Hattie Rabbit wishes her mother had the feet of a chicken (so she could scratch up worms), the neck of a giraffe (so she could reach leaves at the top of the tree), and the trunk of an elephant (so she could act as a shower). But then Hattie realizes she wouldn't have a soft, furry mother if her wishes came true.

In the second story, Hattie mistreats her friends by selling them worthless products. But in the end she learns that friends are more important than money.

Other fine books in this series are:
MOTHER RABBIT'S SON TOM
HATTIE BE QUIET, HATTIE BE GOOD

Heyward, Du Bose, il. by Marjorie Hack. **THE COUNTRY BUNNY AND THE LITTLE GOLD SHOES** (Scholastic, 1975)

Mother Cottontail proves she is wise, kind, and swift. Therefore, old Grandfather chooses her to be the fifth Easter bunny, and she earns the little gold shoes.

Kraus, Robert. **DADDY LONG EARS** (Windmill Books, 1970)

Daddy Long Ears has 32 bunnies to raise by himself. He does a wonderful job despite his many problems.

Kroll, Steven, il. by Janet Stevens. **THE BIG BUNNY AND THE MAGIC SHOW** (Holiday House, 1986)

A few days before Easter, Wilbur decides he's tired of being the Easter bunny. He takes a job with a magician but doesn't like the work. When he's fired, he happily returns to delivering Easter eggs.

Leedy, Loreen. **THE BUNNY PLAY** (Holiday House, 1988)

The bunnies put on a musical version of LITTLE RED RIDING HOOD. They work hard learning how to act, direct, design the set, make costumes, and publicize their play.

Mangas, Brian, il. by Sidney Levitt. **A NICE SURPRISE FOR FATHER RABBIT** (Simon & Schuster, 1989)

When Father Rabbit's train is delayed because of a snow storm, his two children, Sonny Bunny and Honey Bunny, plan a tea party to welcome him home.

Mangas, Brian, il. by Sidney Levitt. **YOU DON'T GET A CARROT UNLESS YOU'RE A BUNNY** (Simon and Schuster, 1989)

For Halloween, Mother Rabbit makes a duck costume for Honey Bunny, and a bear costume for Sonny Bunny. Their costumes are so good no one believes they are really rabbits, but eventually the pair do get their favorite treats—carrots.

Manushkin, Fran, il. by Diane de Groat. **LITTLE RABBIT'S BABY BROTHER** (Crown, 1986)

Little Rabbit isn't sure she wants a new baby in her family. The baby might take her room and bed. Worse, Mother and Father might not have enough time for two bunnies. But Little Rabbit learns that her fears are groundless and that being a big sister is a good thing to be.

McLenighan, Valjean, il. by Vernon McKissack. **TURTLE AND RABBIT** (Follett, 1981)

In this modern adaptation of "The Tortoise and the Hare," Turtle challenges her friend Rabbit to a race along First Street in the center of a city.

Parish, Peggy, il. by Leonard Kessler. **TOO MANY RABBITS** (Macmillan, 1974)

Miss Molly loves her pet rabbits, but when they rapidly multiply, she decides the rabbits must go.

Quackenbush, Robert. **FUNNY BUNNIES** (Clarion Books, 1984)

The Bunny family checks into a small hotel room. Lucy goes for a swim. Her relatives stay in the room to rest, where they are soon joined by workers who come to fix everything from the sink to the lights. The room gets so crowded that when Lucy returns and opens the door, everyone falls out. Another zany book by the same author is:

FUNNY BUNNIES ON THE RUN

Sadler, Marilyn, il. by Roger Bollen. **P. J. FUNNYBUNNY IN THE PERFECT HIDING PLACE** (Western, 1988)

P. J. and his buddies (a pig, a beaver, and a raccoon) invite the girls (a rabbit and a duck) to join them in a game of hide-and-seek. The girls hide so well, it's dark before they're found.

Sadler, Marilyn, il. by Roger Bollen. **THE VERY BAD BUNNY** (Random House, 1984)

P. J.'s family believes he is very bad because he spills the syrup, tangles his brother's yo-yo, and cuts up his father's newspaper. When cousin Binky comes for a visit, however, they all agree that Binky is the worst bunny of all. Another adventure of lovable P. J. is:

THE SPOILED BUNNY

Sonnenschein, Harriet, il. by Jurg Obrist. **HAROLD'S RUNAWAY NOSE** (Simon & Schuster, 1989)

Harold's mother tells him his nose is running. Harold runs off looking everywhere for his nose—into the garden and through the house. Just as Harold gives up hope of ever finding his nose, it turns up where he never thought to look.

Stevens, Carla, il. by Consuelo Joerns. **RABBIT ON BEAR MOUNTAIN** (Scholastic, 1980)

Raccoon, Woodchuck, and Skunk tell Rabbit she's too little to hike up Bear Mountain with them. Rabbit shows them who's the best hiker by reaching the top of the mountain first. Other delightful books by Carla Stevens include

RABBIT AND SKUNK AND THE BIG FIGHT

RABBIT AND SKUNK AND THE SCARY ROCK

Wayland, April, il. by Robin Spowart. **TO RABBITTOWN** (Scholastic, 1989)

A little girl journeys in a fantasy to Rabbittown. There—in the form of a rabbit—she learns to listen to the softest sound and smell the faintest smell. She's happy until she remembers the people she loves back home.

Wells, Rosemary. **MAX'S CHRISTMAS** (Dial, 1986)

It's Christmas Eve and big sister Ruby won't let Max stay up to see Santa Claus come down the chimney. However, Max is determined to see Santa, and he does. Other books about Max include:

MAX'S BATH
MAX'S BREAKFAST
MAX'S BEDTIME
MAX'S BIRTHDAY
MAX'S FIRST WORD
MAX'S NEW SUIT
MAX'S RIDE
MAX'S TOYS

Wilhelm, Hans. **MORE BUNNY TROUBLE** (Scholastic, 1989)

Ralph, the bunny, is babysitting his bunny sister, but when he's neglectful, she crawls into the fox-infested grass. In the nick of time, Ralph figures out how to find her. An earlier book by the same author is:
BUNNY TROUBLE

Rabbit Finger Plays and Action Verse

BUNNY HOP
Repeat the following verse as long as the children are interested. They may hop forward on the hops or hop in place.

Thump and thump and
   (Thump right foot twice.)
Thump and thump!
   (Thump left foot twice.)
Flip, flop.
   (Flip flop hands as paws.)
Hop, hop, hop!
   (Hop three times.)

MARCHING RABBITS
Do the next action verse after reading TWO HUNDRED RABBITS.

If I had 200 rabbits,
I'd march them up the hill
   (March forward.)
And back down again.
   (March backward.)

Their ears would stand tall,
   (Place hands on head for ears that stand up
   and fall.)
Then take a fall.
They would hop around
   (Hop in place.)
And fall to the ground.
   (Fall down.)

Then I'd march them up the hill
   (March forward.)
And back down again.
   (March backward.)

More Finger Plays, Poems, and Songs

"Bunnies" and "Robert the Rabbit" p. 13 in MOVE OVER MOTHER GOOSE by Ruth Dowell, il. by Concetta C. Scott (Gryphon House, 1987).

"Creeping" p. 16, "A Fat Bunny" p. 25, "Here's Bunny" p. 41, "Little Bunny" page 54, "Little Rabbit" p. 56, "Once I Saw a Bunny" p. 68, and "Tire Bunnies" p. 94 in RING A RING O' ROSES (Flint Public Library, 1988).

"The Rabbit" p. 55 in THE RANDOM HOUSE BOOK OF POETRY FOR CHILDREN selected by Jack Prelutsky, il. by Arnold Lobel (Random House, 1983)

"Mr. Rabbit" and "The Rabbit Skip" p. 10 in POEMS TO READ TO THE VERY YOUNG selected by Josette Frank, il. by Eloise Wilkin (Random House, 1982)

"The Toad and the Rabbit" p. 48 in READ ALOUD RHYMES FOR THE VERY YOUNG selected by Jack Prelutsky, il. by Marc Brown (Knopf, 1986)

"Rumpity, Tumpity" p. 11 in RIDE A PURPLE PELICAN by Jack Prelutsky, il. by Garth Williams (Greenwillow, 1986)

RABBITS, RABBITS, a collection of poems by Aileen Fisher, il. by Gail Niemann (Harper & Row, 1983)

"Little Peter Rabbit" p. 22 in WEE SING by Pamela Conn Beall and Susan Hagen Nipp (Price/Stern/Sloan, 1982)

"Do Your Ears Hang Low?" p. 22, "Little Bunny Foo Foo" p. 32, and "Rabbit Ain't Got" p. 31 in WEE SING SILLY SONGS by Pamela Conn Beall and Susan Hagen Nipp (Price/Stern/Sloan, 1983)

Rabbit Games

THE PETER RABBIT AND MR. MCGREGOR CHASE

Children stand in a circle. Use two balls. Designate one ball as Peter Rabbit and the other as Mr. McGregor. Give the Peter Rabbit ball to a child who passes it around the circle from child to child. Then give the Mr. McGregor ball to another child who passes it around the circle to try to catch Peter Rabbit. If Mr. McGregor catches Peter Rabbit, start over.

PETER RABBIT'S LOST SHOE

Each child takes off one shoe and places it in a designated area, which is Mr. McGregor's garden. It works well to play this game in a gym, with the shoes put in a circle chalked on the floor. One child is Mr. McGregor who stands in the circle with the shoes. At the signal to go, the children try to get their shoe back without Mr. McGregor catching them. If Mr. McGregor does catch a child, the child must put the shoe back and try again. Play until there is only one shoe left.

RABBITS IN THE FOREST

Pretend the room is a forest and all the children but one are rabbits hiding in it. The remaining child plays the part of the boy who blows his whistle as suggested in the story TWO HUNDRED RABBITS. When the whistle is blown, the children (rabbits) come out of the forest, line up and march as the boy continues playing. Supervise as needed, but if possible let the children work out the best way to play this game successfully. Make the march as long as you like. Encourage the children to play this game independently.

RABBIT EXERCISES

Read MORNING, RABBIT, MORNING to illustrate how rabbits run and play and do their own special activities. Ask the children to be "rabbity" by following along as everyone does the exercises and activities as suggested in the story. It would be best to divide this activity into two sessions. It would be too much to do all at once. Play background music while exercising.

Rabbit Dramatic Play

THE TORTOISE AND THE HARE

Materials: red flags on sticks; signs reading "Tortoise vs. Hare," "Bear's House," and "Mouse's House"; two race bibs; blue paper for a pond; rabbit ears headband; turtle shell; string

Directions: This can be a group project with everyone helping to make the props and set up the race course.

Begin by making the props. The red flags can be made from paper or cloth and attached to sticks that are stuck into the ground. Make the signs by hand or by using a computer. The bibs are simply sheets of white paper labeled "H" and "T" and attached to the actor's costumes with safety pins. Cut a "pond" from blue paper. A piece of string serves as the starting line.

Follow the directions in Rabbit Crafts for making the rabbit ears. A turtle shell can be made by cutting an oval shape from green poster paper. Draw the markings on the back with a pen or crayon. Roll to make the edges curve and attach a ribbon or yarn at the neck and waist to hold it in place. Make the shell about 14 by 19 inches.

When all the props are ready, set up the race course on the playground and stage the race. You will need a hare, a tortoise, a bear, a mouse, and a starter. The other children can play animals—costumed or not—who cheer on the tortoise. Hopefully, the children will be able to stage the race again and again without any supervision. For younger children, the props should be made ahead of time.

FOOLISH RABBIT'S BIG MISTAKE

To dramatize this story, you will need children to play the following parts: a) one sound effects person who drops the apple, b) three rabbits, c) two bears, d) an elephant, e) several snakes, and f) a lion.

Place the characters along a pathway in the order of their appearance in the story. The storyteller reads or tells the story as the children do the acting. Encourage the actors to make up their own dialogue. It's a good idea to let half the children do the acting while the other half serve as the audience. Then change roles and do the performance again.

See Rabbit Crafts for tips on making props.

Rabbit Crafts

FOOLISH RABBIT'S BIG MISTAKE PROPS

Materials: four 8½ inch wide paper sacks; white, pink, gray, brown, and orange construction paper; scissors; glue; patterns; socks; felt scraps; pink yarn

Directions: You will need three rabbits, two bears, one lion, one elephant, and several snakes to dramatize this story.

Use the patterns that follow to create the masks. Cut off the open end of the sack to make it eleven inches long. Glue the mask onto the sack. Trace the face pattern onto the mask 1¼ inches from the bottom. Open out the sack and cut both the mask and the paper sack for the head opening.

Put the mask on over the head to portray one of the animals.

Make as many snakes as you like by gluing felt eyes and a yarn tongue onto the end of a green or brown sock. Slide the sock over your hand and arm and wiggle around to make the snake move.

LITTLE RABBIT'S LOOSE TOOTH ENVELOPE

Materials: envelope pattern, scissors, glue

Directions: Make the envelope by copying or tracing the pattern or by duplicating it on a copy machine. Cut out and construct by folding on all the dotted lines. Place glue on the two side tabs and glue to the bottom section.

You might like to make multiple copies which the children can take home to use as a prop for retelling the story to their parents. They might also use the envelopes when they lose their own teeth.

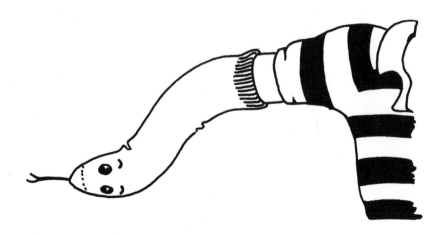

RABBIT EARS

Materials: white and pink construction paper, scissors, glue, stapler, patterns

Directions: Cut a headband from white construction paper that measures 1½ x 23 inches. Overlap and staple together to fit the child's head. Use the pattern to make the ears and staple onto the headband.

The rabbit ears can be worn for dramatizing stories, playing games, performing action verses, and while reading rabbit books.

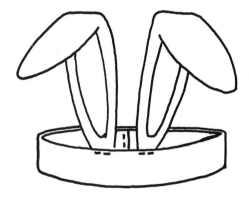

LET'S MAKE RABBITS FLANNEL BOARD CHARACTERS

Materials: wallpaper scraps, white paper, pencil, orange and green construction paper, scissors, glue, flannel, rubber cement

Directions: Trace LET'S MAKE RABBITS characters or use an opaque projector.

Make the pencil rabbit and carrot with white paper and pencil. Make the cutout rabbit with scraps of wallpaper glued together and the cutout carrot with orange and green construction paper. Glue a piece of flannel onto the back of each character with rubber cement. The children will enjoy using them to retell the story.

RABBIT HAND PUPPET

Materials: fine-line felt marker, ribbon

Directions: Draw a rabbit face on the back of your hand. Around your wrist tie a bow using the ribbon. Extend the little and index fingers, and your hand is now a rabbit puppet that goes with you wherever you go. Use it for telling rhymes and singing songs.

Paper Bag Masks

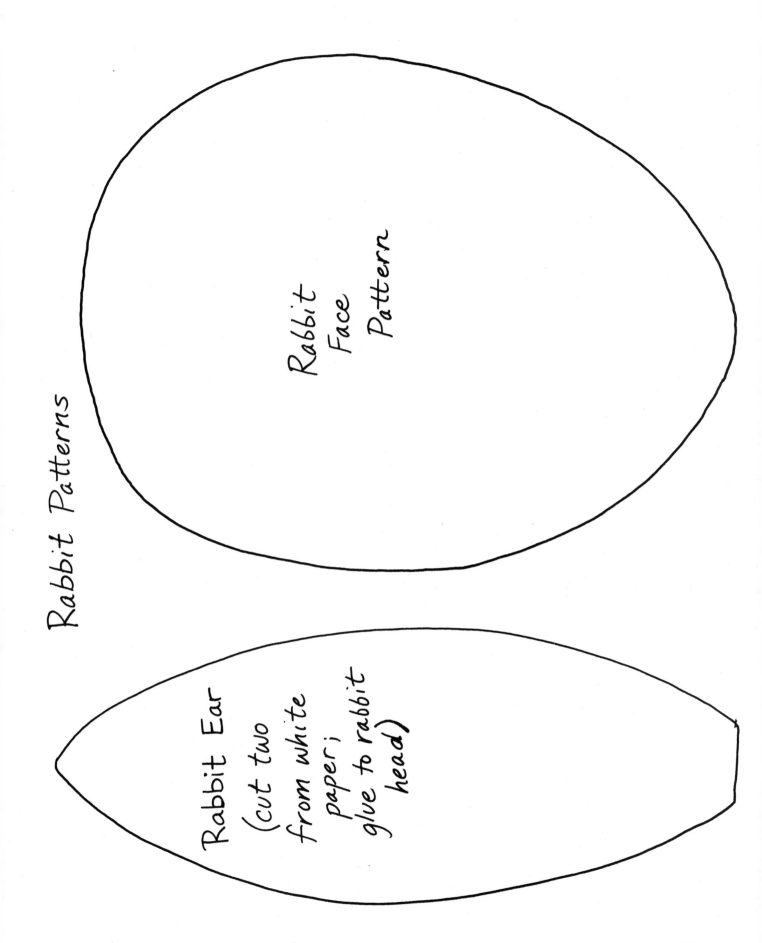

Rabbit Patterns

Rabbit
Face
Pattern

Rabbit Ear
(cut two
from white
paper;
glue to rabbit
head)

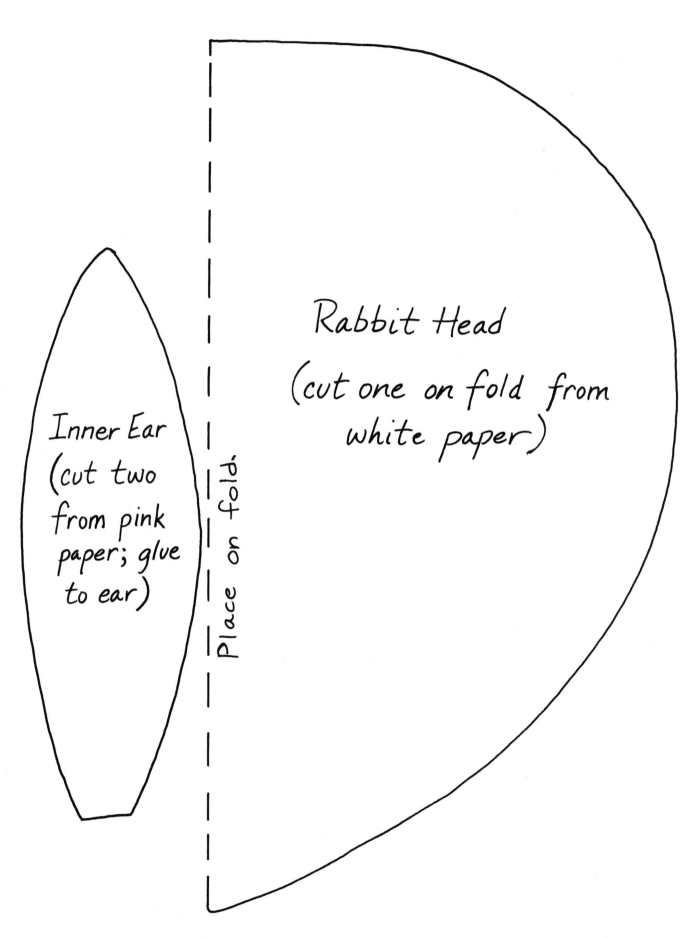

Inner Ear
(cut two
from pink
paper; glue
to ear)

Place on fold.

Rabbit Head
(cut one on fold from
white paper)

194

Bear Patterns

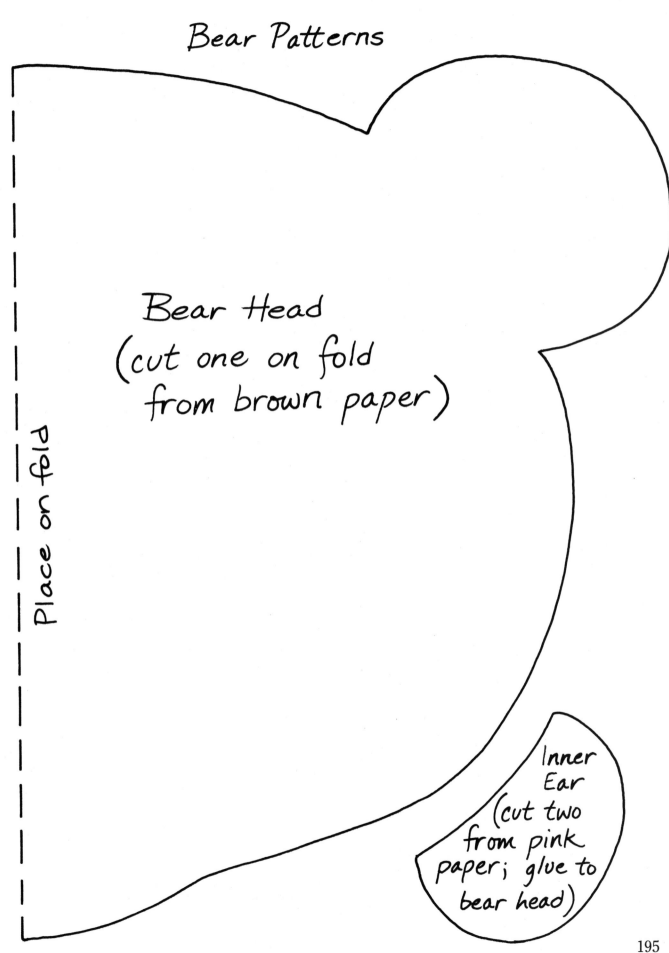

Place on fold

Bear Head
(cut one on fold
from brown paper)

Inner
Ear
(cut two
from pink
paper; glue to
bear head)

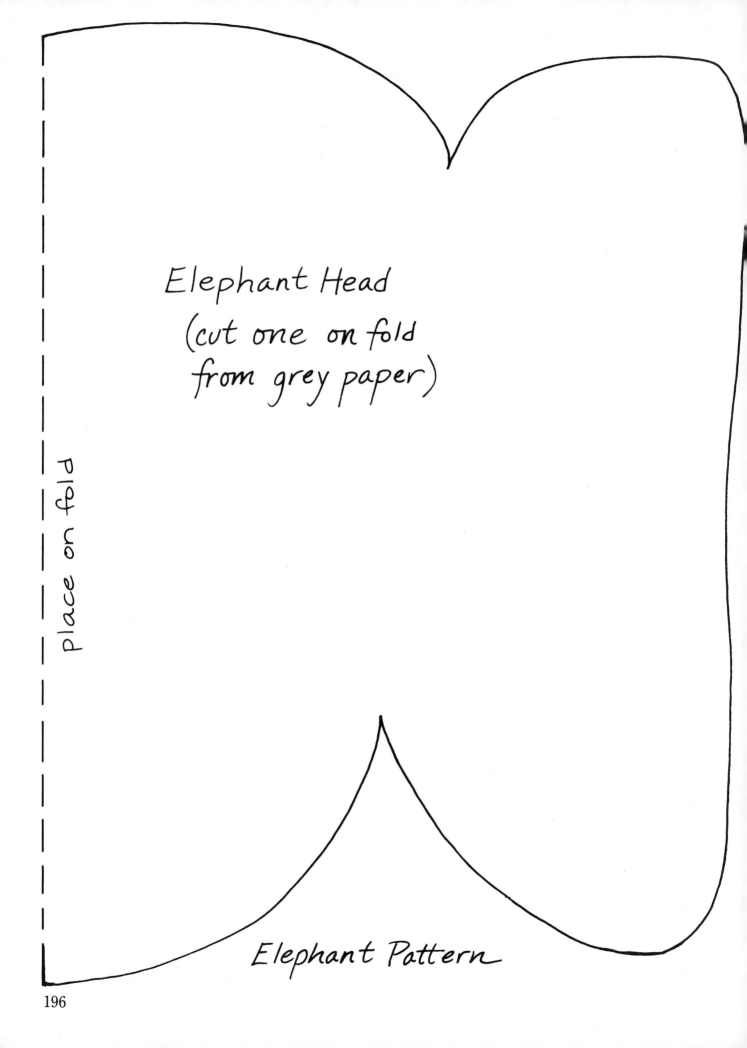

place on fold

Elephant Head
(cut one on fold
from grey paper)

Elephant Pattern

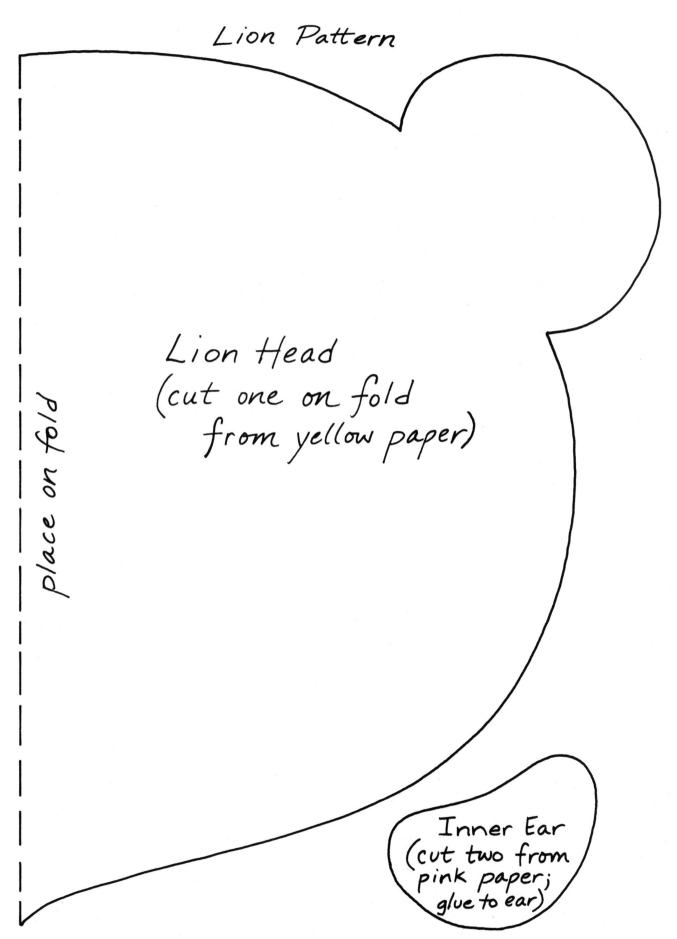

Lion Pattern

Lion Head
(cut one on fold
from yellow paper)

place on fold

Inner Ear
(cut two from
pink paper;
glue to ear)

Tooth Envelope

(glue)

(glue)

Dear Tooth Fairy,

In this envelope you'll find
A little tooth that was mine.
While I'm asleep and dreams are made,
Please come and make a trade.

Love,

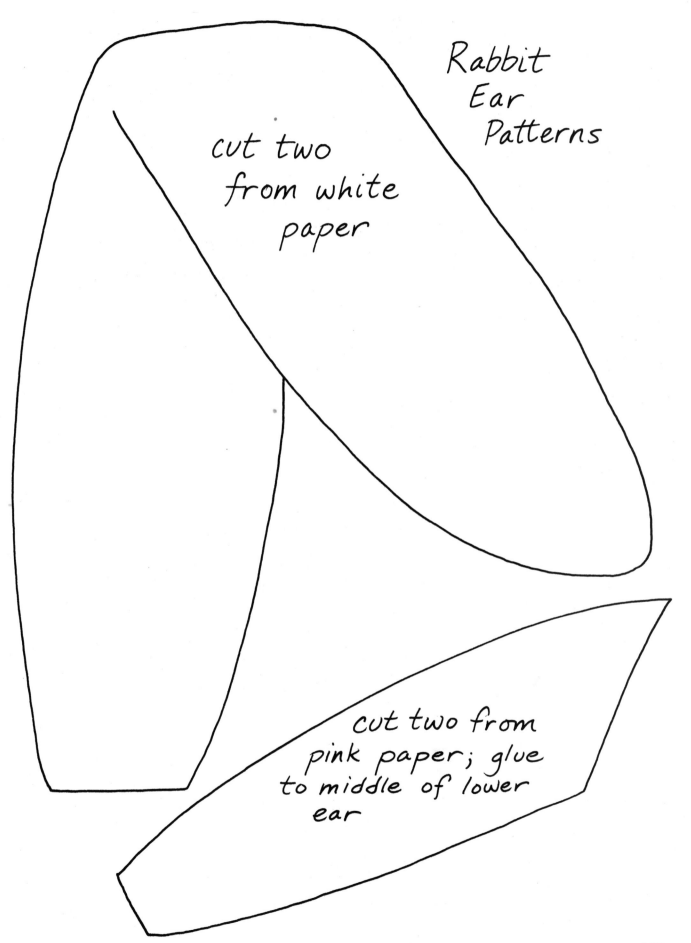

Rabbit
Ear
Patterns

cut two
from white
paper

cut two from
pink paper; glue
to middle of lower
ear

Rabbit Snacks

CARROTS

Serve carrot sticks or a whole carrot with the green stem still attached as if it were just picked from Mr. McGregor's garden. It should be washed and peeled, of course.

RABBIT SALAD

Serve the following "Rabbit Salad" as a healthy snack. The older children will enjoy creating their own rabbits.

Ingredients: lettuce leaves, pear halves, raisins, pink gumdrops, whole almonds, cottage cheese

Directions: To make an individual salad, place a crisp lettuce leaf on a plate. Put the pear half upside down on top of the lettuce. Make a rabbit face on the narrow end of the pear by using the raisins for eyes, a gumdrop for the nose, almonds for ears, and cottage cheese for the tail.

RABBIT CAKE

Make a rabbit cake as the children watch, telling them about the ingredients and how important it is to measure correctly. Have everything ready ahead of time. The children can help add the ingredients and help with the stirring and other activities. Then they will feel as if the cake is their own.

Ingredients:
1½ cups of sugar
¾ cup margarine
2 eggs
1½ cups finely shredded carrots
⅓ cup water
1¾ cups flour
1½ tsp. baking powder
1 tsp. cinnamon
½ tsp. soda
½ tsp. salt
½ cup chopped nuts (optional)

Directions: Cream sugar and margarine. Blend in eggs and shredded carrots. Combine flour, baking powder, cinnamon, soda, and salt. Add to the creamed mixture alternately with the water. Add nuts if desired. Grease bottom of 9 inch square pan. Add batter and bake at 325 degrees for 35 to 40 minutes. Serve warm.

RESOURCES

BOOKS

Bauer, Caroline Feller. CELEBRATIONS (H.W. Wilson, 1985)

Bauer, Caroline Feller. HANDBOOK FOR STORYTELLERS (American Library Assoc., 1977)

Bauer, Caroline Feller. THIS WAY TO BOOKS (H.W. Wilson, 1983)

Beall, Pamela Conn and Susan Hagen Nipp. WEE SING (Price/Stern/Sloan, 1982)

Beall, Pamela Conn and Susan Hagen Nipp. WEE SING AND PLAY (Price/Stern/Sloan, 1985)

Beall, Pamela Conn and Susan Hagen Nipp. WEE SING SILLY SONGS (Price/Stern/Sloan, 1983)

Catron, Carol Elaine and Barbara Catron Parks. SUPER STORY TELLING (T.S. Denison, 1986)

Courson, Diane, il. by Elizabeth Nygaard. LET'S LEARN ABOUT FAIRY TALES AND NURSERY RHYMES (Good Apple, 1988)

de Paola, Tomie. TOMIE DE PAOLA'S MOTHER GOOSE (Putnam, 1985)

Dowell, Ruth I., il. by Concetta C. Scott. MOVE OVER, MOTHER GOOSE (Gryphon House, 1987)

Evans, Joy and Jo Ellen Moore. FUN WITH BOOKS (Evan-Moor, 1987)

Evans, Joy and Jo Ellen Moore. MORE FUN WITH BOOKS (Evan-Moor, 1987)

Flint Public Library. RING A RING O'ROSES: FINGER PLAYS FOR PRE-SCHOOL CHILDREN (Flint Public Library, 1026 E. Kearsley St., Flint, MI 48502, 1988)

Glazer, Tom. EYE WINKER, TOM TINKER, CHIN CHOPPER. (Doubleday, 1973)

Hearne, Betsy. CHOOSING BOOKS FOR CHILDREN (Delacorte, 1981)

Ingram, Victoria. LANGUAGE ARTS AND CRAFTS: ANIMALS. (Monday Morning Books, 1987)

Kimmel, Margaret Mary and Elizabeth Segel. FOR READING OUT LOUD! (Dell, 1983)

Landsberg, Michelle. READING FOR THE LOVE OF IT (Prentice-Hall, 1987)

Maquire, Jack. CREATIVE STORYTELLING (McGraw-Hill, 1985)

Oppenheim, Joanne, Barbara Brenner and Betty D. Boegehold. CHOOSING BOOKS FOR KIDS (Ballantine, 1986)

POEMS TO READ TO THE VERY YOUNG selected by Josette Frank. il. by Eloise Wilkin. (Random House, 1982)

Prelutsky, Jack, il. by Garth Williams. RIDE A PURPLE PELICAN (Greenwillow, 1986)

Prelutsky, Jack, il. by James Stevenson. THE NEW KID ON THE BLOCK (Greenwillow, 1984)

THE RANDOM HOUSE BOOK OF POETRY FOR CHILDREN selected by Jack Prelutsky, il. by Marc Brown (Random House, 1983)

READ-ALOUD RHYMES FOR THE VERY YOUNG selected by Jack Prelutsky, il. by Marc Brown (Knopf, 1986)

Silverstein, Shel. A LIGHT IN THE ATTIC (Harper & Row, 1981)

Silverstein, Shel. WHERE THE SIDEWALK ENDS (Harper & Row, 1974)

Sitarz, Paula Gaj. PICTURE BOOK STORY HOURS (Libraries Unlimited, 1987)

Trelease, Jim. THE READ-ALOUD HANDBOOK (Penguin, 1982)

Wendelin, Karla Hawkins, and M. Jean Greenlaw. **STORYBOOK CLASSROOMS** (Humanics, 1986)

White, Mary Lou, editor. **ADVENTURING WITH BOOKS.** (National Council of Teachers of English, 1981)

PROPS

A Child's Collection, 155 Avenue of the Americas, New York, NY 10013

Creative Teaching Press, P.O. Box 6017, Cypress, CA 90630-0017

Folkmanis, Inc., 1219 Park Avenue, Emeryville, CA 94608

Peaceable Kingdom Press, 2954 Hillegass Avenue, Berkeley, CA 94705

Trudy Toy Company, Norwalk, KY

INDEX